ALGOMA CENTRAL RAILWAY

1 Winter Wonderland—Agawa Canyon

O S NOCK

Bachelor of Science (Engineering, London)
Chartered Engineer
Fellow of the Institution of Civil Engineers
Fellow of the Institution of Mechanical Engineers
Past President, Institution of Railway Signal Engineers

ALGOMA CENTRAL RAILWAY · SAULT STE MARIE
ADAM & CHARLES BLACK · LONDON

First published in 1975 by
A & C Black Limited
4, 5 & 6 Soho Square
London W1V 6AD
© 1975 Algoma Central Railway

ISBN 0 7136 1571 0

Printed in Great Britain by
Butler & Tanner Ltd
Frome and London

Contents

Acknowledgments

The photographs reproduced in Plates 6d, 17b, 20, 23a and 24a are by Omer S A Lavallee of Montreal; those in Plates 27a, 28, 29, 30, 31a, 35, 36, 38, 40a, 41, 42b, 44b and c, 46 and 47 are by the author, and the remainder are by courtesy of the Algoma Central Railway.

Colour plate 3 is from an original oil painting by Russ Porter in the possession of Russel H Rankin, by whose courtesy it is reproduced.

The remaining colour plates are by courtesy of the Algoma Central Railway and the author.

The cartoons of the 'Black Bear' are from drawings by Dennis Purvitis, formerly in the Lands and Forests Department of the Algoma Central Railway.

The maps, engine diagrams and gradient profiles have been prepared by Mrs C Boyer of Chippenham, England, in collaboration with the author, from documents kindly furnished by the Algoma Central Railway.

Illustrations

Illustrations

DIAGRAMS

Preface

A few years ago I was asked by the publishing firm of A & C Black Ltd of London, England, to write a series of books on the railways of the world. I had already written extensively about those of the United Kingdom, about their history, equipment, operation and their railroad men; but this was an altogether wider-ranging assignment. By the year 1971 the first two volumes in this new series, dealing respectively with Southern Africa and with Australia were finished and I was at work on the third, to be devoted to Canada. It was then that I was introduced to Sir Denys Lowson, Bart, then Chairman of the Algoma Central Railway. He not only arranged for me to go to Sault Ste Marie to see the railway, and obtain information for my book on the railways of Canada, but he asked me to consider doing a book solely about the Algoma Central—not in the ordinary World Railways series but a 'special'. Just before Christmas that same year at a very pleasant social gathering in London, England, I met Len Savoie, President of the Railway, Jack Thompson, the Vice-President and General Manager, and members of the Board of Directors.

It was however not until the following summer that I was able to visit the Algoma Country, and then with my wife, I enjoyed three delightful days on the railway. In the business car *Agawa* in the company of Jack Thompson, Tom Gillespie the Comptroller, and their wives, we traveled the length of the line, and later I was able to study many historical documents in the head office at Sault Ste Marie. I left that fascinating and historic city convinced that there was ample material for a full-length book, and I received the 'go-ahead' at a meeting in London late in 1972. It was then arranged that I should return to Canada in the fall of 1973 to travel the railway, see the glorious coloring of the trees in the forests at that season, and journey in the ships of the company. But a serious, though fortunately transient illness, prevented my going at that time and my visit was postponed until the opening of the shipping season, in 1974. So I spent an enthralling month on location, when the winter snows were only beginning to melt, and when there was still a great deal of ice on Lake Superior.

But there was no icy chill about the welcome I received from everyone on the Algoma Central Railway, and the writing of this book, to which I had looked forward for many months with pleasurable anticipation, became a positive 'labor of love'. From the President, Len Savoie, downward, the officers and staff of the company gave of their time and experience with the most wholehearted enthusiasm. Everywhere it was not only the formal help that one might have expected toward the execution of a project initiated by the Chairman of the Company, there was a spontaneous friendly interest by everyone I met, from senior assistants who sometimes produced hidden treasures of historical interest that their bosses did not know existed (!) to the bright young secretaries who always seemed to have tea or coffee ready at the appropriate moments. It was indeed a happy experience for me. Elsewhere in the book I have told of some of the great characters I met 'out the line'.

I was in Sault Ste Marie at the time of the Annual General Meeting of the Company in April 1974, presided over by Sir Denys Lowson himself; I was invited to attend and subsequent events that day reminded me of the occasion nearly 40 years earlier when the Great Western Railway of England celebrated the hundredth anniversary of its Incorporation in a grand luncheon in the Great Hall of the University of Bristol. Then the Chairman of the Company, Sir Robert Horne, quoting from a letter of an old friend, said: 'All England seems to have a friendly family feeling for the Great Western'. Having attended that Annual General Meeting, in April 1974, talked to some of the shareholders, and met many prominent local men at a dinner held the same evening I felt that the same sentiments could be expressed in Sault Ste Marie, where everyone seemed to have a 'friendly family feeling' for the Algoma Central Railway.

During my stay I was able to visit some of the great companies that, like the railway, had their origin in the fabulous Clergue 'empire' at the beginning of the twentieth century; and I am much indebted to Jack Barber of the Algoma Steel Corporation, to Alf Askin of the Abitibi Paper Company and to Bill Hogg of the Great Lakes Power Company for arranging for me to see round their fine plants. I have to thank also Bob Curran, Managing Director of the *Sault Daily Star*, for allowing me to study the old files of that newspaper and for providing some interesting photographs. Here again I found the staunchest support for all activities of the Algoma Central.

My most patent debt however is of course to Sir Denys Lowson himself, for his invitation to do the job and for the very generous assistance he provided to help me to do it.

Since this book was written Sir Denys Lowson, who is mentioned throughout the text, retired as Chairman of the Board and Director of the Company. Sir Denys made a highly significant contribution to the growth and welfare of Algoma Central Railway over a period of many years, commencing with his work as a member of the Bondholders Committee, and continuing with his efforts on behalf of the shareholders during the reorganization of the company in 1958–9.

Sault Ste Marie,   O S NOCK
Ontario

November 1974

Introduction

My first visit to the Soo was brief. It was just long enough to travel the length of the Algoma Central Railway and absorb enough of its remarkable character to write a single chapter in a book trying to cover most of Canada's railways. I came to the Soo for a much longer stay on the last day of March 1974. In Toronto the day had been very grey with thick low cloud, and a searing north wind. There were pockets of snow remaining here and there; and when I left, toward evening by air, it was a pleasure to climb through that thick cloud into the sunshine again, and see the sun gradually sink in a cold sky. But by the time we were nearing the Soo, in the gathering twilight, the clouds were rolling away, and we could see the land below deeply covered in snow. The highways showed up clear, and in the distance the lights of the Soo were twinkling. It was a beautiful sight. The snow made areas of demarcation between land and water, and I could see the narrowing channel of the St Mary's River. We were flying in from the Michigan side, and the whole geography that bequeathed upon the Soo its unique situation, and potential for development, was spread out below us—looking exquisitely beautiful in its covering of snow, and in the clear and frosty night air. We flew out toward the west, to the level ground where the airport is, and touched down, dead on time, with the lightness of a feather. It was a good beginning, fitly rounded off by the warmth of welcome I received from Jack Thompson, Vice-President and General Manager of the Algoma Central Railway, who was at the airport to meet me.

That aerial view made me determined to see more of the city that was to be the base of my operations for at least a month—more that is than the railway network of the Algoma Central; for this railway and its modern business allies, which were at one time all members of the fabulous Clergue Empire, literally made the Soo, just as they sustain the Soo today. And so I sought out all these closely interconnected activities, and can commend to the reader the aerial view on Plate 1; because that fairly epitomizes the situation of the allies of the Algoma Central Railway, in the Soo at any rate. The whereabouts of the three great companies, Algoma Steel, Abitibi Paper and Great Lakes Power, can all be seen in this one picture, together with the great international highway bridge leading to the USA. It does not however give the whole picture—indeed one could hardly expect a single photograph to do that. It shows only the Canadian lock, passing beneath the arched span of the bridge; nor does it show the St Mary's Rapids which are just out of the picture to the left. The American locks are still farther to the left, and it is through them that the great ships of the Algoma Central pass on their way between Lakes Superior and Huron. The Canadian lock is too small for the giants of the present fleet.

That is not all. One day toward the end of my visit I had been viewing the plant at the generating station of the Great Lakes Power Company, and afterwards walked out on the ground beside the Canadian lock. It was a sunny afternoon, but nearing the end of April the wind was still blowing icy cold off Lake Superior, and I was glad to be wrapped up well. But out there I felt indeed in the very presence of Canadian history. I saw the monument to Etienne Brulé and his companion Grenoble commemorating the date, 1622, when they were the first white men to see the St Mary's Rapids, and Lake Superior out beyond. On the Round Tower, which now forms a part of the generating station, there is a plaque noting that it was in 1674 that Sault Ste Marie first appeared on any map—that of Louis Joliet, the explorer. The place was lonely on that cold windswept afternoon, and it did not need very much stretch of the imagination to picture the setting up of the old trading posts, first by the North West Company and then the first establishment of the Hudson's Bay Company there in 1821.

Reverting to that aerial photograph another feature may be described. Beyond and beneath the International Bridge, where it crosses the lock leading to the Great Lakes Power Company's establishment, is a bridge crossing the water at quite low level. This is the track of the Canadian Pacific's American subsidiary, the Minneapolis, St Paul and Sault Ste Marie, the 'Soo Line', to quote its official title. There is a swing bridge to carry this line over the Canadian lock, but when it reaches the American locks, two of them abreast, the first is crossed by a two span lifting bascule bridge, and the second by a vertical lift bridge, similar to those over the St Lawrence Seaway canal on the outskirts of Montreal. On the Canadian side that line swings round in a wide circle to reach a passenger station in the northern part of the city. Passenger service on the CPR is now limited to a single Budd rail car between the Soo and Sudbury; but freight traffic is considerable, particularly in newsprint, from the Abitibi Paper Company into the USA via the Soo Line. Taken all round the Soo is one of the most fascinating geographical areas one could find anywhere, and is a fit setting for the great story I have to tell.

CHAPTER ONE

The 'Soo' and Its Founder

In the year 1608 the great French explorer and colonizer Samuel de Champlain discovered the tremendous estuary of the St Lawrence. Its magnitude, and the wide
and potentially fertile valley into which it led raised hopes that this might be the
beginning of a route 'westward to the far east' lying between the wastes of the
Arctic and the heat of the tropics across the Panama isthmus. It was the life ambition
of many an explorer to find such a route, and having established himself in the upper
valley of the St Lawrence, he claimed the entire land for France—without realizing
anything of the extent of the country into which he was probing. He was rewarded
in 1612 by being appointed Governor of Canada, with a Royal Commission enjoining
him to seek every means to find an easy route to China and the East Indies from the
St Lawrence basin. Naturally exploration lay along the waterways. Unconscious of
what lay to the north, his men skirted the almost limitless wilderness of the Canadian
Shield, and they had soon penetrated westward as far as Lake Huron. An old French
map of the period shows however that while they had established the northern
extent of this lake, which they called *Mer Douce*, they were evidently unaware of the
extent and shape of its southern reaches, and Lake Michigan had not then been
discovered at all.

It was however in pressing westward from Lake Huron, up the fast-flowing river
that debouched into it, that in 1622 a young Frenchman in Champlain's company,
Etienne Brulé, came upon one of the great sights of primeval Canada, where flowing
between dense and magnificent forests, the river came thundering over rapids,
lowering its level by some 20 ft in a very short distance. This was no spectacular
waterfall, but a scene of breathtaking splendor nevertheless, and Etienne Brulé is
believed to be the first white man who ever saw it. The Indians knew it well enough,

and the Ojibway tribe skilfully shot the rapids in their canoes, and with the traditional way of life of the Indian worked with nature, rather than making any attempt to subdue or harness it for their own needs. The rapids—Sault Ste Marie, 'the Falls of St Mary'—remained an obstacle on the way to the west for nearly two hundred years after Brulé first discovered them, and the canoes of voyagers heading toward Lake Superior had to be carried upstream past the rapids to gain the higher level of what the early French cartographers called the *Grand Lac*. The natural obstacle made Sault Ste Marie a staging point on what became one of the earliest trade routes to the west; and if it did not prove the starting point of the 'easy' way to China, it was soon being used for another, and very profitable traffic, the fur trade.

In 1673 the Jesuit priest Pere Marquette founded a mission near the rapids, where little more than an Indian settlement had hitherto existed, but before many years were out the French had great rivals in the fur trade, and trade rivalry led eventually to military activity, and the war with England that ended with General Wolfe's capture of Quebec in 1759 and Amherst's capture of Montreal in 1760. The subsequent transfer of Canada to Great Britain opened the French river and lake route to a host of adventurers, and Sault Ste Marie still stayed on the 'main line', as it were, which led from Ottawa to Lake Nipissing, via French River to Lake Huron, thence through Sault Ste Marie to Lake Superior, and to Grand Portage. A man who was to become a driving force in the fur trade, Alexander Mackenzie, came to Montreal from Stornoway, Isle of Lewis, in 1776. The inconvenience of having to carry the large canoes used by the fur traders past sections of waterway that were not navigable was met by digging canals, and the Northwest Company dug one of the earliest of these at Sault Ste Marie in 1797, but a further factor now began to enter into the scene. During the American War of Independence, Canadian sentiments had mostly been on the side of the British government at home, and the end of the war left strained relations along the American-Canadian frontier. Sault Ste Marie was a 'front-line' post, and the St Lawrence waterway, and the chain of lakes, rivers, and canals leading eastward from it were vital for frontier defense. This was emphasized in the war of 1812 with the United States, in which the canal at Sault Ste Marie was destroyed.

The coming of the railway age put Sault Ste Marie in an interesting position. Its geographical situation seemed to mark it down as a natural junction—a bridgehead and exchange point between the railways of Canada and of the United States, though at first the vast, virtually unexplored nature of the country west of the St Lawrence basin, and the establishment of existing trade routes only along the river valleys and through the lakes, made early development toward the mid-west slow. But the historic decision of 1881 to build the Canadian Pacific Railway galvanized the whole of Western Ontario into vigorous debate, if not necessarily action, while the members of the famous Syndicate debated among themselves the route the new railway should take. I have referred already to the Canadian 'Shield'. It is difficult to convey, in so many words the extraordinary wilderness of rock, swamp, and stumpy forest that

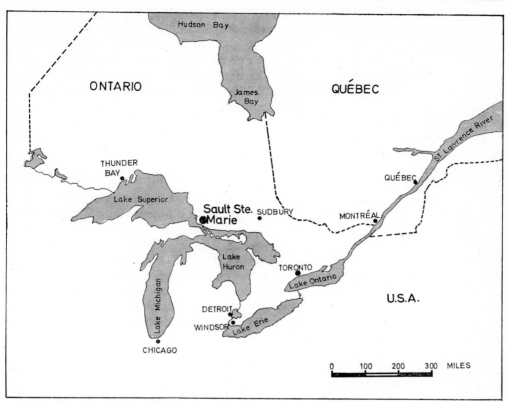

1 Location of Sault Ste Marie—'The Soo'

extends for thousands of square miles westward from the St Lawrence basin, and northward from the Great Lakes, and it is no wonder that prospectors sought to avoid it. To traverse it gave little hope of intermediate traffic being developed; to build a line through it was likely to involve great engineering difficulties. And it so happened that within the Syndicate entrusted with the building of the Canadian Pacific Railway there was one man who was ready with a very neat alternative.

The four partners in the Syndicate, George Stephen, Donald A Smith, R B Angus and J J Hill had together rescued the half bankrupt Chicago, Milwaukee and St Paul Railroad, put it on its feet and become multi-millionaires in the process, and to Hill in particular the obvious way to take the CPR to the west was down the old fur trade route via Lake Nipissing to Sault Ste Marie, over the river and into United States territory, and round the southern shores of Lake Superior, to pass through Duluth. It was a proposal that would bring a great deal of additional traffic to lines in which

23

he was already interested, and would avoid all the engineering difficulties of construction, on the direct line westward across the 'Shield' that had been proposed by the first man to survey a route for the CPR—Sandford Fleming. To his fellow members of the Syndicate, however, Hill's proposal to go south of Lake Superior through United States territory was quite unacceptable, and the antagonism that ensued ran so deep that Hill withdrew. While it was unquestionably right that the new transcontinental railway should run entirely on Canadian soil, it is an interesting thought that if Hill had had his way Sault Ste Marie would have been on the main line to the west. It would have been a rather roundabout route, and as things turned out, it did come on to a route that was of all-Canadian ownership, if not entirely in Canadian territory.

Sault Ste Marie became connected by a lifting bascule bridge over the St Mary's river with two railways in American territory that were subsidiaries of the Canadian Pacific: the Duluth South Shore and Atlantic, and the Minneapolis St Paul and Sault Ste Marie, the latter of which took Canadian interests right into Chicago. Northward through Michigan also came two great American railways, to terminate at Mackinaw City—the Pennsylvania, and the Michigan Central, which latter became part of the New York Central group. These made connection to the MStP&SSM by ferry to St Ignace. But looking at the situation as it was developing in the 1880s, it was clear that Sault Ste Marie was becoming the Grand Junction of the Great Lakes, with no fewer than five important railways feeding into it, together with shipping connections from the Lakes Superior, Michigan and Huron. It might have remained so, and little more, but for the dramatic intervention of a most remarkable personality: Francis Hector Clergue, who was first made aware of the Sault in 1894. At this stage I must introduce the name by which the City of Sault Ste Marie is now universally and popularly known. As a schoolboy reading history and geography, I became aware of a place described by my tutors as 'Soosamaree'—to give it the phonetic spelling. It was not until I came to travel in Canada that I learned how it is now always known as 'The Soo'; and except on ceremonial occasions, as it were, 'The Soo' it will be for the rest of this book.

Now we must turn away from South Western Ontario for a while to look at the early career of the man who completely changed the status of 'The Soo' from a 'grand junction' of railway, road, and shipping routes to a major industrial city. No more unlikely a tycoon had ever existed, up to the year 1894 that is. Clergue was then 38 years of age, and his chequered career had been a series of spectacular 'might have beens', nearly all of which had ended in financial failure. His father, Joseph Hector Clergue had emigrated from France in 1840, during the reign of Louis-Philippe, the Bourbon Duke of Orleans, who had succeeded Charles X, deposed at the time of the mini-revolution of 1830. It was a time of general unrest and upheaval in Europe, and J H Clergue, one of a large Huguenot family, sought peace and tranquillity in America. He found it in the humble calling of a hairdresser in Brewer, Maine, and it was there that his eldest son Francis was born in 1856. After schooling at Bangor he studied law at what was then Maine State College, and at the early age of 20 he was called to the bar. It was soon evident that he was a man of very different stamp from his father, having nothing of reticence, contentment with his environment, or frugality. Not that Francis Clergue was a firebrand, or a radical—far from it; he has been described as a dreamer, but one possessed of boundless optimism and the deepest regard for the wellbeing of his fellow men. At College, in his popularity with both students and teachers, he had revealed definite powers of oratory that were to lead him, early in life, into a series of remarkable, albeit unsuccessful enterprises.

His professional work and early partnership in the legal firm of Laughton, Clergue, and Mason soon gave place to bolder ventures. He had the flair for scouting out a novel idea, and then, using all his personal charm and flow of oratory, to secure substantial backing for it. Unfortunately having got a promising scheme 'off the ground' he does not seem to have had the business acumen to negotiate the next, and subsequent moves, nor the perception to see where the weaknesses in these schemes lay. The chronicle of enterprises that went wrong, between 1880 and the early 1890s, is enough to show the extraordinary diversity of his interests. There was the Bangor street railway, which by his earlier standards was fairly successful, and he followed this with an electric power station on the Penobscot River, four miles above Bangor. This, in a way, was prophetic of the great developments with which this book is concerned, but this early hydro-electric venture was financially unsuccessful. Clergue himself rode out the failure, and in fact increased the esteem won by his personality. At one time he was city solicitor of Bangor, but then he became deeply involved in a much more fanciful project.

Noting the interest and success created by the Mount Washington cog railway, the first in the world, and one that is still operating with steam locomotives, he enterprised a similar railway on Mount Desert Island, up the side of Green Mountain. In connection with this a steamboat service was introduced, and two hotels were built to accommodate summer visitors. The whole thing was a disastrous failure—so disastrous that Clergue left New England altogether, and for a time sought 'Old' England instead. His next project was for the construction of shipyards, dry docks and a bank at Mobile, Alabama, and for this he managed to attract a large amount of English capital, in the City of London. It ended in the biggest financial crash that he had so far experienced, and led to the comment: 'that Mr Clergue is the greatest word painter in the line of modern promoters is admitted by all the bankers with whom he has ever come in touch'. It was not that his arguments were specious, or dishonest; it was just that his insatiable optimism did not seem to make any provision for the difficulties likely to arise.

Then in 1888 came his first venture into the field of main-line railways, when he announced that he had obtained concessions to build a railway across Persia, of all unlikely countries. Again it would seem that his optimism took no account of the difficulties that might arise, which there included international politics, as well as

25

the more mundane matters of engineering and simple finance. Fortified by a loan of $25,000, he went to Europe, and immediately formed three companies: the Persian Railway and Construction; the Persian Electric Light Company, and the City of Teheran Water Works, each with a capital of a million dollars. It was a magnificent concept, and he appeared to have staunch support, some of it of an international character such as that from Reuters, the great news agency. He learned that the Shah of Persia was to visit St Petersburg at the conclusion of an extensive European tour, and he seized upon this as an opportunity not only to present letters of recommendation from the Secretary of State in Maine, but also to secure an introduction to the Russian Imperial Court.

Railways were then a very delicate issue in Russia, particularly where her southern frontiers were concerned. East of Persia lay the 'buffer' state of Afghanistan, flashpoint of the keenly conflicting interests of Russia and Great Britain at that time. Railways were being built southward by the Russians, and north-westward in India against the possibility of a military confrontation in Afghanistan. A railway through Persia could have bypassed the Russian sphere of influence. But before the full strategic significance of Clergue's proposals had been appreciated in St Petersburg he had rather staggered the Shah of Persia by the extent of the industrial projects he advanced. A railway undoubtedly had some points of attraction, but a high-powered electric light installation, and large waterworks were another thing altogether. The Shah was not at all sure that he wanted this sudden influx of industry. But the matter was settled conclusively by the Russians. Clergue may have been eloquent in talking to bankers, and investors, but international politics was something quite new to him, and he was quickly out-maneuvered. In February 1889 the Russian Minister to Persia, Prince Dolgoruki, obtained a document from the Shah granting to Russia first refusal of any railway concession for a period of five years; and as if to slam the door finally against any future overtures from Americans, or anyone else, an agreement was made with Russia in November 1890 positively prohibiting the construction of *any* railways in Persia—a situation that remained unchanged for nearly 40 years.

Clergue returned to Bangor, Maine, and apparently quite undismayed by the ruin of his plans in Persia, began launching plans for diverting the waters of the Penobscot River to build huge dams and electric power plants. By now however his eloquence was beginning to fail him. Investors were becoming increasingly aware of the consistent failure of his enterprises, and he decided reluctantly to leave his native state of Maine. At this critical point in his life it is interesting to look briefly at the character of the man himself. He was so unlike the upstart tycoons of the Railway Mania period in England, for example. He was a most sincere man, not seeking personal wealth, but one with a vision that could be epitomized in the original aims of the Institution of Civil Engineers in harnessing the forces of nature for the benefit and convenience of man. Hydro-electric projects figured again and again in his early schemes that foundered, perhaps because he was in advance of his time in making provision for electrical power before the industries were there to use it, or before their modest operations justified the additional capital outlay. He certainly scared the Shah of Persia by the magnitude of his proposals. It is said that his aim was 'to wield the power of Sovereign over an industrial empire'. He was nicknamed variously *Napoleon* and *Monte Cristo*, both more in sarcasm than praise; but of the Clergue of 1894, penniless, and in the depths of failure, one thinks of Rudyard Kipling's stirring verses '. . . if you can trust yourself when all men doubt you, and make allowance for their doubting too . . .'.

And so Clergue went to work for a company of financiers looking for investment opportunities, and as if he had not had his fill of disappointment he searched along the St Lawrence basin for sites likely to favour hydro-electric development.

I have seen it suggested that Clergue came by chance to the Soo: that a chance conversation in the train caused him to break his journey to the west, and have a look around. From the detailed but yet unpublished history of the Algoma Steel Corporation that I have been privileged to study, it is evident that this was not the case. J J Kehoe and H C Hamilton, who had been concerned with the establishment of the Ontario and Sault Ste Marie Power Company, were on their way to Toronto by train, when Kehoe fell into conversation with a certain H B Foster, who it turned out lived in Bangor, Maine. Kehoe told him of the troubles experienced with hydro-electric development at the Soo. Foster was interested enough to take some notes, and with Hamilton also drawn into the conversation Foster promised to talk to some friends in Bangor who he thought might be interested. In fact, Foster went straight to Clergue, and as a result, in the late summer of 1894 Clergue went to meet Hamilton in Toronto. On hearing of the situation Clergue immediately realized the immense potentialities of the Soo, and in some secrecy he and Hamilton worked out a plan for a take-over.

Secrecy was considered necessary in the preliminary stages, because the town of Sault Ste Marie owned more than 12,000 shares in the unsuccessful Ontario and Sault Ste Marie Water Light and Power Company, and it would have been undesirable for any rumors of a take-over to begin circulating prematurely, and as yet Clergue had not seen the place for himself. But by September of that year his plans were sufficiently matured for him to take one of the CPR steamers, and alight at the Soo. Still keeping up the cloak of secrecy he and a colleague took rooms in one of the hotels under assumed names, and it was not until 1 October 1894 that he came fully into the open and addressed a town meeting. It was then a quiet little place with a population of about 3000, and over a small gathering his eloquence once again won the day.

Before that first visit to the Soo was over he had concluded a contract with the town: in return for assuming the town's debt on the unfinished and abandoned hydro-electric works, he was granted conditional title to the installations. It is probably an exaggeration to say that at that time he had scarcely a penny to his name; but in the fire of his own enthusiasm he had no doubt of his ability to obtain

27

the necessary backing. From his lengthy, widespread, and mostly bitter experience he had learnt much wisdom to mingle with his enthusiasm, and it is perhaps significant that he sought out capitalists in New York and Philadelphia, who had not previously been associated with any of his former enterprises. Between them he managed to raise the $225,000 necessary to buy out the half finished installations at the Soo, and this time, at last, he was on the road to success. The foundation stone of the 'Clergue Empire' had been well and truly laid.

CHAPTER TWO

The Clergue Financial Empire: Build-up and Crash

The years from 1894 onward were to witness a phenomenal industrial development centered upon Sault Ste Marie, and it is of great interest to study the technique adopted by Clergue in its build-up. It was not a preconceived, co-ordinated whole from the outset, but rather the result of a series of what might be called 'chain-reactions'. He started in much the same way as in most of his earlier ill-starred projects. Then when it was clear that to ensure its success one or more links in the chain were missing, he immediately conceived another enterprise to provide the 'missing link'. The difference between his earlier ventures and the build-up at the Soo was that he achieved a remarkable early success. It all sprang from his taking over the power installations, and setting out to enlarge their capacity. Like the town authorities before him, he anticipated that once more power was available, many manufacturing concerns would spring up, eager to use it. But nothing happened, and Clergue was immediately faced with trying to find work for the power he was about to generate. It was the first step in the chain reaction. The Soo was then, as now, very much a town on its own, and he began an immediate study of the neighborhood. Northward, and along the shores of Lake Superior there were abundant spruce forests, and if the logs could be floated down to the Soo there would be all the essentials for a wood-pulping activity.

With his usual flair for projecting new ideas, he quickly obtained the necessary backing to set up the necessary works and equipment. The Sault Ste Marie Pulp and Paper Company was formed, and using red sandstone excavated from the locks and canals, handsome buildings were erected on land adjacent to the Rapids.

The pulp mill began operation in 1896. It was one of the largest in the world, and in common with practice everywhere else at that time, it produced what was termed wet pulp, containing 50 to 55 per cent water. The extent of Clergue's production at the Soo began to hit older firms in the business and his competitors countered by lowering their prices by 25 per cent. Clergue naturally looked to means of reducing his own costs, and came up against one of the established features of the wood pulp trade, that the buyer paid only for the dry content in any consignment. The manufacturer had to pay freight charges for the water content. Clergue set about designing a machine that would extract the water from the pulp, but could get no paper machinery manufacturer, either in the USA or Canada, to make it. One and all declared that it was quite impracticable. Clergue sensed quickly enough that there were vested interests as well as prejudice behind this attitude, and in his usual spontaneous way decided to make the machine himself, and he set up a separate machine shop and foundry at the Soo to do it. At the same time of course he built the new establishment large enough to cope with other general engineering work as well. The chain reaction was working smoothly and producing profitable results, and it was soon to lead him farther afield.

To improve the quality of his wood pulp product, and to enable him to compete in wider and still more profitable markets, he came to considering sulphite pulp. This idea arose from observing operations at the nickel-ore mines at Sudbury. Sulphur dioxide was a waste product of the operation of roasting the ore, and this could be used for making sulphuric acid, which was needed for the production of sulphite pulp. He approached the Canadian Copper Company to try and arrange for purchase of their waste sulphur, and when they refused, he promptly bought two nickel deposits of his own, near Sudbury, to provide the sulphur he needed. His involvement in the nickel business was at first no more than incidental, but in his own expansionist style he set up a large chemical laboratory at the Soo, primarily to produce sulphuric acid, but which afterwards became invaluable in later projects. The nickel mines near Sudbury, which he named *Gertrude* and *Elsie*, after two of his sisters, were the reason for one of his involvements in railways. It was not quite the first in point of time, but it is convenient to mention it at this stage. In 1888 a charter had been granted to a so-called Manitoulin and North Shore Railway Company, which had been planned originally to connect Manitoulin Island with the mainland, and up to the time when Clergue arrived at the Soo, its charter had been extended to authorize a northward connection to join the Canadian Pacific main line at Sudbury. Clergue realized that this was just the outlet he needed from the Gertrude and Elsie mines, to bring the ores to the coast, whence they could be shipped to the Soo. In 1900 however he obtained a new Dominion of Canada charter, not only to construct the line from Sudbury to Little Current, on the mainland opposite to Manitoulin Island, but to cross the island, and then operate a ferry service across Georgian Bay to Tobermory. From there he hoped to arrange a service, independent of the Canadian Pacific Railway, into Toronto. The section actually built and operated, from Sudbury to Little Current, later became the Algoma Eastern Railway.

2   Location of the Helen Mine

Construction on the Manitoulin and North Shore began in 1900, but three years before that had come the discovery that transformed the whole set-up at the Soo. Logging activity to provide raw material for the pulp mills was proceeding in its quiet and traditional way, and although Clergue had more than once cast eyes toward the far north and the activities of the Hudson's Bay Company, nothing had so far transpired to set another chain reaction going toward better transport to the north. The country was extremely rugged, densely wooded, and virtually devoid of population. The main line of the Canadian Pacific Railway ran northwestward at first from Sudbury along a route hacked out of truly virgin country. There were adventurers always on the look out for gold, and one such, an Indian, Ben Boyer by name, was prospecting in the region of Michipicoten, in 1897, when he came upon something unusual. In his own words, told to the newspaper *Sault Star* sometime later, he said:

> I was on top of what seemed to be a mountain. Across the lake was a swath of brownish red that ran from the water's edge to the top of the cliff . . . I had found a vein 300 ft wide, and 100 ft high from the water edge.

Not having any money to exploit his discovery, Boyer cut a lump of the ore, took it to the Soo, and showed it to Clergue. Realizing that they might be on the track of a most valuable deposit, he sent one of his brothers, Ernest V Clergue, to examine what Ben Boyer had found, and in 1898 the deposit was purchased. It was named the *Helen* mine, after yet another of Clergue's sisters, and proved one of the largest that had then been discovered in Canada. Its discovery gave an added impetus to early ideas of a railway to Hudson's Bay, because although the Helen mine was relatively close to Michipicoten harbor, and the ore could be shipped thence to the Soo, this was an operation that could be done only in the summer, when Lake Superior was not frozen over. Furthermore, although I have referred to Michipicoten as a 'harbor', it was then little more than a landing for canoes, and those characteristic flat-bottomed boats used on the Great Lakes known as 'scows'. A railway was essential, and on 11 August 1899, under a Dominion charter, the Algoma Central Railway Company was incorporated. It was conceived as a feeder service, to the various industries developing at the Soo, to haul pulpwood and pine logs to the pulp company and to convey iron ore from the Helen mine. Construction began later in 1899 at two points, firstly northward from the Soo itself, and secondly from Michipicoten to the Helen mine. For this latter all materials, rolling stock and men had been transported to Michipicoten by boat and scow from the Soo.

Although projected to run roughly north and south mainly through the rock, swamp, and lake country of the Canadian shield, and although not expected to aid colonization to any extent, both the Dominion and Ontario governments assisted by way of land grants. To Clergue himself the possibilities of this railway were limitless. He conceived the idea of conveying fresh fish from Arctic waters to the cities of the USA, and having done so, in the customary chain reaction from his enthusiasm,

Plate 1 Aerial view showing, center, the Abitibi Paper mills, left foreground, the power station (across the river) of the Great Lakes Power Company, the International Highway bridge to the USA, spanning the entire picture, and, upper right, part of the Algoma Steel Corporation plant

Plate 2   PIONEER DAYS
ON THE LINE

a   Transport by canoe

b   A camp community

c   Womenfolk inspecting
track formation

Plate 3 SKILL IN TRESTLING

a A bridge at Mile 70

b A typical example of a sharply curved viaduct

PLATE 4   THE FIRST LOCOMOTIVES AT WORK

a   Engine No 1 on a construction train

b   Engine No 3 on one of the original trestles

Plate 5   EARLY DAYS IN THE ALGOMA STEEL CORPORATION

a   The railway yards at Steelton showing the old locomotive roundhouse in the left foreground

b   A view in the first rail mill of the Steel Company

Plate 6
VINTAGE
STEAM
LOCOMOTIVES

a   4–6–0 No 1 bought for $2800 in September 1899

b   0–6–0 No 19: one of two switchers bought new from the Canadian Locomotive Co in 1902

c   4–8–0 No 26: one of two bought in 1903 from the Iron Range and Huron Bay Railway

d   2–8–0 No 30: one of Class 'C2' purchased new from the Montreal Locomotive Works in 1911

Plate 7   MICHIPICOTEN HARBOR—THE BEGINNINGS

a   In 1900 the dock facilities shown above were in use at Michipicoten Harbor. Twelve timber hopper-type loading bins handled the ore into vessels, through the chutes shown. Upon later discovery and development of larger deposits of ore adjacent to the original Helen Mine, it became necessary for the railway to construct modern electrical power ore loading facilities in 1939

b   Panoramic view, showing the steamer *King Edward*, leaving on an early passenger run

Plate 8 SOME EARLY STEAMSHIPS

a The celebrated *Minnie M*

b The *King Edward*, built Hull, England, in 1902

c The *Leafield*, built Sunderland, England, in 1892

d The *Thomas J Drummond*, built in Scotland

Plate 9 STEAMSHIP LINE BROCHURE OF 1909

a Front cover, showing the *King Edward*

b Inland attractions!

a   Culvert under construction to enable trestle at Mile 67 to be filled in

b   Pile trestle at Mile 69, built partly in 1901 and finished in 1910

c   Round timber trestle at Mile 142

Plate 10
LINE IMPROVEMENTS

Plate 11
EFFECTS OF FLOODING

a   A bridge washed out and the rails left hanging

b   Damage to a trestle

c   A location completely destroyed and washed sideways into a river

Plate 12 OUT ON THE LINE

a Constructional days in country north of the Soo

b Aerial view of Brient, showing locomotive coaling plant, water tank and Y for turning locomotives

Plate 13   CONSTRUCTION IN THE WINTER

a   Laying excavation stakes for trestle foundations
    at Mile 104, with men up to their necks in snow

b   The snowy approach to a trestle

Plate 14   ROYAL TRAIN—IN 1920

a   The Prince of Wales on the rear platform of the business car at the Soo

b   The two 4–6–0 locomotives 104 and 103 polished and ready to haul the train

Plate 15   DEVELOPMENTS AT MICHIPICOTEN

a   A view in July 1929, showing new dock under construction

b   A wide aerial view showing one of the larger ships alongside the new dock, after the coal bridge had been installed. Dredging in progress in the outer harbor

Plate 16   MEN OF ALGOMA

a   Francis H Clergue

b   Sir James Dunn

c   E B Barber

d   Sir Denys Lowson, Bart

Plate 17   MONTREAL RIVER VIADUCT

a   One of the 4–6–0 locomotives, Class 'T1' with a 3-coach southbound passenger train

b   Photo taken from a northbound train in October 1950, hauled by 2–8–2 engine No 81

Plate 18   TRESTLES TO BE REPLACED—1917

a   Bent frame trestle at Mile 50, built 1901

b   Bent pile trestle at Mile 74, built 1902

Plate 21   FILLING IN THE TRESTLES

a   Train of special discharge cars in action

b   Loading the discharge cars

Plate 22   INSPECTION CARS—THEN AND NOW

a   The old style

b   The modern 'automobile'

Plate 23   LATER STEAM LOCOMOTIVES

a   No 100, a 4–6–0 from Canadian Locomotive Co, 1912

b   One of the two 'Santa Fe' type of 1929

c   No 60, 2–8–2 purchased from the Wabash in 1941

d   No 82, 2–8–2 purchased from the Minneapolis and St Louis, 1940

Plate 24   HAWK JUNCTION

a   The northbound passenger train arrives from the Soo, in 1950, hauled by 2–8–2 locomotive No 81

b   An aerial view, showing Hawk Lake, bottom left, the railway yards, engine house,
water tank, and the branch to Michipicoten, bearing away from the main line

Plate 25   MODERN MAINTENANCE EQUIPMENT

a   The tie-spacer in use

b   The ballast packer

Plate 26   MODERN FACILITIES AT THE SOO

a   Steelton yards, looking north: the ACR main line is seen leading leftward out of the
upper part of the picture; the Canadian Pacific is seen coming in on the far right, and
passing alongside the ACR yards

b   View looking south, with the ACR Steelton yards in the foreground and the Algoma
Steel Corporation plant at top left

Plate 27
STEELTON YARDS

Sand filling plant for
diesel locomotives

b A view of the yards showing trains of cars loaded with timber. The Algoma Steel
Mill in the background

Plate 28   FREIGHT WORKING IN WINTER

a   Maximum tonnage southbound freight passing Regent, hauled by three SD40 3000 hp locomotives. The rails in the passing track, on which the northbound freight was about to proceed are quite invisible

b   Scene during switching operations at Franz, where the CPR main line is crossed

Plate 29   FREIGHT WORKING IN WINTER

a   The line ahead near Frater

b   About to collect a train order, without stopping, at Frater

Plate 30   BLIZZARD CONDITIONS NORTH OF HAWK JUNCTION

a   The locomotives setting back on to the train, after switching operations at Franz

b   What the locomotives of 'No 7' looked like on arrival at Oba!

Plate 31   WINTER IN ALGOMA COUNTRY

a   A view of the rear part of 'No 7' taken from the leading unit, across one of the frozen lakes

b   A freight in the Agawa Canyon beside the completely frozen river

Plate 32 MULTI-HEADED FREIGHT TRAINS

a   Northbound load, hauled by four 'GP7' locomotives

b   A southbound ore train in majestic scenery: note the finely maintained modern track

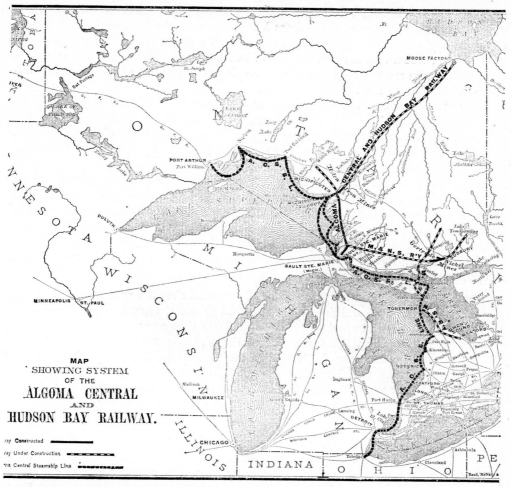

MAP
SHOWING SYSTEM
OF THE
ALGOMA CENTRAL
AND
HUDSON BAY RAILWAY.

~ay Constructed ▬▬▬▬▬

~ay Under Construction ▬ ▬ ▬ ▬

~a Central Steamship Line ●▬●▬●▬●▬●

3 A Railway Map of 1901, showing the optimistic forecast of the extent of the line. The section shown as actually constructed was not completed until many years later. Note also the projected connections to White River (CPR) and of the Manitoulin and North Shore

he changed the title to Algoma Central and Hudson Bay Railway, in 1901. Constructional progress was very slow. Inland from the Soo the country is very rugged and the hillsides so thickly clothed with trees that it must have been extremely difficult for a surveyor to lay his sights on any points very far ahead. Furthermore the ancient rock forming the crust of the shield is intensely hard, and in aligning and

B

levelling the route, much toilsome and expensive cutting work was involved. It was no less difficult on the branch from Michipicoten to the Helen mine. There was no 'skimping' of the work, and Clergue built on the grand scale. At the branch line terminus an excellent harbor was constructed with 4000 ft of wharfage. The syndicate soon had sixteen steamships in service conveying the products of the various enterprises at the Soo to the lower lake ports.

At this stage however the Algoma Central Railway was far from the largest of the Clergue enterprises. The Helen mine became the largest iron ore producer of the day in Canada. The discoverer of the deposit had no notion of its enormous size. By 1900 it was known that it contained four million tons of ore, but later that same year the estimate was increased to thirty millions. The chain reaction process continued. With abundant water power available at the Soo the next step was the establishment, in 1901, of the Algoma Iron, Nickel and Steel Company of Canada. With nickel available from the Gertrude and Elsie mines near Sudbury, Clergue was in a position now to produce high-grade alloy steels. The inauguration of steel production at the Soo was made a gala public occasion. It took place on 18 February 1902, and in describing how the first heat of steel was blown in the Bessemer converter, a reporter of the *Sault Star* wrote:

> The crowd cheered the spectacle. . . . The vessel shot the sparks up to the top of the building and they fell in beautiful showers, a great sparkling curtain. Gradually the sparks gave way to flame that grew whiter with the minutes. In a little while the loudly roaring fire was too white to look at. Then the blower knew the 'cook' in the vessel was done, was cleansed enough to pour. . . . Now it was steel. The first steel ingot ever cast in Ontario began to pour. The crowd cheered again. You may wonder at the crowd, but the sights were enough to move a cigar store Indian to enthusiasm.

Soon that plant was producing a 7 per cent nickel steel, but that was actually too high a nickel content for most requirements. An important contract for nickel steel armour plate was obtained from the famous German armaments firm of Krupp, and they required no more than $3\frac{1}{2}$ per cent nickel. This was the content that later came into considerable use for locomotive coupling rods, connecting rods, and valve gear members. The first rails rolled in Canada were produced at the Soo in May 1902, but according to contemporary reports they were not satisfactory at first. The use of indigenous raw materials was a prime feature in the design of the first two blast furnaces. It was originally intended that they should be fired with charcoal, using timber from the spruce forests on land owned by the Lake Superior Corporation. But this also did not prove satisfactory and they were later fired with coke. The 'Clergue Empire' did not include any coal measures, and so this had to be imported from mines in Pennsylvania. Nevertheless the transport was arranged very economically. The Helen mine was producing far more iron ore than could be used

34

at the Soo, and the surplus was exported in Clergue's own ships to ports on Lake Erie. These ships brought back coal for the blast furnaces as a return load.

Brilliant though all this development undoubtedly was, it had to withstand much criticism, not least from the Conservative opposition to the Liberal Government then in power in Ontario. In 1900 this Government had extended a land grant to the Algoma Central Railway, that included mineral and timber rights, and amounted to 7400 acres for every mile of railway. Except in one respect the requirements of the Government were lenient, because most of them were already fulfilled by Clergue's existing activities at the Soo. The difficult point was that in return for the land grant the railway company was required to bring into the district 1000 new settlers a year, for ten years. The opposition leader in the Ontario Parliament was emphatic that this railway was not likely to promote colonization, though his view was not widely shared at the time. More optimistic forecasts expected that the activities at the Soo would quickly populate what was then termed 'New Ontario', and set up profitable farming along the line of the railway to where it was intended to connect up with the Canadian Pacific in the Missanabie region. But while the construction of the railway brought in a large number of men, at times as many as 4000, few of these remained after the railway was in operation. Worse than this, intermediate traffic in the Algoma wilderness was at first practically non-existent, and the cost and practical difficulties of construction made progress very slow. The railway was not the only part of the Clergue 'Empire' that was not working out according to plan.

To appreciate the extent of the activities he had started in the six years since his first arrival at the Soo, it is interesting to recall the names of the twelve companies that were actually operating, or at an advanced stage of organization by the end of 1900, under the all-embracing aegis of the 'Consolidated Lake Superior Corporation':

Lake Superior Power Company
Sault Ste Marie Pulp and Paper Company
Tagona Water and Light Company
Algoma Commercial Company
Algoma Central and Hudson Bay Railway
Algoma Central Steamship Lines
Manitoulin and North Shore Railway (later the Algoma Eastern)
Algoma Iron Works
Algoma Steel Company
International Transit Company*
Michigan Lake Superior Power Company
Trans St Mary Traction Company

* This operated the street-car service on the Canadian side and the ferry service between the two Soos.

In connection with the foregoing footnote I should explain that by the year 1900 a sizeable town, also with the name of Sault Ste Marie, was growing up on the American side of the St Mary's River. It is indeed no wonder that a man who had built up such a complex of industry was referred to as 'the greatest industrial miracle-maker on the continent', and as 'the Cecil Rhodes of Canada'. There was however more than a happy turn of phrase in comparing Francis Hector Clergue to Cecil Rhodes. Both in their different ways had a vast vision of empire, and both headed into personal disaster through overreaching themselves.

Clergue's outstanding talents lay in the field of promotion, invention, and development of natural resources; but although he had a keen enough eye for what was likely to make good business, he seems to have had little thought for the details of hard consolidation, once the enterprise was in its first operation. The meteoric rise of his 'empire' at the Soo attracted the widest attention throughout North America, and he obtained subsidies and guarantees from the Dominion Government. But one particular episode shows clearly his lack of hard business acumen. The construction of the rail mill was a pioneer move that should have put him in a commanding position for many years, and in 1900 the government placed a contract with the Algoma Steel Company for 125,000 high quality nickel steel rails, delivery to be made at 25,000 each year for five years. But it was agreed that the price was to be fixed by the prevailing market price *in England*. How Clergue came to accept such an arrangement is indeed hard to understand. First of all no nickel steel rails were then in ordinary main line service on the British railways, and the English market price for rails was likely to be basically lower than the sophisticated product of the Soo. Furthermore the prices were fixed for a year, regardless of market trends, and at the very beginning of the contract in 1900, the price of steel rails fell from $35 per ton, to $26 within six months. To make matters worse, Clergue had taken the contract before the plant was fully operable, and he was not able to begin regular deliveries until the middle of 1904.

Before that however the whole financial edifice of the Consolidated Lake Superior Corporation had collapsed. The year 1902 saw the zenith of its prosperity. It was Clergue's policy to see that each new industry contributed to the success of the others. For a man trained as a lawyer he had an astonishing flair for surmounting technical difficulties in all his various companies; but there was one overriding consideration behind each new development. He might invent, and devise, but to carry out these innovations more and more capital was needed. It was all very well to utilize, and even to market every by-product of the factories, but such projects required expensive machinery, and still more capital to install it. The situation rapidly being attained was that all the companies within the Corporation were very busy selling to each other, but not selling anything like enough to the outside world to sustain the enormous capital investment involved. Nevertheless there was a fine facade of prosperity in the Soo. The construction of new factories in the tremendously hard sandstone excavated from the canals, the building of locks and railways had transformed the entire appearance of the area. No longer was there a river rushing

36

over the rapids between dense forests. On both banks of the St Mary's River there were all the outward signs of a very prosperous industrial empire.

Though by the year 1903 there must have been many among Clergue's closest associates who were beginning to waver in their enthusiasm, all seemed well among his enormous work force until the falling off of orders for steel led to the closing down of some of the factories. This was the first shock. Up till the year 1901 most of the financial support had come from wealthy investors in Philadelphia, but with alarming suddenness there developed a recession in confidence in this city, and Clergue had to look elsewhere for support. He negotiated a loan of $5 million from Speyer and Company, of New York. Then came a serious set-back at the rail mill. Some rails supplied to the Canadian Northern proved to be unsatisfactory and the astute partners in that railway, Messrs MacKenzie and Mann, cancelled their orders with the Algoma Steel Works, and bought instead, at a very low price, rails that had been dumped in Canada by a German manufacturer. The Algoma Steel Works had to close down, but far worse than this, the Corporation as a whole found itself completely without funds, not only to pay off the loan to Speyer and Company but to pay the wages at the factories that were still working. The lumberjacks employed in the forests, felling trees for the pulp, were kept waiting for their wages, long after the time when payment was due. The situation both in the Soo itself and in the outer areas was becoming explosive.

At that time the labor force was not organized into trade unions, but the Canadian lumberjack was not a workman to be trifled with, or to be fobbed off with promises; they were kept in the bush camps until supplies were exhausted, and then they were brought into the Soo. They were in an ugly mood, and quickly joined forces with the more violent of the workmen who had been thrown out of employment by the closing of the factories. Real trouble began on 28 September 1903, when a combined force of lumberjacks and town workmen numbering about 1300 marched to the head offices of the Corporation to demand their wages. They found only locked doors, with a notice posted that the Corporation was unable to pay them. What had begun as no more than a strong and very justified protest soon turned to unleashed fury. Those 1300 workmen became a riot mob. They smashed every window within reach; doors were broken down, office staff were driven up to the first floor, missiles came crashing in through the broken windows, and it is difficult to say what might have happened to the staff had not one or two of them had rifles on hand, and fired some warning shots. Realizing they could make no further headway at the offices, the rioting spread to the town. The river ferry was threatened, and when an order went out to close the bars, whisky was brought over from the American side of the St Mary River in rowing boats. The local militia was called out, but could make little impression, and it was only when a force of regular soldiers from Toronto was brought upon the scene that order was finally restored.

The riot, alarming though it was, and called a 'disgrace' by financial interests remote from the Soo, was no more than a slight incident against the magnitude of

37

the general collapse. The Government of Ontario, and indeed of the whole Dominion, could not stand aside. A total of some 7000 voting Canadians were employed in the various subsidiaries of the Consolidated Lake Superior Corporation; these could not be abandoned, any more than could the magnificent power plants and manufacturing facilities that represented so much capital investment. Its producing capacity was a national asset that could not be allowed to fall into decay. The Algoma Central Railway had been laid for no more than 56 miles north from the Soo, also for 15 miles from Michipicoten to the Helen mine, and for a further 5 miles to a second iron ore mine, the Josephine. Its prime object was quite unfulfilled, and there was no money to proceed any farther. The route had been surveyed over the intervening 114 miles necessary to complete the line from the Soo to Michipicoten, but all work came to a halt with the financial crash of 1903. The railway was then in operation as a logging road between Mile 56 and the Soo, and carrying ore from the mines to Michipicoten Harbor, and that was all. The railway, together with all other companies in the Consolidated Lake Superior Corporation, went into liquidation. The Dominion Government stepped in with a loan of $2 million to settle unpaid wages, and other pressing obligations, and then the painful process of reorganization was commenced. Clergue passed from the scene, and so far as the Algoma Central Railway was concerned, the Lake Superior Corporation became the holding company, owning all the capital, amounting to $6,750,000 bonds and $10 million stock. The situation remained stagnant from 1903 until 1909; but in the latter year certain London financiers became interested, and a more forward-looking reorganization of the many activities at the Soo began. The effect on the railway was profound, because plans were then made to provide capital not merely to fill in the unfinished link, but to carry the main line northward to a junction with the National Transcontinental Railway, then under construction. At this stage it is time to leave the wider ramifications of the one-time 'Clergue empire', and concentrate upon the early history of the railway itself.

CHAPTER THREE

On the Line—Early Days

It was a wild and untamed country through which the pioneers of the Algoma Central Railway hacked their way to the north. If it had been simply a case of connecting the Helen and Josephine mines with the Soo, one can imagine that the easiest way would have been to go round the coast. There would probably have been some tough work in rock cutting, as the Canadian Pacific had found on the north shore of Lake Superior, west of Heron Bay, and some sharp intermediate gradients; but as it was, the Algoma Central climbed over 300 ft before it was 5 miles out of the Soo. However much its critics might decry this feature of its origin, the railway was intended as a colonizing catalyst, and the location of the land grants approved by Statute of the Ontario Government in 1900 show clearly what was expected in this way. The allocation amounted to 7400 acres per mile of line built, amounting to 1,632,632 acres. The preamble to the original Act of 1900 included these words:

> . . . and whereas such railway will run through a country not hitherto accessible for the purpose of habitation and its construction is rendered difficult and costly by reason of the nature of the territory to be traversed by it; and whereas, owing to the undeveloped character of the country through which it will pass, the traffic of the railway for some time to come will be limited to carrying timber and mineral ores and will not be of sufficient value to produce a revenue on the capital invested therein, and whereas the said territory, though rich in natural resources, cannot be made available to the people of the Province, or to new settlers without the facilities for transportation provided by a railway . . .

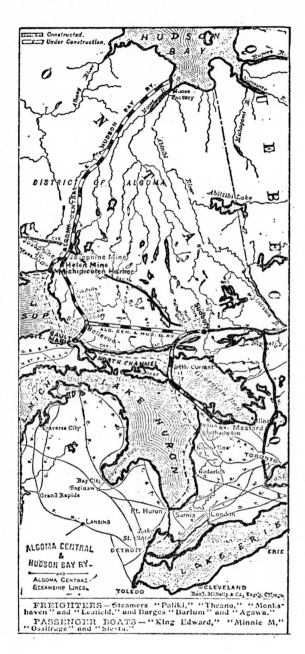

4 Another curious map of 1905 showing a different projected route to Hudson Bay

This, indeed, was putting the situation mildly. Today one has to travel by air over this territory to appreciate something of its extraordinary nature: covered with dense forest; studded with innumerable lakes, large and small, intersected and linked up by rivers, that were so many turbulent mountain torrents. But there was no such thing as aerial reconnaissance in 1900, let alone the facilities that now exist for accurate aerial survey. At first the waterways were the only means of penetrating this region, and it was by canoe, hard step by hard step, that the pioneers probed their way into the interior. They braved storms on the larger lakes, negotiated numerous rapids on the mountain rivers, and carried their crafts by manual portage where they could not be navigated. Moreover the country did not follow ordered layout of mountain ranges; it was a mad jumble of intensely hard rocks, with their lower slopes so clothed with trees that one could scarcely see where there were clefts, to make a possible track for a railway. At the same time those back at the Soo were constantly urging for completion, while at the same time stressing the need for a route of minimum constructional costs. And with these strictures, added to the difficulties of the country itself, it is not surprising that the surveys were done less thoroughly than was desirable; curves and gradients were severe, to avoid excessive cutting and embankment work, and when it came to actually laying the track, it certainly had the character of a logging road, rather than of a potential main line. It was suggested that the AC&HBR stood for All Curves and High Bridges Railway.

By the year 1903, when the financial collapse of the Clergue 'empire' occurred, the railway from the Soo had reached Mile 56. It is a vivid reflection upon the nature of the intervening country, and of the twists and turns the line had to take to make a way through it that 'end of steel' was only 42 miles from the Soo, as the crow flies. It was not that any great deviations to left or right of the direct line were concerned; it was just a continuous series of 'wriggles', with the altitude above the level of Lake Superior see-sawing up and down between 469 ft at Heyden, 178 ft at Searchmont, 510 ft at Achigan, 625 ft at Ogidaki, 541 ft at Mashkode and up to 851 ft. at Mekatina, just before which the line had entered into the Land Grant area containing the temporary terminus. I may add that the water level in Lake Superior is 602 ft above sea level, so that at Mekatina the line was at the considerable altitude of 1453 ft. In the meantime Clergue was as optimistic over colonization as he was over all his other enterprises. In 1902 he said: 'The settlers are rushing in as fast as we can get lots opened up for them. These settlers are coming mainly from the older provinces, the States, and the British Isles. Scandinavians, of whom much was expected, have not appeared in large numbers yet'.

Even in the Soo however there were some inclined to poke sly fun at Clergue's enthusiasm, and a writer in the newspaper *Sault Star* suggested that some of the station names along the railway, such as Ogidaki, Mashkode, and Mekatina, were 'devised by a Welshman who talks Russian with the Aberdeen inflection', and that they were 'primarily designed to keep the coming Scandinavians at home', adding

P. & T. No. 11.

Cancelling

P. & T. No. 8 and Supplements.

THE ALGOMA CENTRAL AND HUDSON BAY RAILWAY COMPANY.

LOCAL PASSENGER TARIFF

BETWEEN

STATIONS ON MAIN LINE.

EFFECTIVE SEPTEMBER 10th, 1901

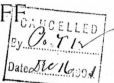

CANCELLED
By Co. T. N.
Date Dec 16 1904

BETWEEN	SAULT STE. MARIE, ONT.	TAGONA	BRICK YARD	ROOT RIVER	GRANITE QUARRY	AWERES	HEYDEN	ISLAND LAKE	VANKOUGHNET	BELLEVUE	WILDE	GOULAIS	WABOOSE
Sault Ste. Marie, Ont......													
Tagona........	.05												
Brick Yard.....	.10	.05											
Root River....	.40	.35	.30										
Granite Quarry	.45	.40	.35	.10									
Aweres........	.60	.55	.50	.20	.15								
Heyden.......	.65	.60	.55	.25	.20	.10							
Island Lake....	.80	.75	.70	.40	.35	.20	.15						
VanKoughnet..	.90	.85	.80	.50	.45	.30	.25	.10					
Bellevue.......	.95	.90	.85	.55	.50	.35	.30	.15	.10				
Wilde.........	1.20	1.15	1.10	.80	.75	.60	.55	.40	.30	.25			
Goulais........	1.55	1.50	1.45	1.15	1.10	.95	.90	.75	.65	.60	.35		
Waboose	1.80	1.75	1.70	1.40	1.35	1.20	1.15	1.00	.90	.85	.60	.25	
Achigan........	2.15	2.10	2.05	1.75	1.70	1.55	1.50	1.35	1.25	1.20	.95	.60	.35

AND

Children five years of age and under carried free when accompanied by an adult.
Children over five and under twelve years of age to be charged half fare.

150 lbs of baggage allowed on each full fare ticket.

75 lbs of baggage allowed on each half fare ticket.

Excess baggage to be charged for at the rate of (20) twenty per cent of regular fare per 100 lbs. Minimum charge 25 cents.

W. B. ROSEVEAR,

General Traffic Manager.

Issued at
Sault Ste. Marie, Ont., Aug. 29, 1901.

that 'a man who can't recollect the name of the place he wants to go to, has other difficulties besides paying for his ticket'! Nevertheless some settlement was taking place, and it was reported in 1902 that at Gaudette township, north of Searchmont, there were 145 families settled on at least 100 farms.

Some ten years ago a very amusing story was published entitled *Railroading as She Was*, by J W Mills, and it is worth quoting in full. He wrote:

The fact that prior to, and to some extent after, the first world war the Algoma Central Railway was a sort of glorified toteroad catering to the requirements of the Bush Operations of the Paper Company, makes me feel justified in penning this narrative of happenings of fifty years or more ago when the term 'Pangis Turn' signified a round trip from Sault Ste Marie to Mile 68, then the 'end of the steel'.

The gentlemen rough-necks making up the crew were selected by a process of elimination for their ability as fistic performers, also on their capacity for hard liquor, and the handling thereof. This refers to the train crew only and not the engine crew who were considered to be much lower in the social scale and whose limited ability in reading signals sometimes produced results of a startling order. This did not affect their vocabulary, choice samples of which could be frequently overheard by the passengers as they conversed at long range with the rest of the train crew.

At the start of the trip in the Sault the women passengers were isolated in a separate coach at the rear of the train with lumberjacks in the front coaches. This arrangement provided some protection for the former as the only ones they had to fight off were members of the train crew, and clergy, the latter en route to the camps for the purpose of taking up collections for missionaries to be used in converting heathens in various unheard of parts of the world. It was, and is readily admitted that there is only one place for lumberjacks to go consequently religious services were deemed a waste of time.

The writer obtained status on the train crew through his proven ability to make three fast trips to Pete Sundstrom's bar in Searchmont and return with a water pail full of beer each trip, and still be on board when the train pulled out. This agility also assured free transportation.

At Ogidaki the baggageman had set up a barrel in the lake as a target for his .303 Savage, and did his shooting from the baggage car door while the train was in motion. The fact that the barrel was there ten years later is ample proof that Searchmont beer had its good points.

At Chippewa (Mile 51) there was a large tree under which lumberjacks waiting for the Southbound train, could rest in the shade. This tree served two purposes in that when the Northbound arrived from the Sault the returning camp personnel were carefully carried from the train to the tree and placed in the shady area, after all beverages had been removed from their person and luggage. On awakening they quite often decided it was the same day and that they had missed the dang-busted Southbound, and returned to camp. At the end of the month when looking over their pay checks they figured that the thieving pencil pusher had short-changed them several days, and accepted the situation as inevitable.

A strenuous effort was always made to get to the Company headquarters at Pangis prior to the noon meal time, usually with success and after lunch and just prior to departure time for the Southbound trip the cook was invited outside by one member of the crew to share in a drink, while the other members accumulated enough pastry for the trip to the Sault as well as for the next day. This required careful timing to ensure that the last drink was shared just before the train pulled out, and prior to the cook's return to the cookery.

In the early 1900's a woman was put on a pedestal and was treated as a fragile piece of humanity to be carefully approached, handled, and babied. This was borne out on one trip when the Southbound train loaded with passengers ground to a sudden complete stop upsetting the equilibrium of a few pails of berries and disturbing the tranquillity of two plump matrons who were in line at the door labelled 'Women'. Inquiries as to the stop and subsequent backing up revealed that the Conductor's current girl friend had put her head out the window and her hat had blown off. The Conductor, gentleman that he was, promptly pulled the emergency cord and after backing the train about five miles the hat was retrieved. The fact that it had blown under the train and a large stuffed bird, probably a pigeon, nestled in the crown as a decoration, looking as though it had run into a load of No. 6 shot, was neither here nor there.

Incidentally I would add that the method of handling women as described in the preceding paragraph did not apply to women on farms who enjoyed the same status as horses, except that instead of sleeping in a stall, they had the privilege of living in the farmhouse, eating oatmeal instead of oats.

A wonderful spring at the North end of the Bellvue trestle called for another stop while the engineer and fireman went for a drink, and smoke before continuing on to the Sault. This stop occurred on the Southbound trip only as an ample supply of beverages was available from the Sault as far North as Pangis.

Timetables were available but were used mostly for wrapping garbage from the caboose, and a table four or five years old was likely to be a better guide than one for the current year. Arrival and departure times were anybody's guess. Stops were unscheduled and frequent, and in some cases overlapped creating some confusion in the cab due to the

Algoma Central Railway Co.

Until further notice, trains of the Algoma Central Railway will arrive and depart daily, as follows:

MAIN LINE.

No. 1.	March 1st, 1901.	No. 2.
... p m lv.	Sault Ste. Marie Or... ...	7 30 p m
...5 p m "	.... Root River........	7 00 p m
... p m "	Granite Quarry..... "	6 50 p m
... 40 p m "	...... Awres.... "	6 35 p m
...5 p m "	.... Heyden, ... "	6 25 p m
2 20 p m "	.... "	6 05 p m
2 45 p m "	.... "	5 30 p m
3 00 p m ar.	.... Silver Creek	5 15 p m

Trains depart and arrive at Sault Ste. Marie Pulp and Paper Co. Terminal.

W. B. BOSEVEAR,
General Traffic Manager

engineer's idea that if he whistled for one stop, he would have to back up to whistle for the next.

There was no dining car, however, it was always possible to get a good feed of berries by walking alongside the train, or ahead of it, and getting back on board when it caught up.

Things have changed on the A.C. Ry. since the 1905's and in some instances an improvement can be noticed—however, in arriving at the present state of efficiency they have lost the glamor that made them attractive.

We of the old school are very fortunate in having memories of an era which will never return. It was damn poor business but it was fun.

It may be added that in 1901, Goulais, on the river opposite to Searchmont, was the limit of regular service, but by the spring of 1902 the 'Pangis Turn' was working. The 56-mile journey from the Soo was *scheduled* in five hours, but how long they actually took may be guessed at from Mills' story! After the peak year of 1902 there seems to have been a cut-back, for in 1903 regular passenger trains were running only to Trout Lake, and in 1904 after the financial crash at the Soo, passenger trains did not run beyond Ogidaki. As can be imagined the original equipment was not elaborate, and of the 13 locomotives with which the railway opened for business 11 had been bought up secondhand. Seven small 0–4–0 tender engines had been purchased from the Chicago, Burlington and Quincy, and 4 larger engines of the 4–6–0 type from the Lehigh Valley, but more detailed reference to the steam locomotive stock of the line is made in a later chapter. At this stage it may be added that 4 more locomotives of the 2–8–0 type were purchased from the Baldwin locomotive Company in 1902. One of these was a two-cylinder compound, and the other three, of similar general proportions, were two cylinder simples. The early stock was completed in 1903 by purchase from the Iron Range and Huron Bay Railway of two rather curious, and distinctly 'vintage' 4–8–0s.

On 23 May 1901, the name of the railway was changed to Algoma Central and Hudson Bay, and just before this was officially proclaimed, the Chief Engineer, W Z Earle, had despatched one of his staff, C F Hannington by name, to examine the country north, with a view of extending the line to Hudson Bay. At that time of course operation on the line had barely started, and the passenger service from the Sault extended at first only to Goulais, and then to Ogidaki, in the year 1901. Hannington's remit was to start at Missanabie, where the projected line of the Algoma Central was to cross the Canadian Pacific main line to the west, and then to work northward to Moose Factory, at the southernmost point of Hudson Bay, in the gulf known as James Bay. The log of Hannington's exploration begins on 13 May 1901, when he left the Sault to arrive at Missanabie on the following day. The distance, as the crow flies, is about 125 miles, so the difficulties of transport in the Algoma district can be well appreciated. Hannington reported:

Missanabie is a small village situated on Dog Lake, on the main line of the CPR; is made up of a Hudson's Bay Company store, railway station, post office, church, boarding house, and about a dozen dwelling houses, occupied for the most part by half breeds.

Dog Lake is about 20 miles by 12 miles wide, and it contains many islands. The shores are, as a rule, low rocky ridges running in all directions, many of them being mere mounds, and between these ridges are generally swamps or small lakes, all of which empty into Dog Lake and then south into Lake Superior. The timber around the lake has to a large extent been destroyed by fire and is of little value . . .

The extent to which the country was quite devoid of population must be emphasized. Hannington had no more than three settlements on which to base his expedition. These were the posts of the Hudson's Bay Company at Missanabie, on the Canadian Pacific main line, at New Brunswick House, at the northern end of Brunswick Lake, and at Moose Factory, on the island in the broadening estuary of the Moose River about 10 miles inland from where it debouches into James Bay. Hannington's itinerary led him over rough country from Missanabie to Brunswick, and then from the outlet of the lake to where the stream joined the Missinaibi River. This was then known as the Moose River, and he followed this right down to Moose Factory. Today, I might mention, it is only the lower part of this large river, from its confluence with the Mattagami, that is called 'Moose River'. The sketch map on page 48 shows the route taken, while at various points probes were made to right and left of the guiding water-course, examining the quality of the timber and the likelihood of mineral deposits. The total distance from Missanabie to Moose Factory by the route traveled was roughly 314 miles, but the explorer and his party, from leaving Missanabie to his return there four months later, traveled no less than 1530 miles—810 by lakes and rivers, and 720 by land portage. On the outward journey the party paused at no fewer than 37 camps, of which he could give names only to five. All the rest were, in 'the midst of nowhere', as the saying goes. The map takes the story of railway development in Northern Ontario considerably ahead of the time of which I am now writing, and shows that things did not work out quite as the men of the Algoma Central contemplated as far back as 1901. Then there was only one transcontinental railway in Canada, and the station of Missanabie, where there was a depot of the Hudson's Bay Company, was a natural starting point for the exploration. It was then assumed that this would be the intersecting place of the Algoma Central with the CPR. Reading between the lines of his report one can sense that Hannington was not very enthusiastic about the countryside, though he concluded that there would have been little difficulty in getting a good direct line from Missanabie to Moose Factory, 'without making it an expensive one to build . . .' to quote his own words. Of the only intermediate place on the route he wrote:

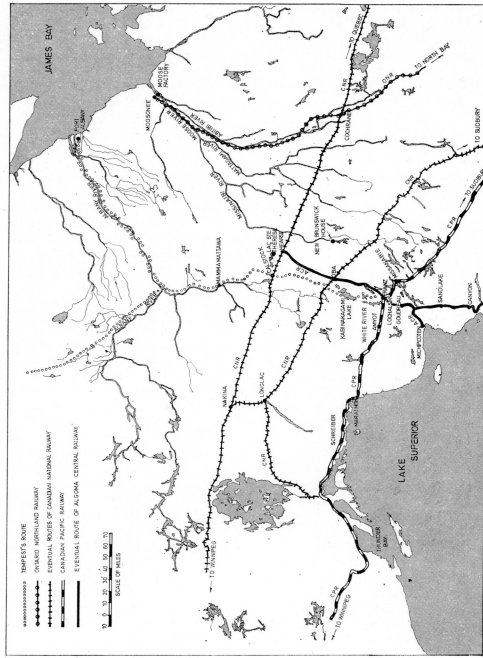

5 Explorations to Hudson Bay. At the times these were made by Hannington from Missanabie to Moose Factory and by Tempest from Lochalsh to Fort Albany and beyond, the lines of the CNR were not constructed, nor also was that of the Ontario Northland Railway

Coming down the west arm the route turns into the main Brunswick Lake at Fairy Point, but why it was so named, I cannot even guess, as it is simply a bare, rocky point, without any beauty whatever. Fairy Point is 23·9 miles from Missanabie by direct canoe route, and from this Point up east arm is 7 miles. I sent out two sick Indians from here, after having done my best to cure them, leaving the load to be picked up when the canoe returned. From this to Brunswick Lake Post at 36·6 miles the north shore has been swept by fire nearly the whole distance. There are clumps of good spruce and poplar here and there but these make a very small percentage of the whole. On the south side of the lake there is more green timber, and on both sides the country flattens out and the rocky ridges and mounds to a great extent disappear. At the Brunswick post of the Hudson's Bay Company, there is a fine garden in which are grown excellent vegetables, though corn as a rule is cut down by early frosts, before arriving at the green corn stage. Strange to say there are very few fish in Brunswick Lake, though Crooked Lake is good in that way so far as pickeral and pike are concerned. There are about 100 Indians at this Post but no houses except those belonging to the Hudson's Bay Company. These Indians live by hunting and fishing and leave the Post about the end of August, to be gone until spring, when they return with their furs. The country is burnt in most places from one to three miles inland, but there are some places where good timber is to be found. The general level of the country is from twenty to forty feet above the lake and after rising to that elevation there are only slight dips to some muskeg or stream, and arise again on the other side. I do not think there are any high summits between any of the streams from here on and the country is an easy one for railway work.

There is a further fascinating sidelight upon the country to east and west of the Missinaibi River in one passage from Hannington's report:

On Monday, 10 June, I made an examination of the Chegokwitaugen River for 16 miles and found it good valley, a flat country covered with very good spruce and a few pine, with a rapid river in many places. Game is very plentiful on this stream. I shot a yearling caribou and an otter. Numerous tracks of moose and caribou (but no beaver) are abundant. The caribou was large enough to give us a supply of fresh meat, without its being wasted and it was very good. I turned back from this exploration on account of log jams, several of which I cut through, but the last was too formidable.

Then again he writes:

From Camp No. 12 I explored the Ozuskotassie River for 14 miles and found it a rapid stream, well timbered along the banks, and for a distance back of from ½ to 1½ miles. From top of ridge the country is nearly level, rising very gradually through a beautiful farming country until the muskeg is reached. Every river in the country is the same, timbered along the banks and for some distance back, then muskeg which is moss, muck and clay upon which a few stunted spruce and tamarac grow. Following on across this muskeg if you strike another belt of timber, you may be sure you are approaching another stream which has drained part of the muskeg and allowed timber to grow. Gooseberries and currants, honeysuckles, clematis and roses grow in great profusion.

The place names have a way of repeating themselves, and when earlier explorations moved the names were transferred to the new localities. Some time after leaving the Hudson's Bay Company post at New Brunswick, he came to Old Brunswick, of which he wrote:

The greater part of the timber on the shores of Old Brunswick Lake was burnt years ago, and they are now covered with a growth of small poplar and spruce. There is some good spruce at the western end or side of this lake, but it is not very valuable so far as I could see. The country is flat and the line from Missanabie to Moose Factory would strike here from the west arm of Missanabie Lake without any difficulty. This Lake is full of pickeral and pike, but no trout. The old Post is deserted and burnt down and the site is a wilderness of raspberry bushes and weeds. The only thing left standing is one chimney, which the swallows have taken possession of and seem to enjoy. Following down Brunswick River, I came across two moose feeding upon the grass along the edge of the river; they were not afraid and their confidence was not misplaced. One was the largest moose I ever saw, the other also large, but not monster.

Toward the northern end of the survey Hannington reported:

From Camp No. 29 at the 224th mile to Camp No. 30 at the 234th mile, the condition of things along Moose River is bad, there being only 2 miles in 10 not burning, and I have no doubt the whole country will be destroyed unless we have rain, which seems unlikely. At the 229th mile is a new Hudson's Bay Company Post which is kept open and managed by Moose Factory from fall until spring. At this point the muskeg is 550 feet away on west side and 1800 feet on east and the timber was very good up to this muskeg, though it has since been burned. Between Camps 30 and 31 there is a great deal of fire. The muskeg closes in and at the 239th mile commences immediately on top of bank 95 feet high, on east side and runs back for miles. At Camp No. 31 it is 1800 feet to muskeg on the east side at an elevation of 65 feet above River. This is at Strong Rapids, why so called I do not know, as in most parts of it there is not enough water to float a canoe.

Camp No. 32 is at the 251st mile, and there is good spruce and poplar along River to this point. 600 feet to 2000 feet is the muskeg. There are fires raging in many places and I fancy the whole belt of timber will be destroyed. The River is worse and worse, more and more shallow. General level of country at 261st mile is 70 feet above river.

Camp No. 33 is at the mouth of Matawgami River which enters from east at 265th mile and is a very large deep stream, larger a great deal, in every way, than the Moose, which we have been following. Splendid spruce and poplar along the Moose to this point. Banks are 25 feet above River and gradually rise to 90 feet in one mile; 1½ miles to muskeg on west side and 1500 feet on east. The soil is excellent and the red currants growing wild are equal to any I ever saw cultivated. I examined the Matawgami River for nearly 20 miles and found very little timber, the greater part having been burned, but it is a fine agricultural country for the entire distance. This river averages 700 feet in width and is not so swift as the Moose has been. In the 20 miles traveled we paddled up stream 7 miles, which was a novelty after so much poling. I believe, however, there are some bad rapids further up and one 5 mile portage, otherwise the easier canoe route would be from Chapleau down the Chapleau River to its junction with Matawgami and so on to the Moose.

When he finally arrived at Moose Factory, and was made very welcome by the Hudson's Bay Company's men, Hannington extended his survey considerably to seek out likely traffics for the railway, if it was ever built, and was surprised to find that some fairly obvious sources of revenue seemed to be completely neglected. It is astonishing to recall also that the sole means of communication with the outer world was a ship that arrived *once a year* from England! Hannington reported:

There are vast quantities of silt being brought down the Moose River from the Abbitibi, which is very muddy, so muddy in fact, that one cannot see the bottom even in the shallowest water. Bars are constantly being formed under existing circumstances, but of course if the water could be confined to one channel, this trouble would be materially lessened. The ship which arrives annually in August from England bringing yearly supplies to Hudson's Bay Posts around the bay, (of which Moose Factory is the headquarters) lies 21 miles out where there is 30 feet of water, until partly unloaded, when she moves in to the outer bar where her unloading is completed. At the outer roads where there is no shelter of any kind, and the ship is in constant danger of being cast away and broken up by wind storms; this being so much the case that the Hudson's Bay Company now intend to make a supply depot on Charleton Island, 44 miles from the outer roads and 65 miles from Moose Factory. This island is from 25 to 30 miles long and affords safe protection from wind and storm, and from here the different posts, Moose Factory, Albany, Ruperts, Hannah Bay and so on, will be supplied by a small steamer of light draught (probably a stern wheeler) able to navigate these shallow waters. The Hudson's Bay people tell me there is no harbor at Albany on the West, but Hannah Bay to the east is far superior to Moose Factory in that way, and that Rupert House at the north of the Ruperts River is the best of all and can be made a good harbor at slight expense.

There are whales and seals in James Bay, and outside of these the Hudson's Bay Company know nothing of what can be caught in these waters. They have been established since 1670 and have not yet tried for codfish, though there are banks in the Bay similar to those off the coast of Newfoundland and there is no reason why these fish should not abound. The shores of James Bay are flat and marshy as a rule, and vast numbers of wild fowl are to be had. One of the staple articles of diet is salted wild goose, large quantities are laid down in Autumn for winter use. There is a church at Moose factory under the charge of Bishop Newnham, called Moosonee, also school house, Bishop's Court and so on. There are about 500 Indians at this post, all of whom belong to the church of England. The annual ship was daily expected while I was at Moose, but I left before her arrival, in fact, as it turned out the day before.

As it happened it was the Ontario Northland Railway, and not the Algoma Central that eventually laid their tracks into Moosonee, and when I went there in 1972 it still bore the air of a remote outpost, with no land communication except by rail. One can smile however at the concluding sentence of Hannington's report:

> The trip was most tiresome and monotonous and as I said before I was more than glad to see the main line of the CPR again!

The financial difficulties of the Clergue syndicate, and the ultimate collapse of the entire edifice in 1903 not only postponed indefinitely any prospects of fulfilment of the '. . . and Hudson Bay' part of the railway's title, but brought to a halt completion even of the line between the Sault and Michipicoten Harbor. Gone was Francis Clergue's dream of running nightly fish trains from Hudson Bay over the international bridge at the Sault to Minneapolis and Chicago. In the difficult years from 1903 to 1908 additional track was laid to bring the 'end of steel' from Mile 56 to Mile 68, but no other work was done north of that point. In the meantime the railway situation so far as transcontinental lines was changing. In 1905 work had begun on the construction of the National Transcontinental Railway—1800 miles of single-tracked road through virgin country then devoid of all trade, agriculture and industry, from Moncton, New Brunswick, through Quebec, and thence in a straight line westward to Winnipeg. This new railway, which was being projected with great enthusiasm, ran athwart any line that the Algoma Central might

TIMETABLES 1901 and 1905

| TRAIN No 1 | | | Miles | TRAIN No 2 | |
1901	1905			1901	1905
9.00 am	9.00	SAULT STE MARIE	0	6.30	6.50
9.05	9.03	Tagona	1	6.22	6.45
9.25	9.19	Root River	8	6.08	6.28
9.32	9.22	Granite Quarry	10	6.05	6.26
9.45	9.27	Aweres	12	6.00	6.20
9.50	9.29	Heyden	13	5.58	6.18
10.08	9.34	Island Lake	16	5.47	6.11
10.09	9.39	Vankoughnet	18	5.41	6.05
10.11	9.44	Bellevue	19	5.39	6.00
10.28	9.57	Wilde	24	5.26	5.47
10.41	10.06	Silver Creek	28	5.13	5.33
11.05	10.16	Searchmont*	31	5.00	5.23
11.45	10.30	Wabos	36	4.08	5.14
12.15 pm	10.46	Achigan	41	3.40	4.56
1.0	11.10	Ogidaki	48	3.15	4.35
	11.50	TROUT LAKE	56		4.00

* In 1901 known as Goulais
Note 1901 details taken from the *Sault Star* of 28 November 1901

have built in order to reach Hudson Bay; and when active measures began in 1909 to complete the Algoma Central, the traffic possibilities that might develop from connection with the National Transcontinental were very much to the fore. Before referring to the important further surveys of 1911–12 however, the circumstances in which the management of the Algoma Central were changed must be explained, in the following chapter.

Sault Ste. Marie, Ont, Aug 15/07

CIRCULAR P– 7– 16

TO AGENTS

BERRY PICKER'S EXCURSION will be run from Sault Ste Marie to Trout Lake and return, on Tuesday Aug. 20th., Thursday Aug. 22nd, and Saturday Aug. 24th, at the following rates:—

ALL STATIONS Sault Ste Marie to Searchlight, inclusive, 50 cents round trip.

ALL STATIONS Searchmont to Trout Lake inclusive, $1.00 round trip.

Use regular Excursion tickets form S. E. and Ex. 1.

T. J. Kennedy
Traffic Manager

CHAPTER FOUR

The Years of Uncertainty

The financial collapse at the Sault in 1903 had naturally been a great shock to all those employed in the various Clergue enterprises, not least to those on the Algoma Central Railway. While manufacturing concerns are inevitably subject to the waxing and waning of trade, there was a tradition of stability in railway employment, even amid all the vicissitudes of a rapidly developing country like the Canada of 70 years ago that seemed to put it on a rather higher plane, especially when there was the spectacle of abounding prosperity on the Canadian Pacific. The central reorganization of the Clergue enterprises brought new hope to the Sault, and ushered in a period of extreme activity on the railway; but for those concerned with management it was a time of great anxiety and uncertainty. Francis Clergue had lost control, and disappeared from the scene, and things remained virtually stagnant until 1909. In the meantime, in 1908, W C Franz had been made General Manager of all companies, representing the Philadelphia interest, the owners of the first stock sold in the Sault industries. It was a year later that an English group with funds received from a bond issue sold in London acquired control of all the Clergue companies. But what of Clergue himself? One cannot be other than inquisitive to know the fate— if one might call it so—of a personality who had done so much to create a first rate industrial complex at the Sault.

He went to Europe and travelled extensively, particularly in Czarist Russia, where he is said to have made many friends in high court circles. He had retained the presidency of the Waterbury Tool Company in Connecticut, and used his personal influence to interest both the French and Russian Governments in a heavy gun turret that had been developed by his company; and in the early stages of World War I he organized the production of munitions on a considerable scale in Connecticut.

It was, as in so many of his earlier enterprises, his misfortune to back lost causes, and one does not need to dwell upon the consequences of a large contract for shells that he obtained from the Czarist Government of Russia. This contract was apparently too large to be carried out in his own factory at Connecticut, and was sub-let to the Canadian Car and Foundry Company, of Montreal. This company had an assembly and shipping depot at Kingsland, New Jersey, and much of this material was destroyed in a fire, early in 1917. The complications that ensued, both from the loss of the material, and the elimination of the client for whom it was destined involved litigation that was not resolved until nearly twenty years later. By that time Clergue himself was nearly eighty years of age, and he died in 1939 after spending the later part of his life living quietly in Montreal.

It was nevertheless at the Sault itself that the final and ultimate tribute was paid to Francis Hector Clergue, when the Public School named after him was opened in March 1952. In concluding a notable speech at the opening of this school, Earl Orchard, Chairman of the Sault Ste Marie Board of Education, said:

> Mr Clergue lost control of the enterprises, and a few years afterwards retired from the scene of his labors here to promote others elsewhere. At no time, however, did these later undertakings approach the size and grandeur of the schemes he set going in the Algoma wilderness. This was the scene of his greatest efforts, his greatest triumphs, his greatest failures. Francis Hector Clergue belongs and will ever belong to Sault Ste Marie, our Founder and First Citizen. It is against his background here that he may well be called a mighty Builder of Canada.
>
> Francis H Clergue was a man ahead of his time. It has taken the better part of fifty years for the industries he fathered and the city he foresaw to come into their own. Among other things, Clergue has been called 'the greatest industrial miracle worker on the North American continent', and 'Cecil Rhodes of Canada'. Greater than anything that may be said of him, greater than the industries which are his monument, is the significance of this school which we open in his name today. When the bricks and mortar of his industries have become dust and the steel columns are but flakes of rust, the influence of the teachings and the learning that will be done in this school will be going on and on at increasing rate and with increasing scope in the lives of boys and girls, men and women. We are proud today to officially name this the Francis Hector Clergue Public School. In this school, as in all the schools under our jurisdiction, we look for the spread of the ideals of Christianity and democracy, those two great principles which must go hand in hand in the building up of our Canada and our modern world.

It is pleasing to recall that two years before his death, when he had already attained the age of 81, he returned to the Sault, to attend a testimonial banquet. That was the first and only time that many who were then benefiting from his earlier enterprises saw him in the flesh.

But to return to the year 1909, when the English financial group secured control of all the Clergue enterprises, the policy became one of concentrating attention on the development of the Steel Company, using the money received from the sale of the Pulp and Power companies for this purpose. The position of the railway was markedly affected by these reorganizations, though the new owners were anxious enough to complete the line. A new first mortgage bond issue was made of $10,080,000, of which $3,000,000 was used to clear the old bonds of $6,750,000 and the balance of $7,080,000 allocated to completion of construction of the line. But the trust deed limited the cost to $30,000 a mile—not a large sum in such a rugged terrain. Between the years 1903 and 1908 no more than 12 additional miles of track had been laid, bringing the 'end of steel' to a point 68 miles from the Sault, and before any further work was done, the new management obtained a report from F H McGuigan, a consulting engineer from Toronto. He reported favourably, and with the aid of the finance previously mentioned, construction was restarted in earnest.

In 1909 the route had been surveyed, and grading completed to the point of connection with the Michipicoten branch, then referred to as Josephine Junction; but the majority of bridges and trestles on the section beyond the 68th mile had not been constructed. The first work undertaken was the locating of a line from Hawk Lake, where the surveyed line to Josephine turned westward, to make connection with the Canadian Pacific main line. It is interesting to find that this new survey headed almost due north from Hawk Lake to cross the CPR at Hobon Lake, and not to the northeast, at Missanabie where Hannington had set out on his exploration to Moose Factory 8 years earlier. This new section was taken through rough virgin country, but though much intersected with small rivers, lakes, and stretches of muskeg the locating engineer, S Keemle, was able to get a line with a maximum gradient of 0·6 per cent (1 in 166). Even so the estimated cost was $38,000 per mile, complete with track and all structures. Although this was above the norm set by the trust deed of 1909, it was no doubt hoped to secure cheaper construction on the more northerly part of the line, judging from the reports in Hannington's survey. It is interesting however that the first new work after 1909 should have been directed to connecting up the Michipicoten branch with the CPR, as the most likely source of early revenue. In May 1910 a contract was placed with the O'Boyle Bros Construction Company, of Sault Ste Marie, for this 30 mile section, from Hawk Lake to Hobon Lake.

Three months later another contract was placed with the same company for the completion of the original line from Mile 68 to Josephine Junction, a distance of 170½ miles. This was far from a straightforward job. Although most of the grading had already been done, the unfinished works were generally in poor shape, with embankments settled and the ground unstable, while in some of the cuttings there had been slips. The contract with O'Boyle's required everything to be brought up to an acceptable standard, all bridging completed, together with the ballasting and the track laying. There was one exception in respect of the bridging; that was the large curving viaduct over the Montreal River, 91½ miles north of the Sault, and the subject of a separate contract. Further work taken immediately in hand was the completion of the line from Michipicoten Harbor. The only part of this that had been regularly worked, and was in reasonable condition, was the 19 mile stretch from the Helen mine to the harbor. The upper 10 miles, to Josephine Junction, had been unused for some years. It was in very poor shape. The ties were rotten, and such ballast as there had been originally was useless. The whole section required complete renewal, and this was done by the engineer's department of the Algoma Central Railway, with some help from the O'Boyle company.

This section involved a good deal of tiresome work in construction. A contemporary report explains that the labor available was scarce and generally poor, and the supervisors had to fight a running battle with bush fires, whisky (!), and all the incidentals arising from them. There was some heavy cutting work and steep gradients in constructing the branches to the mines, with a maximum of 2½ per cent (1 in 40) in favor of the loaded trains. The use of timber trestling for viaducts, though common enough in the pioneer days of Canadian railways, was a constant source of anxiety at times of bush fires. On the new section of line from Hawk Lake to Hobon there was some quite heavy work, with much cutting in rock and numerous small bridges, though here the work, sub-let to two different contractors, was reported as 'exceptionally well done'. On 10 January 1912 track laying was completed, and provided for the first time a railway connection from the Michipicoten district to the main network of Canada, via the CPR at Hobon Lake. The actual junction was made at the north end of the lake, and across its narrowing waters the two railways are running roughly parallel to each other for the last 2 miles before the junction. It was named Franz after W C Franz, who was made General Manager of all the companies in the former Clergue 'empire' in 1908. Although a junction of such significance the visitor from Europe would probably be surprised to find it is no more than a grade crossing of two single-tracked railways, deep in the forests, with hardly a habitation in sight, other than those directly connected with the two railways.

In the meantime work was proceeding slowly on the main line from the Sault, north of Mile 68, and by May 1911 track had reached the Montreal River, at the 91½ mile. Here a deep ravine had to be crossed. The work here had been taken account of in the first surveys of the line, and a spectacular steel viaduct had been designed as early as 1902 by the firm of Boller and Hodge, of New York. The contract for its erection was let to the Canadian Bridge Company. It is 1550 ft long, and 130 ft high, and it is located near to the great falls of the Montreal River. It lies in very difficult country, and as the alignment required had to be curving, in addition to its great length and height, it presented a remarkable piece of construction. It consists

of tower girders, supported on steel legs with concrete pedestal piers and end abutments. In all there are thirteen 30 ft tower girders, and one 40 ft, the last mentioned
being situated on an island in the middle of the river. The longest intermediate girder
has a span of 85 ft, but five others are 75 ft span. This fine structure was designed
to the Dominion Government specifications, for class I loading, and track was laid
across the viaduct in October 1911.

North of the Montreal River to the junction with the northern part of the line
at Hawk Lake construction work made slow progress. An exceptional amount of
bridging and trestling was needed, and some of the bridges were very large. Roads
in the vicinity were non-existent; the rock-strewn rivers could not be used for
transport of building materials, and so practically everything had to be brought up
by rail, and construction carried out immediately ahead of the 'end of steel'. For this
reason only one bridge could be built at a time. The local timber generally was not
suitable, and most of that used for trestling and piling was British Columbia fir. In
reporting on the progress of the construction in August 1912, R S McCormick,
Chief Engineer of the railway, commented:

> The old line from Sault Ste Marie to Hawk Lake Junction is through a
> most difficult country to build in, and while the location secured was good
> on the whole, the line is badly handicapped with heavy grades and sharp
> curvature. To improve this grade and alignment would require extensive
> relocating, which for the present is not contemplated. The route, however, is
> very picturesque and travelers have a treat in rugged scenery awaiting them
> on the opening for traffic of the Algoma Central north of the 'Soo'.

Even so, one hardly imagines that even the most optimistic of the railwaymen of
60 years ago could have foreseen the tremendous popularity of the present day
excursions to the Agawa Canyon. The line from the south to Hawk Lake Junction
was completed about the middle of 1912.

The new owners were not unmindful of the full title of their railway—'Algoma
Central and Hudson Bay', and in May 1911 an expedition to Hudson Bay was
organized 'to ascertain the merits of various points on the coast, as outlets to the
Algoma Central Railway, ascertain the feasibility and cost of a Railway and Waterway, or Railway, to such points, and to take cognizance of the timber, rock, out-
crops and agricultural lands encountered on the route'. The Chief Engineer, R S
McCormick, entrusted this expedition to a young engineer of outstanding ability,
J S Tempest, who was called upon to display a rare mixture of pluck, fortitude and
powers of endurance, in addition to engineering skill, in the course of an odyssey
that lasted from May 1911 till February 1912. It was literally an expedition, a repeti-
tion of Hannington's epic of 1901, only much longer, and extended into the depths
of the Canadian winter. There was, however, one important difference. Constructional work had started on the National Transcontinental Railway, and that great,
but unfortunate enterprise had fixed a divisional point at a new settlement named

Hearst, roughly 90 miles north-north-east of Franz. Work was still in an early stage; but it seemed logical for the northward extension of the Algoma Central to make for this point, rather than head for Brunswick Lake and the course of the Missinaibi River, as in Hannington's original survey. After all, Hearst was only 20 miles west of the Missinaibi River crossing on the line of the National Trans-continental, and could provide an equally good starting point for the northward continuation of the line to Hudson Bay. One point needs to be mentioned here in respect of terminology. The bay itself is always written in the singular, but the historic company whose Charter was granted by King Charles II is the Hudson's Bay Company.

Tempest began his expedition from Lochalsh, a station on the Canadian Pacific main line about half way between Franz and Missanabie. There was a track of sorts across country from Goudreau, on the Algoma Central, and besides having a post office and a station on the CPR Lochalsh had the advantage of lying at the head of a chain of lakes, extending for no less than 16 miles to the north, and enabling the first part of the trip to be made in relative comfort by canoe. The party leaving Lochalsh consisted of eight men: an Ontario land surveyor, a geologist, a cook, four packers and canoe men, and Tempest himself. The cook and the canoe men were Indians. The report covers 55 pages of closely typed description, and is a fascinating document in itself; but here I can be concerned only with those parts that affect the eventual build-up of the Algoma Central Railway. They made for the great expanse of Kabinagagami Lake—now spelt Kabinakagami—and then followed the river of that name, until they reached the route of the National Transcontinental Railway, not at Hearst itself, but about 20 miles to the west where the Kabinakagami River was crossed, near to the present station of Calstock. There Tempest met the engineer in charge of construction on the 'TCR', as it was then referred to, and later some of the contractors' engineers. In his report he wrote:

> They each had a splendid garden and were most enthusiastic over the possibilities of the country from an agricultural point of view.
>
> While in the neighborhood I tramped over a lot of country and found many big stretches of good clay land that had been almost completely de-nuded of trees and brush by the ever recurring forest fires. There is no doubt this will be an important agricultural country some day.

From this locality Tempest's exploration led toward the Albany River, and eventually to its mouth, at Fort Albany, on Hudson Bay. How his route differed from that of Hannington in 1901 can be seen from the sketch map. He had however barely started on his travels when he arrived at Fort Albany at the end of June. His subsequent adventures in which he eventually reached York Factory on 7 January 1912, 'the end of all our difficult traveling', has no significance toward the later history of the Algoma Central Railway. But when he writes in conclusion that from York Factory he was able to hire trains of big strong husky dogs to traverse the ensuing

600 miles—*six hundred miles!*—to near Winnipeg, and that was 'easy' traveling, one can only imagine what some of his earlier journeys had been like. That 600 mile 'last lap' took him just four days inside a month.

To return to actual construction work, detailed surveys were in progress north of Franz, and Louis Whitman, the locating engineer, was able to get a good route with the same maximum gradient and curvature as between Hawk Lake and the junction with the CPR. The country traversed was rough for the first 30 miles north of Franz; north of this however the line enters the great clay belt of Northern Ontario, and the grading work was light. The difficult work at the southern end balanced this however, and the overall cost from Hawk Lake to the National Trans-continental line at Hearst averaged out at almost exactly the $30,000 per mile provided for in the estimates of 1909. This section included the crossing of the Canadian Northern Ontario Extension, then under construction, at a junction eventually known as Oba. This meant that the Algoma Central would intersect no fewer than three transcontinental routes, though the wisdom of the optimistic projection of two additional lines, in the period now under discussion, was doubted by many, even in that highly expansive period. It was generally agreed that a second transcontinental line, to compete with the Canadian Pacific, was desirable; but when the Grand Trunk and the Canadian Northern failed to agree, except to promote two rival lines, those who took a more detached view of things had grave doubts. But the Algoma Central attempted to 'cash in' on the situation with enthusiasm. Connection to one highly prosperous transcontinental line was good enough in itself; connection to two more unfinished ones held out the prospects of good traffic in conveying materials to both Oba and Hearst. As with the Algoma Central itself, there was little chance of furnishing supplies at intermediate points. Every-thing had to go in through the 'end of steel'.

On the northernmost stretch of the Algoma Central there were very few bridges and none of any great size except for a bay crossing of Oba Lake, where four pile trestles were driven, one of them being 1302 ft long with the deck 10 ft above the thing of a disappointment, and never came up to the standards achieved by the ear-liest 2–8–0s, 21–24. Such was the general position of locomotive operation up to the time when the work of completing the line through to Hearst was taken in hand. water. The rest of the bridging consisted of pile structures. The largest was the crossing of the Mattawishquia River, 700 ft long, near Hearst. In a report dated August 1912 McCormick rather dismissed as of little interest the bridge work north of Franz; but in my own travel on the line I found much that was unusual and fascinating, particularly to one brought up on British conditions. Three hundred acres of farmlands were opened by the Algoma Central Railway for settlement, near Hearst, in 1913. The company built colonization roads, was pleased with the nearly stoneless soil in the great clay belt, and offered farmers $4 a cord for pulpwood that they cut on their own land while clearing it. (A cord is about 85 cubic feet of solid wood.) At first the settlers paid no more than $1 an acre, but when there were 20 farms in any one settlement, the later arrivals had to pay $2 an acre. The line into Hearst was opened for traffic in 1914, and the Algoma Central Railway as we know it today was complete. It had opened up a large and wild area; it had helped to map it, and to develop it, and in what continued to be a very critical period it proved the major integrating force in the Algoma District. Through the hard times that followed the crash of the Clergue 'empire' and the financial crises that continued for a number of years the investors got no dividends, but the trains never stopped running.

Before telling of what happened to the Algoma Central soon after the outbreak of war in 1914, the situation on the two new transcontinental lines must be briefly recalled. The Canadian Northern was not in a good position even before it embarked on its chimerical twofold extensions, westward to Vancouver and eastward to Sudbury. Despite the success of the first lines built by those remarkable promoters MacKenzie and Mann the railway had not, up to 1912, paid any dividend on its ordinary shares, and out in the west the company found itself short of several hundred million dollars necessary to complete the line to Vancouver. With the western end unfinished little traffic had begun to flow on the Ontario extension. It had been arranged that the Grand Trunk would work the National Transcontinental, but that company was by 1914 wishing it had never heard of extensions to the far west. Its protégé, the Grand Trunk Pacific, constructed from Winnipeg to Prince Rupert could not even earn its operating expenses. East of Winnipeg the optimistic views of some of the men who had built the National Transcontinental proved to be ill-founded. The intermediate traffic was not there, and the Grand Trunk handed it back to the Dominion Government. The situation was difficult. Both the Grand Trunk and the Canadian Northern had been encouraged to build the lines, and they were urgently needed for heavy through loads of wartime traffic.

This situation naturally reacted upon the Algoma Central. The traffic that was expected to come from the connections at Oba and Hearst did not materialize, and in December 1914 the railway went into receivership. The trains nevertheless continued to run. The plight of the National Transcontinental, the Grand Trunk Pacific, and of the Canadian Northern were matters of national urgency, to which the Dominion Government had to give attention; but the Algoma Central was a relatively small concern by comparison. While the steel works at the Sault had become the largest in Canada, and the pulp and paper works were important the railway was not the only means of outward transport, though a vital enough carrier of ore between the mines in the Michipicoten area and the Sault in the winter, when the lakes were frozen. There had been a time when a rumor circulated that the Canadian Pacific would take it over; but through all its troubles the Algoma Central remained independent, and in 1916 it was taken over by a bondholders' committee. This group controlled the operations of the company through three additional reorganizations and innumerable minor crises until the year 1959, when a re-financing cleared the last of the outstanding debt and interest arrears.

CHAPTER FIVE

Steam Locomotives

The Algoma Central Railway opened for business in 1899 with eleven locomotives, all bought up secondhand, and not a great deal of dimensional information about them is available. But from some old photographs, line drawings have been prepared by way of a preface to the set of drawings reproduced from the official diagram book illustrating all the remaining types of steam locomotive owned by the company. These diagrams include some locomotives of the Algoma Eastern Railway, which as related earlier began as the Manitoulin and North Shore Railway, and became a part of the Clergue 'empire'. But the Algoma Eastern was acquired by the Canadian Pacific in 1930, and its motive power affairs passed out of the ken of Sault Ste Marie from that time onward. Before passing on to the drawings, and the details accompanying them, it will be convenient to give a summary list of the Algoma Central steam locomotives, and their diverse origins (see page 64).

None of the locomotives purchased secondhand from American Railways were to the least extent modern. The '60' class obtained from the Wabash had been built in 1912–13; the '70' class, from the Virginian, were Baldwin products of 1910, while the '80' class had been built by the American Locomotive Company in 1915–16. The two 'Santa Fe' type, purchased new from the Canadian Locomotive Company, in 1929, were of advanced design, as will be appreciated from the specification printed on page 71, but from all accounts the long coupled wheelbase as originally designed did not take kindly to the incessant and severe curvature of the line, and at first they suffered from heavy tire wear on the leading pair of coupled wheels. Engine No 52 of the Algoma Eastern, classified by that railway as Class 'C1' was the same design as ACR Class 'C2'. Similarly AER Class 'C2' was the same as Class 'C3' of ACR. The only locomotive class of the Algoma Eastern, prior to 1922, that was essentially different from the similar types of the Algoma Central, was the AER Class 'C3' of 1921—a powerful 2–8–0 of approximately 50,000 lb tractive effort, of which two were built by the Montreal Locomotive Works in 1921.

ALGOMA CENTRAL LOCOMOTIVE SUMMARY

Class	Engine Nos	Type	Date acquired	Condition	From
—	1–4	4–6–0	1899	Secondhand	Lehigh Valley RR
—	5–11	0–4–0	1899	Secondhand	Chicago, Burlington and Quincy RR
SI	19–20	0–6–0	1902	New	Canadian Locomotive Company
CI	21–23	2–8–0	1902	New	Baldwin Locomotive Company
CI	24	2–8–0 Compound	1900	New	Baldwin Locomotive Company
—	25–26	4–8–0	1903	Secondhand	Iron Range and Huron Bay Railway
MI	27*	2–6–0	1907	New	Montreal Locomotive Works
'C2'	28–37	2–8–0	1911	New	Montreal Locomotive Works
'C3'	38–42	2–8–0	1913	New	Canadian Locomotive Company
Santa Fe	50–51	2–10–2	1929	New	Canadian Locomotive Company
'60'	60–64	2–8–2	1941–2	Secondhand	Wabash Railway
'70'	70–71	2–8–2	1943	Secondhand	Virginian Railway
'80'	80–85	2–8–2	1940–3	Secondhand	Minneapolis and St Louis RR
'TI'	100–104	4–6–0	1912	New	Canadian Locomotive Company

* Sold to the Algoma Eastern Railway.

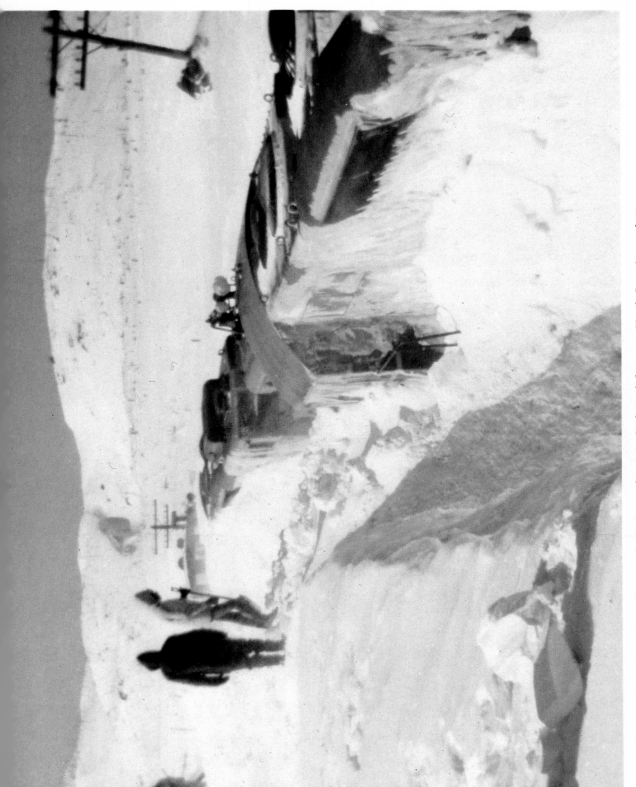

2 Locomotives of an ore train completely snowed up on the branch between Hawk Junction and Wawa

3   First snow in the Canyon: a loaded ore train beginning the steep climb to Frater hauled by 2–8–2 locomotive No 70

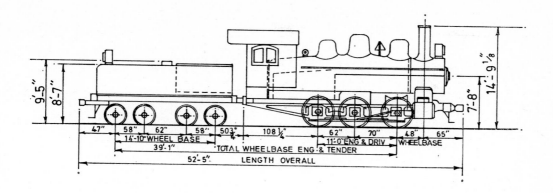

CLASS 'SI' Road Nos 19 and 20
Built by Canadian Locomotive Co (Kingston) 1902

BASIC DIMENSIONS:

Cylinders	dia	18 in	Tractive effort	28,080 lb
	stroke	26 in	Factor of adhesion	4·37
Driving wheel	dia	4 ft 3 in	Cylinder horsepower	1078
Boiler pressure		200 lb per sq in	Boiler/cylinder hp	79·3%

BOILER:

		HEATING SURFACES: sq ft	
Belpaire firebox	96⅛ in × 41 in	Tubes	1304
Outside dia 1st course	4 ft 8 in	Firebox	138
Inside dia 2nd course	5 ft 2⅝ in	Total	1442
Distance between tube		Grate area	27·3
plates	10 ft 5 in	Boiler horsepower	855

RUNNING GEAR ETC:

Driving wheels	centers	3 ft 8 in dia
	outside	4 ft 3 in dia
Tender wheels	outside	2 ft 9 in dia
Driving axle box journals		8½ in × 10 in
Tender axle box journals		4¼ in × 8 in
Engine frames	4 in wide, at 3 ft 10 in centers	
Slide valves	maximum travel 5½ in	

WEIGHTS AND CAPACITY:

Engine in working order	54·8 tons (Imperial)
Tender in working order	40·1 tons (Imperial)
Coal capacity	6 tons
Water capacity	3800 gallons (Imperial)

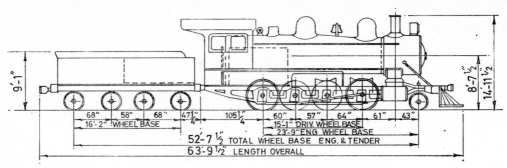

CLASS 'C1' Road Nos 21–23 and 24
Built by Baldwin Locomotive Works, 1900

BASIC DIMENSIONS:

		Engines 21–3 (simple)	Engine 24 (compound)
Cylinders	dia	21 in	$15\frac{1}{2}$ in and 26
	stroke	30 in	30 in
Driving wheel dia		4 ft 8 in	4 ft 8 in
Boiler pressure	lb/sq in	200	200
Tractive effort	lb	40,200	35,200
Factor of adhesion		3·94	5·1
Cylinder horsepower		1340	1180
Boiler/cylinder hp		78·5	108

BOILER:

Wagon top—crown bar
Firebox — 42 in × $120\frac{1}{8}$ in
Outside dia 1st course — 5 ft $6\frac{5}{8}$ in
Inside dia 3rd course — 6 ft $2\frac{1}{2}$ in
Tubes, 321 total, 2 in outside dia
Distance between tube plates 13 ft 6 in

HEATING SURFACES: sq ft

Tubes	2253
Firebox	202
Total	2455
Grate Area	35·1
Boiler horsepower	1050

RUNNING GEAR ETC:

Driving wheels	centers	4 ft 2 in dia
	outside	4 ft 8 in dia
Leading wheels	outside	2 ft 6 in dia
Tender wheels	outside	2 ft 9 in dia
Driving axlebox journals		$8\frac{1}{2}$ in × 11 in
Leading axlebox journals		$6\frac{1}{2}$ in × $14\frac{1}{2}$ in
Tender axlebox journals		5 in × 9 in
Engine frames		4 in wide at 3 ft 8 in centers
Valves engines 21–23	slide	
engine 24	Piston: $5\frac{5}{8}$ in travel, $\frac{7}{8}$ in lap	

WEIGHTS:

Engine, in working order	81·7 tons (Imperial)
Tender, in working order	43·9 tons (Imperial)
Coal capacity	10 tons
Water capacity	3750 gallons (Imperial)

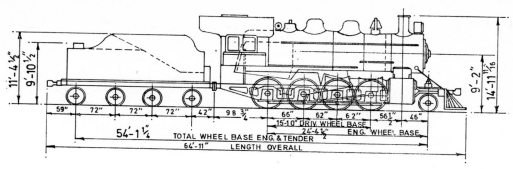

CLASS 'C2' Road Nos 28–37
Built by Montreal Locomotive Works, 1911

BASIC DIMENSIONS:

Cylinders	dia	$22\frac{1}{2}$ in	Tractive effort	38,800 lb
	stroke	28 in	Factor of adhesion	4·31
Driving wheel	dia	4 ft 8 in	Cylinder horsepower	1640
Boiler pressure		180 lb per sq in	Boiler/cylinder hp	100·4%

BOILER:

Extended wagon top
Firebox $96\frac{5}{8}$ in by $65\frac{1}{4}$ in
Inside dia 1st course   5 ft 9 in
Inside dia 3rd course   6 ft 4 in
Tubes, 240–2 in outside dia
        24–5 in outside dia
4–3 in outside dia arch tubes
Distance between tube plates 14 ft $2\frac{1}{2}$ in

HEATING SURFACES: sq ft

Tubes	1774·6
Superheater flues	443·4
Arch tubes	24·7
Firebox	159
Superheater	308
Combined total	2709·7
Grate area	43·7
Boiler horsepower	1646

RUNNING GEAR ETC:

Driving wheels:	centers	4 ft 2 in dia
	outside	4 ft 8 in dia
Leading wheels	outside	2 ft 6 in dia
Tender wheels	outside	2 ft 9 in dia
Driving axlebox journals (main)		$9\frac{1}{2}$ in × 12 in
Driving axlebox journals (front)		
(back and intermediate)		9 in × 12 in
Leading axlebox journals		6 in × 11 in
Tender axlebox journals		$5\frac{1}{2}$ in by 10 in
Engine frames	$4\frac{1}{2}$ in wide at 3 ft 7 in centers	
Valves	piston, 11 in dia, 6 in max travel, 1 in lap	
Motion		Walschaerts

WEIGHTS AND CAPACITIES:

Engine, in working order	87 tons (Imperial)
Tender, in working order	57·2 tons (Imperial)
Coal capacity	10 tons
Water capacity	5000 gallons (Imperial)

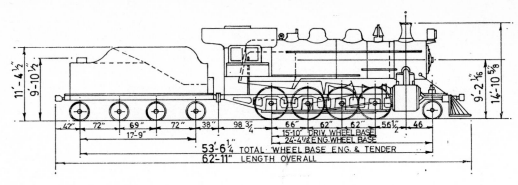

CLASS 'C3' Road Nos 38–42
Built by Canadian Locomotive Company, 1911

BASIC DIMENSIONS:

Cylinders	dia	22 in	Tractive effort	41,100 lb
	stroke	28 in	Factor of adhesion	4·26
Driving wheel	dia	4 ft 8 in	Cylinder horsepower	1742
Boiler pressure		200 lb per sq in	Boiler/cylinder hp	93·9

BOILER:

		HEATING SURFACES:	sq ft
Extended wagon top		Tubes	1773·6
Firebox	96 in × 65¼ in	Superheater flues	443·4
Outside dia 1st course	5 ft 10½ in	Arch tubes	24·5
Outside dia 3rd course	6 ft 5 9/16 in	Firebox	161
Tubes 240–2 in outside dia		Superheater	153
24–5 in outside dia		Combined total	2655·5
4–3 in outside dia arch tubes		Grate area	44
Distance between tube plates 14 ft 2½ in		Boiler horsepower	1636

RUNNING GEAR ETC:

Driving wheels	centers	4 ft 2 in dia
	outside	4 ft 8 in dia
Leading wheels	outside	2 ft 6 in dia
Tender wheels	outside	2 ft 9 in dia
Driving axlebox journals (main)		9½ in × 12 in
Driving axlebox journals (front)		
(back, and intermediate)		9 in × 12 in
Leading axlebox journals		6 in × 11 in
Tender axlebox journals		5½ × 10 in
Engine frames	4½ in wide at 3 ft 7 in centers	
Valves	piston 11 in dia, 6 in max travel, 1 in lap,	
	3/16 in lead, 1/16 in exhaust clearance	
Motion	Walschaerts	

WEIGHTS AND CAPACITIES:

Engine, in working order:	89·5 tons (Imperial)
Tender, in working order:	61·5 tons (Imperial)
Coal capacity	10 tons
Water capacity	5000 gallons (Imperial)

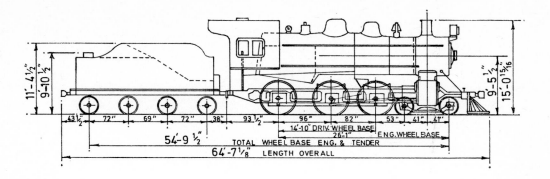

CLASS 'T1' Road Nos 100–104
Built by Canadian Locomotive Company, 1912

BASIC DIMENSIONS:

Cylinders	dia	22½ in	Tractive effort	34,400 lb
	stroke	28 in	Factor of adhesion	4·08
Driving wheel	dia	5 ft 3 in	Cylinder horsepower	1640
Boiler pressure		180 lb per sq in	Boiler/cylinder hp	103·4%

BOILER:

Extended wagon top

		HEATING SURFACES: sq ft	
Firebox	70 in × 104 in	Tubes	1789
Outside dia 1st course	5 ft 10⅜ in	Superheater flues	447
Outside dia 3rd course	6 ft 5 9/16 in	Arch tubes	26·2
Tubes 240–2 in outside dia		Firebox	180
24–5 in outside dia		Superheater	153
4–3 in outside dia arch tubes		Combined total	2595·2
Distance between tube plates 14 ft 4 in		Grate area	50·5
		Boiler horsepower	1695·5

RUNNING GEAR ETC:

Driving wheels	centers	4 ft 8 in dia
Driving wheels	outside	5 ft 3 in dia
Bogie wheels	outside	2 ft 7 in dia
Tender wheels	outside	2 ft 9 in dia
Driving axlebox journals (main)		9½ in × 12 in
Driving axlebox journals (front and back)		9 in × 12 in
Bogie axlebox journals		6 in × 10 in
Tender axlebox journals		5½ in × 10 in

Engine frames   4½ in wide at 3 ft 7 in centers
Valves   piston 11 in dia, 5¾ in max travel, 15/16 in lap,
            5/16 in lead

Motion   Walschaerts

WEIGHTS AND CAPACITIES:

Engine, in working order	85·1 tons (Imperial)
Tender, in working order	56·8 tons (Imperial)
Coal capacity	10 tons
Water capacity	5000 gallons (Imperial)

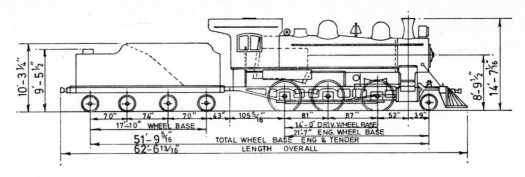

CLASS 'M1' Road No 27 (later No 50 Algoma Eastern)
Built by Montreal Locomotive Works, 1907

BASIC DIMENSIONS:

Cylinders	dia	20 in	Tractive effort	28,410 lb
	stroke	26 in	Factor of adhesion	4·38
Driving wheel	dia	4 ft 8 in	Cylinder horsepower	1199
Boiler pressure		180 lb per sq in	Boiler/ cylinder hp	80·56%

BOILER:

		HEATING SURFACES:	sq ft
Extended wagon top		Tubes	1636
Firebox	$90\frac{1}{8}$ in × $62\frac{1}{4}$ in	Arch tubes	19·6
Inside dia 1st course	4 ft 9 in	Firebox	126
Outside dia 3rd course	5 ft 6 in	Total	1781·6
Tubes 255–2 in outside dia		Grate area	39
3–3 in outside dia arch tubes		Boiler horsepower	966
Distance between tube plates 12 ft 4 in			

RUNNING GEAR ETC:

Driving wheels	centers	4 ft 2 in dia
Driving wheels	outside	4 ft 8 in dia
Leading wheels	outside	2 ft 6 in dia
Tender wheels	outside	2 ft 9 in dia
Driving axlebox journals (all)		$9\frac{1}{2}$ in × 10 in
Leading axlebox journals		6 in × 10 in
Tender axlebox journals		5 in × 9 in
Engine frames		$4\frac{1}{2}$ in wide at 3 ft 7 in centers
Valves		slide, $5\frac{1}{2}$ in max travel
Motion		Stephenson's link

WEIGHTS AND CAPACITIES:

Engine, in working order	65·2 tons (Imperial)
Tender, in working order	46·2 tons (Imperial)
Coal capacity	10 tons
Water capacity	5000 gallons (Imperial)

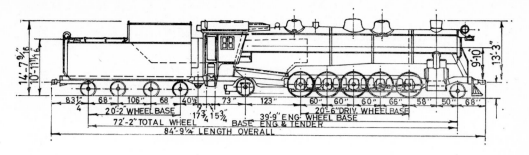

CLASS 'SANTA FE' Road Nos 50–51
Built by Canadian Locomotive Company, 1929

BASIC DIMENSIONS:

Cylinders	dia	24 in	Tractive effort	60,250 lb
	stroke	28 in	Factor of adhesion	4·3
Driving wheel	dia	4 ft 9 in	Cylinder horsepower	2590
Boiler pressure		250 lb per sq in	Boiler/cylinder hp	100%

BOILER:

Extended wagon top

Firebox	$114\frac{1}{8} \times 84\frac{1}{4}$ in	
Inside dia 1st course	6 ft $2\frac{5}{8}$ in	
Outside dia 3rd course	7 ft 2 in	
Tubes 146–$3\frac{1}{2}$ in outside dia flues		
44–$2\frac{1}{4}$ in outside dia		
Distance between tube plates 19 ft 3 in		

HEATING SURFACES: sq ft

Tubes	3059
Water tube and syphons	89
Firebox	258
Superheater	1500
Combined total	4906
Grate area	66·7
Boiler horsepower	2590

RUNNING GEAR ETC:

Driving wheels	centers	4 ft 2 in dia
Driving wheels	outside	4 ft 9 in dia
Leading wheels	outside	2 ft 6 in dia
Trailing wheels	outside	3 ft 7 in dia
Tender wheels	outside	2 ft 9 in dia
Driving axlebox journals (main)		$11\frac{1}{2}$ in $\times$ 13 in
Driving axlebox journals (front)		9 in $\times$ 12 in
Leading axlebox journals		$6\frac{1}{2}$ in $\times$ 12 in
Trailing axlebox journals		9 in $\times$ 14 in
Tender axlebox journals		6 in $\times$ 11 in
Engine frames		6 in wide at 3 ft 5 in centers
Valves		piston, 14 in dia, max travel $8\frac{3}{4}$ in, pal $1\frac{1}{4}$ in, lead $\frac{1}{4}$ in
Motion		Walschaerts

WEIGHTS AND CAPACITIES:

Engine, in working order	151·5 tons (Imperial)
Tender, in working order	93·5 tons (Imperial)
Coal capacity	15 tons
Water capacity	9500 gallons (Imperial)

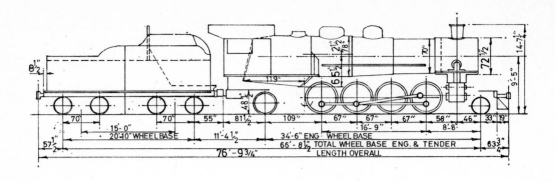

CLASS '60' Road Nos 60–64
Purchased from Wabash Railway Co, 1941–2

BASIC DIMENSIONS:

Cylinders	dia	$25\frac{1}{2}$ in	Tractive effort	54,408 lb
	stroke	30 in	Factor of adhesion	3·8
Driving wheel	dia	5 ft 4 in	Cylinder horsepower	2459
Boiler pressure		210 lb per sq in		

BOILER:

		HEATING SURFACES:	sq ft
Firebox	$108\frac{1}{8} \times 84\frac{1}{4}$ in	Tubes	2202
Outside dia 1st course	5 ft 10 in	Flues	902
Outside dia 3rd course	6 ft 6 in	Arch tubes	26
Tubes 201–2 in outside dia		Firebox	180
30–$5\frac{1}{2}$ in outside dia		Superheater	740
4–arch tubes 3 in outside dia		Combined total	4050
		Grate area	63

RUNNING GEAR ETC:

Driving wheels	centers	4 ft 8 in dia
Driving wheels	outside	5 ft 4 in dia
Leading wheels	outside	2 ft 9 in dia
Trailing wheels	outside	3 ft $8\frac{1}{4}$ in dia
Tender wheels	outside	3 ft 0 in dia
Driving axlebox journals (main)		11 in × 12 in
Driving axlebox journals (others)		$9\frac{1}{2}$ in × 12 in
Leading axlebox journals		6 in × 12 in
Trailing axlebox journals		7 in × 14 in
Tender axlebox journals		$5\frac{1}{2}$ in × 10 in
Valves		piston, 14 in dia, max travel 7 in
Motion		Walschaerts

WEIGHTS AND CAPACITIES:

Engine, in working order	119 tons (Imperial)
Tender, in working order	70·7 tons (Imperial)
Coal capacity	13 tons
Water capacity	8500 gallons (Imperial)

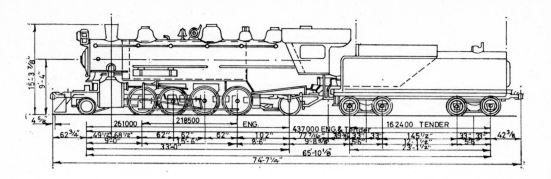

CLASS '70' Road Nos 70–71
Purchased from Virginian Railway Co, 1943

BASIC DIMENSIONS:

Cylinders	dia	24 in	Tractive effort	56,000 lb
	stroke	32 in	Factor of adhesion	3·91
Driving wheel	dia	4 ft 8 in	Cylinder horsepower	2076
Boiler pressure		200 lb per sq in		

BOILER:

		HEATING SURFACES: sq ft	
Firebox	102 in × 72 in	Tubes	2148
Inside dia 1st course	6 ft 7⅛ in	Flues	949
Outside dia 3rd course	6 ft 10 in	Arch tubes	
Tubes 188–2¼ in outside dia		Firebox	189
34–5½ in outside dia		Superheater	
4–arch tubes 3 in outside dia		Combined total	4041
		Grate area	51

RUNNING GEAR ETC:

Driving wheels	centers	4 ft 1 in dia
Driving wheels	outside	4 ft 8 in dia
Leading wheels	outside	2 ft 6 in dia
Trailing wheels	outside	3 ft 0 in dia
Tender wheels	outside	2 ft 9 in dia
Driving axlebox journals (main)		10½ in × 12 in
Driving axlebox journals (others)		9½ in × 12 in
Leading axlebox journals		—
Trailing axlebox journals		6 in × 11 in
Tender axlebox journals		5½ in × 10 in
Valves	piston 13⅝ in dia, max travel 6 in, lap 1 in, lead ¼ in, exhaust lap 1/16 in	
Motion		Walschaerts

WEIGHTS AND CAPACITIES:

Engine, in working order:	116·5 tons (Imperial)
Tender, in working order:	72·5 tons (Imperial)
Coal capacity	13 tons
Water capacity	7750 gallons (Imperial)

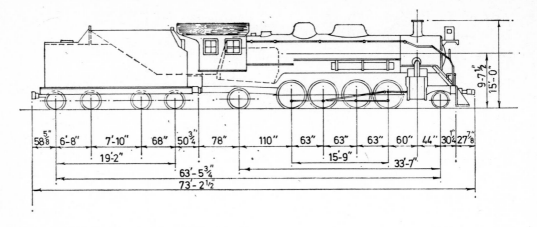

CLASS '80' Road Nos 80–85
Purchased from Minneapolis and St Louis RR, 1940

NOTE: There were slight variations in weight between individual engines of this class, but dimensions tabulated were common to all

BASIC DIMENSIONS:

Cylinders	dia	24 in	Tractive effort	49,800 lb
	stroke	30 in	Factor of adhesion	3·99
Driving wheel	dia	4 ft 11 in	Cylinder horsepower	2076
Boiler pressure		200 lb per sq in		

BOILER:

		HEATING SURFACES:	sq ft
Firebox	$108\frac{1}{8}$ in × $73\frac{1}{4}$ in	Tubes	1892
Tubes	170–$2\frac{1}{4}$ in outside dia	Flues	872
		Arch tubes	27
	32–$5\frac{1}{2}$ in outside dia	Firebox	204
		Total	2995*
Length of tubes and flues	19 ft	Grate area	55

RUNNING GEAR ETC:

Driving wheels, outside dia	4 ft 11 in
Leading wheels, outside dia	2 ft 9 in
Trailing wheels, outside dia	3 ft 7 in
Tender wheels, outside dia	2 ft 9 in
Driving axlebox journals (main)	$10\frac{1}{2}$ in × 12 in
Driving axlebox journals (others)	$8\frac{1}{2}$ in × 12 in
Leading axlebox journals	$6\frac{1}{2}$ in × 12 in
Trailing axlebox journals	8 in × 14 in
Tender axlebox journals	6 in × 11 in
Valve gear	Walschaerts

WEIGHTS AND CAPACITIES:

Engine, in working order	118·7 tons (Imperial)
Tender, in working order	84·2 tons (Imperial)
Coal capacity	$17\frac{1}{2}$ tons
Water capacity	10,200 gallons (Imperial)

* No particulars of superheater (Schmidt Type 'A') given on diagrams

74

Sept.No.109

Algoma Central Railway Company, Sault Ste. Marie, Ont., Sept.30,1899.

F To James T. Gardner, Dr.
756 Rookery Building,
Chicago, Ill.

1899

Oct	18	For one Locomotive lettered "Algoma Central Railway" and number "No. 1" (Bill No. 545)		2800	00

Checked by C. O.

Approved:

Gen'l. Manager. Auditor. President.

Received Oct. 23/99 from the Treasurer of ALGOMA CENTRAL RAILWAY COMPANY,

----------TWENTY EIGHT HUNDRED----------DOLLARS ($ 2800.00)

in full of the above account.

ALGOMA CENTRAL 2-10-2 ENGINES 50 AND 51 SPECIALITIES AND ACCESSORIES ETC

Westinghouse—ET 6 brake and Sch L air signal
1-8½ cross-compound air pump second course LJ
Air reservoirs 1-20½″ × 72″ LS — 1-24½″ × 80 LS—1-24½″ × 72″ LS
CLC driver brake
ALC power reverse gear
Type BK stoker
Franklin automatic butterfly firedoor
Franklin power grate shaker
Franklin lateral motion driving
Franklin driving box cellar and lubricator
Franklin driving box spreaders and end plates
Franklin radial buffers
Commonwealth constant resistance engine truck

Floating bushing main driving box
Floating bushing trailing truck box
Loco superheater Coy's type 'E' with multiple throttle header
Breco flexible joints on all air and steam heat piping between engine and tender
Hancock air operated cylinder cocks
Steam heat world leslie
Security fire brick arch
Pyle National type 'K' electric headlight equipment
14″ round case incandescent headlight
CN Ry Std NUMBER LAMP ON FRONT OF SMOKE BOX
Pyle National tail lamp TSLG 33-ww on rear of tender
1–Hancock HNL 5000 injector rs only
1–set K–39 Eleso feed water heater with CF pump on third course of boiler
1–world loco double top check on first course of boiler
King metallic packing on piston and valve rods
Franklin unit safety bar between engine and tender
King air sanders with economizee valves
World Ashcroft steam gauge
Couplers engine ARA type 'D' with 11″ knuckle and heat treated knuckle pins
Couplers tender type 'D' Symington swivel butt coupler bottom operated
    with manganese knuckle and heat treated knuckle pins
Draft gear miner class A78–XB with farlow attachment
Tender trucks Symington side frames
Tender truck journal boxes Symington 6″ × 1″
Engine and tender truck wheels solid rolled steel
Commonwealth cast steel water bottom tender frame
Commonwealth cast steel cradle
Commonwealth cast steel delta radial trailing truck
Driving wheels cast steel centers, steel tires held by lip and shrinkage;
    all tires flanged
Lubricators—Detroit 22 3-feed in cab, Nathan 4-feed mechanical for valves and cylinders
Can Nat 2 hopper self dumping ash pan
Can Nat vacuum valves in steam chest
World Ashcroft control gauge and fittings
Safety valves 2–3½″ world consolidated 1–muffled 1–plain
Tender brake cylinder 14″ × 12″ special type 'K'
Engine frames vanadium cast steel
Internal quick acting bell ringer
Johns-Mansville 85% magnesia lagging on boiler and cylinders
Boiler jacket keystone loco jacket steel
Baker valvegear
Alemite grease fittings applied
Gravity coal hopper in tender
Boiler dome designed for internal inspection without removing stand pipe
FBC staybolts in breaking zone of boiler
Dead grates at back
Design of coupler and pilot complies with Board of RR Commissioners' requirements for
    switching as well as road service
Boiler courses, dome and dome liner, high tensile silkon steel
Swanson flange oilers to front wheels

Crosshead wrist, pin lubricated through end of pin
Driving axles hollow bored
Main crank pin hollow bored
Driving springs carbon spring steel
CNR Std short type vestibule cab

The original locomotive allocation can be closely related to the first train services, and the successive extensions of the line north. The service was developed as follows:

Date	Section	Mileage
August 1900	Michipicoten Harbor to Helen Mine	11·6
November 1900	Sault to Bellevue	19
December 1901	Sault to Ogidaki	48
In Year 1903	Track complete to Pangis	56
December 1912	Sault to Franz	194·9
December 1912	Sault to Michipicoten Harbor:	
	a Sault to Hawk Junction	164·9
	b Hawk to Michipicoten	26·3
October 1913	Sault to Oba	244·7
November 1914	Sault to Hearst	295·8

Of engines numbers 1–4, purchased from the Lehigh Valley Railroad, numbers 1 and 3 worked out of the Soo, while numbers 2 and 4 were sent to Michipicoten, by scow. In the years 1909 and 1910 numbers 1 and 3 were rented to the contractors, O'Boyle, then working on the line north of Mile 69. At that time the little 0–4–0 engines 5, 6, 7, 8, 10 and 11 were working out of the Soo, while number 9 was sent to Michipicoten. Number 9 handled ore trains and empties between Helen Mine and Helen Junction.

Of the later engines acquired during this early period the two 0–6–0 tender engines 19 and 20 worked almost exclusively on switching operations in Soo yards. Having no leading wheels they were unsuitable for the incessant curvature of the main line. The four 2–8–0s 21–24 were much appreciated engines. They were nicely balanced, rode well and steamed freely. Two of the simples, numbers 21 and 22, were sent to Michipicoten for working the ore trains from Helen Junction down to the harbor, while 23 and the compound 24 were at the Soo. The two rather remarkable 4–8–0s, 25 and 26, were also at the Soo, but their performance was something of a disappointment, and never came up to the standards achieved by the earliest 2–8–0s, 21–24. Such was the general position of locomotive operation up to the time when the work of completing the line through to Hearst was taken in hand.

In readiness for this, 20 locomotives were ordered new. Fifteen of these were the

2–8–0 freighters 28 to 42 and 5 were the passenger 4–6–0s 100–104. These 20 locomotives formed the mainstay of the main line traffic for upward of 30 years. Their
general appearance and dimensional details can be studied from the drawings and
the tabular matter presented beneath them. The 2–8–0s with their 4′ 8″ wheels were
well suited to freight haulage on the difficult gradients, while their short wheelbase
made them easy on the curves. It could of course hardly be expected that they could
take very heavy tonnages of loaded freight on a gradient like that from Canyon up
to Frater, for example; but at the time when these engines were in their heyday the
mineral haul from the Helen mine was down to Michipicoten Harbor for shipment
rather than as now, by rail to the Soo.

The passenger 4–6–0s, numbers 100–104 with 5′ 3″ coupled wheels, were fast
engines, and there are many tales of their being run up to 60 mph. While at Hawk
Junction I met one of the great characters of the locomotive department, retired
engineer Omer Boucher, who had begun on locomotives as a fireman at Franz, in
1918. He told me how the 4–6–0s were favored on ballast trains, which on the
Algoma Central had to run fast. It is told that Boucher used to run the 50 miles
between Franz and Oba—a relatively straight and not too hilly section—in less than
the hour, with a 4–6–0 and a ballast train. It was two of these engines that were
involved in the incident with the Royal Train at the Montreal Falls viaduct in 1920,
when, as related in Chapter 6, the Prince of Wales suddenly pulled the communication cord in order to stop the train and admire the view. Although the stop itself
was a hazard, seeing that a second train was following close behind, and there was
then no radio communication, as now, the main trouble anticipated was that of re-
starting up the heavy gradient that begins immediately north of the bridge. The train
provided by the Canadian Pacific weighed between 650 and 700 tons, and the two
4–6–0s, 104 and 103, had between them a tractive effort of 63,000 lb—none too
much to start such a load in the awkward circumstances of severe curvature in
addition to heavy grading. I may add that Jack Thompson's father was fireman on
one of these two engines.

The only addition to the motive power stud of the Algoma Central between 1913,
when numbers 38–42 were delivered from Kingston, and reinforcements which
arrived in the form of secondhand American 2–8–2s during World War II, were the
two remarkable 'Santa Fe' 2–10–0s, numbers 50 and 51, built new for the ACR at
the Kingston works of the Canadian Locomotive Company in 1929. The order for
these locomotives was placed after trials had been carried out with a Canadian
National engine of the same type, and the new ACR 2–10–2s had a tractive effort
of 53,000 lb derived from 24″ × 28″ cylinders, 4′ 9″ coupled wheels and a boiler
pressure of 250 lb per square inch. The Kingston 2–8–0s of 1913 had a tractive
effort of 35,700 lb so that the 'Santa Fe's' represented an advance of nearly 50 per
cent in power. At first trouble was experienced with excessive wear on the flanges
of the leading coupled wheels; but then the flanges were removed entirely from
the central pair, and the trouble was largely cured. Frank Hayes the present Master

Mechanic of the railway told that after that change they were 'lovely engines'. They were certainly most handsomely proportioned, and over all sections of the line their maximum rated loads were the same as those now specified for the 'GP7' diesels. But one difference to be noted was that while these big steam locomotives had a weight in working order of 338,800 lbs (151 imperial tons), the diesels that are rated to do the same work weigh only 250,000 lb (111 imperial tons). The load limits are as follows, with class 'B' trains:

Northward		Southward	
Section	Tons	Section	Tons
Steelton–Goulais	1490	Hearst–Hawk Junction	2890
Goulais–Frater	1160	Hawk–Mekatina	1300
Frater–Hawk Junction	1395	Mekatina–Goulais	1440
Hawk–Hearst	2745	Goulais–Steelton	1535

On the Michipicoten branch the lowest ratings of all are to be found, in no more than 930 tons from Brient up to Helen. These were mighty big loads for such a route, and involved an inevitably high coal consumption. As will be seen from the detailed specification for these engines on page 71 they were fitted with mechanical stokers. There was a coaling plant at Frater, and freight trains almost invariably stopped there to re-coal, and clean the fires.

When the onset of World War II brought a considerable increase in traffic over the line, 17 additional freight engines of the 2–8–2 type were purchased secondhand from certain United States railways. The '60' class, of which there were seven, came from the Wabash, and although relatively old units, some dating from 1912, they were fine engines for Algoma Central conditions and were much appreciated. Although having a tractive effort somewhat below that of the 'Santa Fe's' they steamed freely and did their work well. The same could not be said of the two '70' class, a couple of Baldwin-built 2–8–2s from Virginian Railway dating from 1910. They certainly had a relatively high tractive effort of 49,500 lb, but they had a long narrow firebox that was awkward to fire, and to crown all a voracious appetite for coal. After some early struggles the expedient was adopted of putting two firemen on to them, but did not provide the answer, and they had to be withdrawn from main line work and employed instead switching in Steelton yard.

The last steam locomotives of the Algoma Central to be noted are the '80' class. Of these eight locomotives the last two, numbers 86 and 87, were fitted with boosters. They were no youngsters even when they first arrived at the Soo, and although good engines they did not become such universal favorites as the '60' class, judging from conversations I have had with the men who ran them. It is remarkable nevertheless how faithful the engineers and firemen of those days were to the steam locomotive, and how sceptical at first they were of the potentialities of the diesel. Frank Hayes told me that when the first trials of the standard 'passenger' General Motors diesels were in progress on the Canadian Pacific and the Canadian National there were remarks such as: '. . . they may be all right down in the States, but they'd be no good here.' But in Chapter 12 of this book I tell how, as everywhere else in North America, the diesels came to conquer, so rapidly indeed on the Algoma Central that it was the first railway in the whole continent to be completely dieselized. All steam locomotives on the line had been taken out of service by the end of 1952.

CHAPTER SIX

Earlier Days on the Great Lakes

Many years before the Algoma Central Railway was even thought of there was a trading post of the Hudson's Bay Company at Michipicoten. The 'fort' was in a strategic position on an island at the mouth of the Michipicoten River, and in the mid-nineteenth century it was busily engaged in the fur trade. It was indeed the southern terminus of a canoe route leading up the Michipicoten River to the height of land, or watershed, near the present Hawk Junction on the railway, and so down north via the Missinaibi and Moose Rivers to Moose Factory—a route that was closely followed in the earliest explorations toward the proposed extensions of the Algoma Central Railway to Hudson Bay. A record dating back to May 1869 has some significance toward the present story. It is the certificate of shipping, by the agent for THE GOVERNOR AND COMPANY OF ADVENTURERS OF ENGLAND, TRADING INTO HUDSON'S BAY, of five cases of furs 'in and upon the good steamer called the *Algoma*', bound for Collingwood, Ontario. The *Algoma* of 1869 was a quaint little paddle steamer, built by the Niagara Harbor and Dock Company in 1839, and for the first 25 years of her life named the *City of Toronto*. She was originally built for the passenger, mail and packet service between Toronto, Kingston and Prescott; but after various adventures, fire damage, change of ownership and change of name, she was acquired in 1864 by the Lake Superior Royal Mail Line, renamed a second time the *Algoma* and operated between Fort William and Collingwood.

Studying a map of the Great Lakes the remarkably strategic position of the Soo will be quickly apparent, but it must be recorded that even before the first *Algoma* had been withdrawn, in 1888, there had been a second ship of the same name, one of three vessels built on the Clyde in 1883 for the Canadian Pacific Railway, to convey

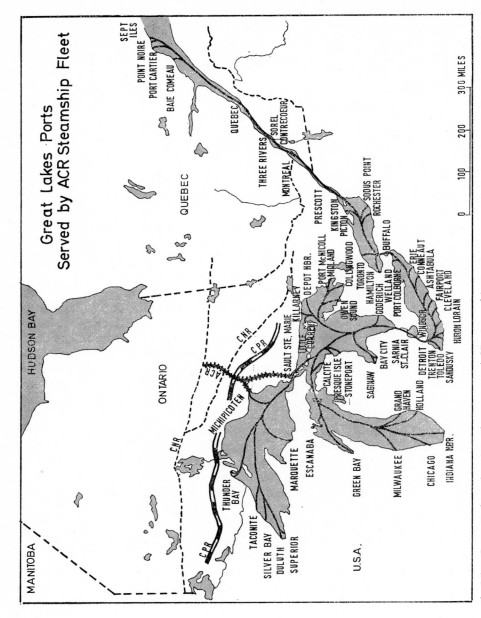

6 The Great Lakes showing the present ACR steamship routes

men and materials for construction of the very difficult section of that great pioneer transcontinental railway along the northern shores of Lake Superior. The three ships *Alberta*, *Athabasca* and *Algoma* began service from what was their home port, Owen Sound, in May 1885. But this *Algoma* had a very short life. At midnight, between the sixth and seventh of November in that same year, in very bad weather, the ship struck a reef at the northeast corner of Isle Royale, within 50 miles of Port Arthur. She broke in two, and 38 lives were lost. The other *Algoma*, the one-time *City of Toronto*, apparently survived the newer ship by three years. The dangers of navigation on the waters of Lake Superior are underlined in later periods of this present story.

The Algoma Central Railway was in the shipping business practically from its inception, and as early as the year 1900 four vessels were purchased. They were necessarily of the ocean-going type, because three of them were built in England, and the other one in Holland, and all had to come across the Atlantic before taking up their Canadian duties. They were needed for transporting men and materials from the Soo to Michipicoten Harbor for the building of the railway line to the Helen mine, and when ore began to move it was shipped from Michipicoten. The four ships purchased were the *Monkshaven*, built at South Shields, England, in 1882; the *Leafield*, built at Sunderland in 1892; the *Paliki*, also built at Sunderland, but in 1889; and finally the *Theano*, built at Rotterdam in 1889. The *Monkshaven* and the *Theano* were purchased secondhand in England, and the other two in the United States. All these ships were of the then conventional ocean-going cargo type, with cabins amidships. They are often referred to as of the turret-type, or whalebacks. None of them were very large, as the following details show, and they were not in any way specialized toward the carrying of the traffic loaded upon them when in the ownership of the Algoma Central Railway:

	tonnage
Monkshaven	2097
Leafield	1454
Paliki	1578
Theano	952

In addition to the conveyance of ore from Michipicoten Harbor there was another task for the Algoma Central Steamships. As told in earlier chapters of this book it was many years after the inception of the railway in 1899 that rail communication between the Soo and Michipicoten was established. There was literally no form of inland transport by road, and so all the people working at the mine, and their families, had to be taken to Michipicoten by water. The Algoma Central therefore purchased three passenger ships, which operated not only between the Soo and Michipicoten, but also to Cleveland, Windsor, and Detroit. Two of these ships the *Ossifrage* and the *Minnie M* were built at yards on the Great Lakes, but the third, the *King Edward*, was a highly picturesque side-wheeler, which in England would be called a paddle steamer, and was indeed built on the Humber, at Hull, in 1902. How this small vessel of no more than 355 tons fared on her voyage across the Atlantic does not seem to have been recorded. At the Soo the *King Edward* and the *Ossifrage* docked near the present Algoma Central Steamships Dock, and the *Minnie M* just below the Canadian Ship Canal.

To those not very familiar with the area it might be imagined that navigation on the Great Lakes would be a comparatively simple and placid business, in calm sheltered waters. But until one has actually been there the geographical statistics of a 'sea' like Lake Superior, Lake Huron, or Lake Michigan do not really strike home. For they are literally inland seas, and they behave like seas. To help European readers to get something of the picture I may add that Lake Superior is very nearly as large as the North Sea. The only difference is that it is composed of fresh instead of salt water; and at times it can be almost as 'cruel' as anything described in the novels of Nicholas Monsarrat. Of the seven vessels with which the Algoma Central Railway inaugurated its steamship business no fewer than four were wrecked—three on the Great Lakes, and one at St Felicite, Quebec. Two of these victims were claimed by Lake Superior, the *Leafield* in 1913, off Angus Island, when she was bound for Thunder Bay with a load of rails. The cargo, and the entire crew were lost. The *Theano* had an even shorter life in the service of the Algoma Central Railway being lost in Thunder Bay in November 1906.

By that time in the year winter conditions are usually closing in upon the lakes. In recalling these early disasters however it must be remembered that these little ships had none of the modern aids to navigation, and that their ocean-type hulls were most susceptible to damage on the shoals and reefs around the shores of these inland waters. In conditions of ice a captain might venture perhaps a little closer in-shore to avoid a large floating mass of ice, and strike rocks. Away from the shores Lake Superior is very deep, but its northern shore is rocky, particularly in the approach to Michipicoten Harbor. Parts of the area are also susceptible to fog. But there were occasions gay and hilarious, as well as tragic, in the early voyages of the Algoma Central Steamships, and the part played by the *Minnie M* in a political escapade centered upon a by-election in 1903 has been immortalized in some very amusing doggerel composed by the purser of the ship after it was all over. One would imagine that there were no such things as closely-regulated electoral registers then in the Algoma country for this coup to be so successful. This is what happened:

THE TRIP OF THE MINNIE M . . . as told by the purser . . .

> Oh, have you heard the stories
> Of the trip of the Minnie M.
> How the Grits did fool the Tories,
> And completely euchred them.

Twas in the bye-election
They had up at the Soo.
The Grits made a selection
Of a drunken shameless crew.

On the twenty sixth of October—
On the bye-election day,
This crowd, not strictly sober,
Sailed up Batchewana Bay.

We had our instruction
To take them there and back,
To save Grits from destruction
By the festive Lumber Jack.

We went for them o'er the river,
And took on liquor at the docks,
The Jacks in the morn did shiver
As we met them up the locks.

But they soon got a reviver
From the stock we took on board,
And no longer gave a stiver
For the shame they did afford.

The Lumber Jacks were jolly,
'Twas a picnic unto them—
This trip of fraud and folly
On the steamer Minnie M.

The cost did not concern them—
That they'ed nothing to do with
There was heelers there to learn them,
How to cast their votes for Smith.

They were each given a slip of paper
With the name they were to vote.
And the Jacks, with wink and caper,
Did their willingness denote.

They said 'If they would swear you,
You need not fear the law,
And let not the Bible scare you,
For the Bible's one of straw.'

We stopped at Michipicoten
And a train stood on the line
To take all who were willing
Up to vote at Helen's Mine.

The whiskey flowed both fast and free,
And some were near undone,
But the votes for Smith were twenty three
Miscampbell he got none.

They brought them back to Michipicoten,
And said 'here's where you vote.'
Of course the thing was rotten
But they did not care a groat,

They went in, for Smith they voted,
Did this drunken, reckless crew,
And the ballot box denoted
They got forty against two.

The heelers came on board again,
Their work that day was through,
And we turned the steamer Minnie M.
With her head towards the Soo.

The Jacks were full and glorious.
Their mirth we could not stem,
And they carried on uproarious
On the deck of the Minnie M.

They got all they demanded
And did all they had to do.
After midnight they were landed
Over at the American Soo.

I've made many trips up there and back,
But this one was the gem,
That time we took the Lumber Jacks
Up on the Minnie M.

Still stranger however was the fact that one of the parties most directly affected gained prior knowledge of what was afoot. In its issue of 29 October 1903, *The Sault Star*, in referring to events about the coming election, had this piece of news:

Then there were some strange doings up the Lake Superior shore. Mr Miscampbell, in an open letter to Attorney General Gibson, when that gentleman was here on Saturday, intimated that there was to be a wholesale personation of voters, at Michipicoten, Wawa, and Helen Mine, and other violations of the Election Act. The steamship Minnie M, as the letter said would be the case, left early Monday morning on a mysterious trip up the Lake, having on board a selected crowd of passengers . . .

Of the first seven ships of the fleet the *Paliki* was the last to remain in service, and she was not sold until 1924. Of the others, the *King Edward* was sold to the Canadian Government during World War I, in 1917, and did duty as a naval auxiliary for two years. The last record of her, still in Government service, was in 1921. The *Minnie M* was sold in 1910, and of the four lost in wrecks the dates of their respective fates were *Theano*, 1906, *Leafield*, 1913, *Monkshaven*, 1914 and the *Ossifrage*, 1919. Among the earlier fleet was an eighth, not hitherto mentioned, that had been purchased in 1902, and the first new vessel owned by the Company. This was the *Agawa*, which was built in that year as a barge at Collingwood Shipyard, and also the first of the Algoma Central Railway fleet to have a name appropriate to the Algoma country. After the loss of the *Theano* in 1906 another bulk-carrier was needed and the *Agawa* was converted to steam in 1907. She then put in 20 years of hard revenue-earning service until, in 1927, she went aground off South Bay, Manitoulin Island, and remained there during the winter. She passed out of Algoma Central ownership, but was salvaged next year by the insurance underwriters, and duly sold by them. Her second, and more colorful career was just beginning!

In 1928 she was renamed the *Robert P Durham* and in 1940 renamed a second time the *Heron Bay*. At that time she was being operated by the Quebec and Ontario Transportation Company, but later she was sold to the Federal Commerce Navigation Co Ltd of Montreal, and used as a salt storage barge at Sept Iles. In readiness for this rather humdrum duty she was renamed a third time, the *Federal Husky*. Then as if this old lady of the Lakes and the St Lawrence had not had a sufficiently varied career, after *sixty years*, she was loaded with scrap at Quebec City in July 1965, and assisted by an ocean tug crossed the Atlantic to put in at Bilbao, Spain, in November 1965, to end her career as it had begun, in the service of the Algoma Central, as a barge.

Between 1910 and 1913, to replace losses and provide more modern units, three ships were purchased. These were the *T J Drummond*, an ocean-going vessel built in Scotland, about which not many statistics are available; the *Uranus*, built at Lorain, Ohio, in 1901, purchased in 1914 and renamed the *W C Franz*; and the *Saturn*, which like the *Uranus* had been built by the American Shipbuilding Company, at Lorain, but a much larger ship with a tonnage of 6000 against 3429. This ship was renamed the *J Frater Taylor* on coming into the possession of the Algoma Central. In 1936 she was again renamed the *Algosoo*. The ocean going capacity of the *T J Drummond* was used for war purposes in 1915, when she carried a shipment of steel billets from the Algoma Steel Corporation from the Soo to France—the longest revenue-earning trip ever made by one of the Algoma Central Railway ships. In 1917 however she was part of an exchange transaction with the Great Lakes Transportation Company by which the Algoma Central Railway received instead the *William S Mack*, a vessel of 5500 net tons, originally built at Lorain in 1901. On entering Algoma Central service, in 1917 she was renamed the *Home Smith*, after the President of the company at the Soo. She was later renamed *Algorail*, and together with the *Algosoo* was the longest survivor of what may be termed the earlier fleet. The *Algosoo* served in all 52 years under the company's flag, from 1913 to 1965, and *Algorail* served from 1917 to 1963. At those latter dates both ships were sold.

At the end of World War I the Algoma Central had six ships in service. These were the old veterans *Paliki* and *Ossifrage*; the converted barge *Agawa* and the three Lorain-built bulk carriers, then named *J Frater Taylor*, *W C Franz*, and *Home Smith;* but by 1927 the fleet was reduced to three, the *Paliki* having been sold, and the *Ossifrage* and the *Agawa* wrecked. The *W C Franz* was concerned in an exciting affair off Whitefish Point, at the outer entrance to Whitefish Bay and the St Mary's River in November 1919. She answered the distress signals of the steamer *Myron* which sank, but was not in time to rescue more than one man of her crew of 16, the captain, who had clung to the roof section of the *Myron's* pilothouse for more than 20 hours. The *Franz* herself was sunk in a collision on Lake Huron in November 1934, a total loss, with consequences to the Algoma Central Railway that are related in Chapter 8 of this book.

The present chapter may well be concluded by telling of the last months of the *Algosoo*, the last vessel of those purchased before 1920 to remain in service. It is an interesting and colourful saga, vividly portraying what can sometimes happen in these inland waters. When 64 years old, and with 52 years of Algoma Central service behind her, she passed upbound through the Canadian Soo Locks on 24 November 1965. She had discharged a load of coal at the Algoma Steamships dock and then headed for the Lakehead to load the final cargo of her career, grain, for Sorel, Quebec. With nearly 2,000,000 miles logged on the Great Lakes, and 14,000,000 net tons of cargo conveyed for the Algoma Central she headed down Lake Superior. The weather was bad, and she had a rough trip down the Lake, and in the night of 27 November, distress signals from her were picked up by the United States coast-guard in Soo, Michigan. In heavy weather off Whitefish Point the *Algosoo's* cargo had shifted, causing her to list dangerously, and she was also in difficulties with her steering.

All modern aids were summoned to her assistance. A cutter, the *Naugatuck*, was sent out, and also a helicopter from the coastguard base at Traverse City, Michigan. The *Algosoo* was escorted by the cutter to Whiskey Bay nine miles above the Soo, Michigan locks, where the tug *John Purvis* took over escort duties to get her safely into the docks of the Algoma Steel Corporation. There the cargo was examined, found to be undamaged, and was righted, and the great old ship continued her final voyage. She passed through the Welland Canal on 4 December 1965 to deliver her cargo at Sorel. From there she went on to her end—to be scrapped at Lauzon, Quebec.

CHAPTER SEVEN

The Bondholders' Control Period: Operation and Engineering

The railway defaulted on its interest payments and went into the hands of Receivers at a difficult moment in history; for the date was December 1914, and war conditions made it impossible for the London Committee to contact the various foreign bond-holders. So, in November 1916 the Receivers were discharged and the Bondholders' Committee appointed a President and Vice-President to operate the railway and its affairs at the Soo. The history of the years that followed—42 in all—falls fairly into two separate categories, namely financial affairs, in which a diversity of business interests strove to gain either control or monetary advantage from the parlous situation of the railway; and secondly purely railway matters, many of which were dictated by the exigencies of the financial position. I am taking the railway operation and engineering matter first.

During the Receivership, J A Goudge, Technical Adviser to the Committee, made an inspection of the whole line, and his report included the statement that it was still only a 'construction road'. In 1914 there were 185 wooden bridges, many of no more than a temporary nature, together with 15 steel bridges on the main line and on the Michipicoten Branch. The roadbed, particularly the section from Franz to Hearst, was inadequately ballasted and had insufficient drainage, and this condition deteriorated still further in 1915 when labor was reduced to no more than a foreman for each section. This resulted in derailments of freight trains occurring almost weekly. The trestle spanning the Bellevue Valley was in such a condition that Receivers' Certificates were sold to raise the money necessary to replace it, in steel.

During World War I however, revenues improved considerably in both the railway and shipping operations, but unfortunately the track could not be properly maintained through shortage of labor and materials. This situation developed because

Canada as a whole had geared up her industries to produce materials needed for the war. In 1918 two trestle bridges in the Agawa Canyon were swept away by pulpwood of the Paper Company. Thaws in the spring, accompanied by heavy rains, washed the logs from skidways into the river, and they were carried rapidly downstream. As a result the main line was closed to all freight traffic between 1 and 14 June. The railway put in a claim for damages, but the Paper Company termed the accident an 'Act of God', and it was therefore not liable, and the ACR's claim failed accordingly.

The period just after the war brought little consolation. The railway carried on, curtailing maintenance and operational expenditures when revenues were low, and increasing them when improved conditions warranted it. Some interesting bridge improvement schemes were nevertheless carried out. As mentioned previously much of the earlier work was little removed from that of a temporary contractor's line. The valleys and creeks were crossed on timber trestle viaducts. Some of these were on considerable curves and were masterpieces in themselves. But as elsewhere in North America, they could not be regarded as more than temporary and in the years 1917 and 1918 a number of them were replaced. An interesting example, typical of the procedure adopted in many cases, was that at Mile 67, built originally in 1901. It is shown in the photograph reproduced on Plate 10. A concrete culvert was built to carry the stream and then the viaduct itself was replaced, or rather buried out of sight, by filling tipped from vehicles on the line above. Another interesting case, also illustrated, was that of the round timber trestle at Mile 142, north of the Agawa Canyon, which had timber fenders to protect the piers in the event of boulders or other obstacles being carried down by flood water. This was replaced by a substantial 10 ft wide culvert.

One event in 1920 had its diverting moments. In that year the late Duke of Windsor, when Prince of Wales, traveled extensively in Canada, and on his way to the west he travelled via the Soo, where he and his party had arrived in a luxurious special train provided by the Canadian Pacific Railway. He was to continue over the Algoma Central to Franz, where the CPR main line was to be rejoined. To haul this heavy train the ACR provided two of its 4 6-0 locomotives, Nos 104 and 103. At Northland the train was stopped to enable the Prince to practise target shooting on a tin can placed on a stump. Home Smith, the President, and G Montgomery, the General Manager, traveled in the special train, while E B Barber, then Vice-President and Comptroller, followed in the ACR business car *Lake Superior*. Nearing the Montreal Falls viaduct, Barber suddenly saw ahead, to his astonishment and alarm, that the special train was standing in the middle of the curve on the high steel viaduct. It transpired that without any warning the Prince had pulled the emergency cord, bringing the train to a stop, in order to stand on the edge of the bridge to look at the undeveloped falls and magnificent view. It has been suggested that the management of the ACR must have heaved a deep sigh of relief when the Royal Train was safely landed into Franz and handed over to the CPR!

By the year 1929 business was looking up somewhat. The Algoma Central Railway had built a coal bridge, and a dock with a length of 550 ft at Michipicoten. The *New York Times* had built a paper mill at Kapuskasing about 60 miles east of Hearst on the former National Transcontinental line, and the Kimberley Clark Company had built a mill for making 'Kleenex' tissue paper. At Smooth Rock Falls a sulphite plant was in operation, and last but not least, the Canadian National Railways used much coal in running its trains both east and west of Oba, and Hearst. At first all the coal for these activities was being hauled from Fort William, but the Algoma Central quoted advantageous rates based on importing at Michipicoten. To Hearst the rail haul was only 157 miles, against 376 from Fort William. The ACR secured the business of the Paper and other companies, but the CNR refused, stating that they had to run the trains in any case, and the coal cargoes were their main traffic. The first coal cargoes were unloaded on the dock at Michipicoten in September 1929. It was at this time that the Algoma Central took delivery of the two very fine 'Santa Fe' type locomotives referred to in Chapter 5.

The years of depression, from 1930 onward, brought some unfortunate recessions in traffic. The Federal Government decided to assist the depressed Nova Scotia coal mines by granting a subsidy of one third of a cent per ton mile on coal shipments to these points, mentioned in the previous paragraph; and although the coal was inferior to that coming into Michipicoten from the United States, the Algoma Central lost a considerable part of its coal traffic. In 1930, the officers of the company, including the London Committee, accepted a 10 per cent reduction in pay, and the repair shops were operated on only three days a week. Cash at one time became so low that to pay wages it appeared that drawing upon the Accident Fund might be necessary to sustain even these attenuated operations. This however did not prove necessary, but lack of adequate maintenance of both equipment and track led to further general deterioration of the property.

In this difficult period the former associated companies of the Clergue 'empire' were frequently working in strong opposition to each other, and in years not long before the outbreak of World War II the Algoma Steel Company, then under the leadership of Sir James Dunn, was very much a thorn in the side of the railway. When the decision was taken to develop the siderite Helen mine, for example, steps were taken by the Steel Company to deprive the railway of the traffic resulting therefrom. The original two-mile spur into the mine, over which no traffic had moved since 1918, required rebuilding in order to deliver heavy ore crushers and other mining machinery to the property and the railway spent a considerable sum restoring track and bridges. In the meantime, however, in some secrecy, surveys had been made by agents of the Steel Company to find an alternative outlet, but with no success.

Then the Mission, across Michipicoten Bay, was considered as a site and matters reached the stage of the Federal Minister of Railways and Canals at Ottawa agreeing not only to have the necessary dredging done, but also to build a road from the sinter plant at Wawa to truck the ore to the proposed dock. Upon hearing of the proposed dredging near the Mission, by the Federal Government, the Algoma

Central contacted the local member of the Government. He was most perturbed that such an undertaking should be contemplated in his area, and in subsequent interviews with the Minister he secured a cancellation of the dredging. This in any case would have been a very costly operation, because of the continual silting from the Michipicoten River into the bay. No alternative was therefore left but to use the railway from Wawa to Michipicoten Harbor and an agreement, dated 28 October 1937, was signed for a contract to move 4 million tons from Wawa into railway vessels at a rate of 50 cents per ton—a triumph for the Algoma Central.

The railway proceeded with the construction of loading facilities and the necessary tracks at Michipicoten and Wawa. From a steel trestle ore was dumped into a storage bin, from which the ore was conveyed by belt into the ships. The capital cost was $236,500, and as it seemed likely that no further contract would be received that amount was written off over the 4 million tons. Sir James Dunn's attitude to the railway had mellowed to the extent that he offered to assist in the financing; but not wishing to be in any way indebted to him at this stage, he was assured that the railway had sufficient funds to do the necessary constructional work at the harbor. The relations between the Algoma Central Railway and Sir James Dunn will be more apparent to the reader after the next chapter.

By 1939 the financial position of the railway had indeed greatly improved, though the condition of track and rolling stock was such that large expenditures were necessary for rehabilitation and capital improvement. The increased revenues were largely attributable to railway and ship earnings, through the production of Helen sintered ore, from coal, and from pulpwood shipments to the United States. This situation enabled the management to carry out important and much needed improvements on the line, including the elimination of further timber trestles by filling, or by steel bridges, and by heavy ballasting particularly on the most northerly 100 miles. The yard area from the excellent gravel pit at Mile 150 produced over 2 million cu yd for this programme. Freight cars were rebuilt in the shops, and an Equipment Trust issue was placed for 350 gondola cars. Secondhand steam locomotives, with greater hauling capacity, were purchased from certain railways in the United States.

During World War II new regulations of the Forestry Department of Ontario required that cross ties should be sawn and not hand hewn. Extensive stands of Jack Pine in the area of Mile 150 on the railway's land grant had provided the greater part of the maintenance requirements, which ran at 80,000 to 100,000 a year. These were hand hewn on two sides under a contract that precluded any form of treatment such as creosoting. The railway therefore purchased and installed a sawmill and built a spur line into a Jack Pine area at Mile 183, and to run the operation an organization under a qualified forestry engineer was set up. Installation of a creosoting plant would have been much too costly and therefore a plant using Osmose was built at Hawk Junction to treat the sawn ties. This treatment, which gives to new ties their greenish appearance, increased the life of a tie by an estimated two to three times. Exhaustion of suitable tie timber in this area resulted in negotiations with the Dubreuil Brothers to produce ties for the railway in an area north of Magpie Junction on the Michipicoten Branch. This remarkable family has steadily built up its operations, and a station named Dubreuilville is located near to the center of their present activity, at Mileage 184·2.

In 1941 the large car shops at the Soo, built originally in 1899, in wood, were destroyed by fire; they were rebuilt in brick, with a much improved layout for operating, and with additional machinery. At the same time Steelton yards were remodelled. It was in this area however that at about the same time there came the final serious threat against the railway by one of its former associates. A proposal was made to install a direct rail connection between the Steel Company's property, adjacent to the Steelton Yards, and the Canadian Pacific Railway. Authority to do this was actually obtained from the Board of Transport Commissioners. The ACR immediately made an application to the Board for a hearing, in order to protect its interests, and a date was duly fixed. The management was confident that no right-of-way for the connection could be made without encroaching upon land of the Terminals Company. But it was war time and a request for the plan was refused on the grounds that its publication would be of assistance to Germany.

The hearing in Ottawa was most unfortunate for the railway, because after presenting the case in the morning the Special Counsel who had been engaged for the case informed the Board that a Federal Government commitment required his departure that very afternoon for Washington. Against the ACR was a formidable array of lawyers representing the Steel Company; Sir James Dunn, as a Quebec barrister, also addressed the Board. To crown all a Senator, in the rearmost row used by the public, rose and made a scurrilous attack on the ACR. The railway prepared and sent to the Commission a rebuttal of the arguments submitted at the hearing by the Algoma Steel Company, including its contention that as Terminal property was involved a plan of the proposed connection should be produced, because it affected the Trustees of Central Terminals under its mortgage, as well as the railway and its Trustees. The Board ordered the Steel Company to send plans to the parties mentioned in the rebuttal, and received a reply that the plans would be sent in about a month. But they were never sent, and no further hearings took place. So, the threatened CPR direct connection into the Steel plant passed into oblivion.

One of the problems of shipping on the Great Lakes is that all operations are suspended during the winter months; the normal procedure for plants taking raw materials on water is to stock-pile during the summer so as to have enough supplies to last throughout the period when the lakes are frozen over. But in the winter of 1950 an all-rail movement to the Soo for Steel plant requirements was needed, because to fulfil contracts practically all sintered ore produced had been exported at the close of navigation. It then became evident that there were big advantages in an all-rail movement. By direct conveyance by ore-car to plant breakage was virtually eliminated, and it resulted in a very substantial increase in blast furnace production, per ton of ore actually mined. Since then all sinter for the plant has been moved by rail.

94

Whatever anxieties may have persistently lain with the Bondholders' Committee in London, and in day-to-day affairs with the management of the railway at the Soo, the marvellous spirit of the ordinary man 'out the line'—as the Scottish expression goes—which I have found consistently on railways all over the world, was nowhere stronger than on the Algoma Central; and it seemed that the rugged terrain, and the availability of equipment that was not then always of the best merely sharpened their determination, and increased their *esprit de corps*. In my journeys over the line I had the privilege of meeting many men whose service extends back to more than 40 years, and of hearing their stories, gay and grave. Among the exciting episodes inevitably connected with a railway through such a countryside and subject, as I experienced in my own travels, to such extremes of weather, I learned how closely the men who ran the trains were—and still are—in touch with social development and industrial activity: how alive to any possibility of attracting any extra traffic, and how cordial and astute in keeping good relations with everyone living within sight and sound of the railway.

I traveled from end to end of the line with Russell Rankin, the present General Superintendent, whose own service extends back around 40 years, including a great diversity of experience, and he was constantly pointing out the sites and significance of past and present activities, but knew all the men concerned personally, and their family connections. But to anyone who had not traveled over the line it must not be imagined that it is a continuous chain of teeming activity. Even today the line traverses vast stretches of virgin forest, where between the few trains the only sounds are those of nature—the crash of a tree felled by beaver, the growl of a bear, the splash of a leaping trout. Through such a land the railway provides a tenuous line of communication, and in the days when dividends were non-existent and money for improvement was scarce the men who ran the trains did a magnificent job of public relations, though they would probably be a bit puzzled to hear it called by such a high-sounding modern name. In their free days they fished the lakes, and shot the partridges, and on the more northerly stretches of the line would perhaps join with some customer in a moose hunt. Hawk Junction, so named from the very beautiful Hawk Lake, grew up as an out-and-out railway colony, deep in what had been primeval forest. And then there was Hearst.

This indeed was an outpost. I have told earlier in this book how the Algoma Central first arrived at Hearst, and of the significance of the connection with the Transcontinental line of the Canadian Government Railway; but no words of mine can truly convey the unique atmosphere of this remarkable town. I met the present Mayor and some of its leading citizens, and while it would be wrong to give the idea that Hearst is a relic of the 'wild west', or of the days of Wells Fargo, this community of 5000 souls has retained much of the pioneering spirit of 60 to 70 years ago in its vigor, its individuality, its abounding good humor, and today not least in its prosperity from the timber trade which places much valuable traffic on the line. And here too the men of the Algoma Central are as well known, and as respected and welcome, as at any place in the 295 miles separating it from the Soo. One of the older servants of the Company expressed all these sentiments in a single sentence: 'Working on the ACR was not a job; it was a way of life'.

No account of Canadian railway life would be complete without a 'bear' story, and so I will conclude this chapter, which has, I fear, been one mostly of stress and strain, on a more lighthearted note. One day the Railway Assistant Superintendent at Hawk Junction was walking the track from Josephine to Mile 3 where a work gang was located. Happening to look back he saw a large black bear loping along toward him. He immediately began to run, but then decided that he could not last the distance to Mile 3 so slid down an embankment, armed himself with good-sized stones and prepared to do battle. But the bear completely ignored him and continued on his way. When eventually the Assistant Superintendent got to Mile 3 he found the bear at the cook-car, waiting to be fed!

4　Launch of the MV *Sir Denys Lowson* at Collingwood shipyard in 1964. The flat-bottomed lake ships are launched broad-side, because of the confined space

5 One of the 'SD40' 3000 hp diesel electric locomotives newly delivered from General Motors plant, London, Ontario

CHAPTER EIGHT

Bondholders' Control and Its Ending: Financial Operations

This chapter could well have as its sub-title the life story of one remarkable man, E B Barber, who joined the Algoma Central Railway as a night timekeeper in the Company's Commercial Dock, in 1905, and who in 1934 was appointed President and General Manager. He was appointed Assistant Comptroller in 1913 just as the Company's fortunes were plunging to their all-time nadir, and when the railway defaulted on its interest payments in December 1914 one might have thought that a man who had already shown such outstanding ability, as to receive exceptionally rapid promotion, would have read the signs writ large in the sky and resigned to seek opportunity elsewhere. But Barber stood firm on the apparently sinking ship and eventually, after *forty-five years* of continuous struggle, saw it emerge into calm and prosperous waters.

This account can conveniently begin with the discharge of the Receivership in November 1916, when the London Bondholders' Committee assumed control of the railway. They appointed R Home Smith of Toronto as President, and George A Montgomery as Vice-President and General Manager, while in 1918 Barber, continuing in the office of Comptroller, was also appointed a Vice-President. A 'Scheme of Arrangement' was drawn up with the Lake Superior Corporation, which included the provision of a maximum net income of $100,000 per year, for working capital, and a sum of $3,000,000 of the preferred shares of the railway, equal to 60 per cent of the shares then outstanding, were issued to the Bondholders' Committee, as fully paid, as trustees for the benefit of the railway and terminal companies bondholders.

The later stages of World War I brought an improvement in the fortunes of the Algoma Steel Company, and the Bondholders' Committee attempted to secure some improvement of the terms under which the Lake Superior Corporation had given its guarantee, under the 1916 'Scheme of Arrangement', but agreement could not be reached, and it was not until the year 1928 that any improvement in the financial position could be negotiated. Then, after lengthy negotiations between the railway, the Lake Superior Power Company, and the province of Ontario, an agreement was concluded providing for power development at the Montreal Falls, which the railway crosses on a lofty curving steel viaduct 92 miles north of the Soo. Because the development could not be made without using railway land for dams, powerhouses and such like, it was agreed that a yearly rental of $25,000 should be paid to the railway for a period of 60 years, less a payment made to the province, as a charge for developed power in excess of 20,000 horsepower. Before this agreement had been concluded the General Manager of the ACR, G A Montgomery, died, and E B Barber was appointed to succeed him.

The year 1928 was an eventful one, financially, for the ACR. A financier named Dodd, from Montreal, had bought up sufficient shares in the Lake Superior Corporation as to secure his election as President, in that year. He started immediately a great campaign of propaganda boosting the future prospects of 'Lake Superior', and was successful in raising the Stock Market quotations for the shares to such a high figure that the ACR, with the approval of the London Bondholders' Committee, demanded immediate settlement of the guarantee made under the 1916 'Scheme of Arrangement'. But Dodd was not carrying his own directors along with him, and when things reached the stage of negotiation, and he and Home Smith of the ACR were traveling to London to meet the Bondholders' Committee, a message was sent from Canada demanding his immediate return, and his resignation. This episode brought the reputation of the Lake Superior Board to a low ebb, and considerable changes were made, with men of greater repute replacing those forced to reign, following the dismissal of Dodd.

Late in 1928 a new attempt was made to secure a settlement of the guarantee, and Home Smith left for London a second time, now accompanied by Sir William Stavert, representing the Lake Superior Board. This time agreement was reached, but not ratified in Canada, and further negotiations took place in 1929. Home Smith and Barber represented the ACR. In the previous year one of the provisions agreed to in London, but not ratified, was that one-third of the Lake Superior assets should be transferred to the bondholders; but in 1929 Barber argued that this transfer should be made to railway assets instead. He asked for this change to strengthen the income of the railway if dividends were declared, and to ensure a close relationship between the two companies. It was then the turn of the London Committee to disagree, and they insisted that the Lake Superior assets should go to the bondholders. Again Barber stood out, arguing that such an arrangement would sever completely the railway connection at the Soo, with the Lake Superior and the Power Company, and release them of any obligation to give traffic to the railway. The negotiations were renewed in England in 1930, and Barber carried the whole burden so far as the

Algoma Central Railway was concerned; and this time, at last, agreement was secured. The terms were covered by twelve clauses, as set out in an appendix at the end of this chapter, and when this, the '1930 Scheme', became effective the prospects for the railway began to look brighter.

Then however came the world-wide slump of the 1930s with a general recession in business, and on top of this one of the Company's steamships, the *W C Franz*, was sunk in a collision in 1934. This reduced the fleet to only two vessels. These ships had furnished substantial earnings, and it was essential to the future of the railway to get more, because only two, each of no more than 5500 tons capacity, would not warrant continuing the operation. It was discovered that two United States vessels, one of 9400 tons capacity and one of 10,500 tons, were in the possession of bondholders following a financial crash in 1930, and after discussions with the attorneys for the owners, agreement was reached for their purchase. The London Committee at first agreed; but then certain other financial commitments alarmed them and approval was withdrawn. Barber sent strong representations to London, by cable, and London then agreed, though with the proviso that the purchase must be financed out of railway funds, because the Committee would not release any funds in its possession. When all was settled it transpired that a sheriff's sale was necessary, and this took place in the lobby of the Buffalo Post Office. The purchase was in every way a fortuitous one, because the earnings from these vessels actually kept the Company going in the lean years of railway operation.

In 1932 another mighty power appeared on the Algoma scene in the person of Sir James Dunn. This remarkable man had originally been attracted to the Algoma country by its speculative possibilities, but he arrived just at a time when Algoma Steel was experiencing the full blast of the economic depression. Bankruptcy, for the second time in its history, was precipitated by inability to pay a coal bill of $62,476, and on 13 August 1932, the furnaces were allowed to cool and the plant closed down. Dunn, far from fighting shy of a very difficult situation, took steps to secure full personal control, and immediately initiated moves for a complete reorganization of the Lake Superior Corporation. Despite the Railway Company's interest, in light of the 1930 Scheme of Arrangement, care seemed to be taken to exclude Home Smith and Barber from any of the discussions and this naturally aroused suspicions in their minds as to Dunn's intentions so far as the future of the railway was concerned. It would have been quite in keeping with his character and past record for him to bid high to secure absolute control. While all this was going on Home Smith decided to resign, having borne immense burdens as President for 18 years, and E B Barber was appointed to succeed him. Smith died in the following year. The divorce of the former Clergue companies at the Soo was now approaching completion. The Paper Company was then owned by the Abitibi Pulp and Paper Company, then in Receivership, and the Power Company was owned by Middle West Utilities, of Chicago.

In 1934 the Algoma Central Railway was entering upon a new period, in which it continued to be controlled by the Bondholders London Committee, with E B Barber as President, at the Soo, and with Sir James Dunn installed as President of the newly reorganized Algoma Steel Corporation. For the next 20 years Barber and Dunn fought a running battle for control of the railway. Dunn started in at once. In his reminiscences Barber has written:

> In 1934 Sir James, accompanied by Harry Gundy, head of an important investment house in Toronto, wished to go to the Helen property and the writer accompanied them in the car *Michipicoten*. During the trip Mr Gundy asked how many tons of steel rails were laid; what did I estimate the tonnage was in steel bridges, and so on, and then remarked 'Jimmy, we should buy up the bonds, sell the steel for scrap and make a fine profit on the transaction'. Later on the trip, Sir James told me he intended to get control of the Railway. He apparently had in mind re-uniting the three remaining Clergue industries and he later made overtures for acquiring Great Lakes Power Company and the Abitibi Mill at the Soo. The Middle West Utilities had been ordered to sell the Power Company at the Soo by the Roosevelt Administration. The President of the Power Company was J A McPhail, who was also a director of the Steel Company. If Sir James had been willing to agree as to terms of sale, a purchase price might possibly have been arranged. This could have been of great value in the future in respect of production costs of steel products and mining operations. The Railway, however, was financially weak and dependent largely on Steel traffics, and was therefore the Company in which control was first attempted.

The 'blow-by-blow' history of the Dunn-Barber confrontations of the next few years make complicated reading, but all the time they are flavored with Sir James Dunn's attempts to secure control of the railway. He attempted to embarrass the company over the question of mileage tax. Under the provision of an Ontario Act, called a 'Mileage Tax', railways operating in the Province were taxed $65 per mile for mainline trackage. The Algoma Central had paid no tax under the Act since its inception, and had not been pressed for payment by successive Governments. But the question got raised in 1934, and there seems little doubt that some back-stage work was done by Sir James, in his contacts with leading members of the Government. Concurrently Sir James promoted, and secured incorporation of a new company, the 'Southern Algoma Railway', which he argued was necessary because the Algoma Central had neither the operational expertise nor the financial stability to meet the needs of the Steel Company. How things were contrived one can only guess, but this was followed by the serving of a writ upon E B Barber personally for payment of mileage taxes and the interest thereon amounting to no less than $1,389,016·19.

Barber went to London in 1936 to give a personal account of all these events to the Bondholders' Committee. Sir James followed, and after the Committee had endorsed the policy Barber had recommended, sought him out and tried to get information, and if necessary to get any decisions reversed; certainly the two men parted on none too happy terms.

There were many complications over land rights, arising from the previous interconnection of the various Clergue companies in the Soo. One developed with a subsidiary of the Steel Company over a magnetite deposit at Goulais held under the regular mining lease of the railway, and great difficulty was being experienced with the Steel Company itself regarding the Terminals right-of-way running through the Steel plant property. But Barber still managed to hold his own, without a major show-down. 'In June 1938', he relates, 'a Steel Company official came to see our Steamship Superintendent, and I happened to enter the office just as he was leaving. After the usual amenities he said he might as well state that he had come to advise the railway would not receive the coal and ore shipments, as Sir James had telephoned from London giving instructions to cut off all traffic possible and "starve the railway". I could have held them to the coal movement', Barber continued, 'but did not wish to enter into a controversy that would further aggravate relations, as the coal movement alone was not sufficiently profitable.' Barber's astute handling of this further attack paid off more quickly than might have been expected, because in the spring of 1939 the ACR vessels were again given Steel Company cargoes of ore and coal without any reference to the 'starvation' incident of the previous year.

By this same year of 1939 however the tax situation between the province and the ACR was becoming more and more of a menace. Adding together Mileage Tax, Land Tax, and Fire Tax a total of $2,276,010·54 was claimed against the railway, and with the improvement in revenue and the promise of greater all-round stability Barber felt that he ought to try for a settlement. The Prime Minister of Ontario, Mitchell Hepburn, who was on the most intimate terms with Sir James Dunn, asked the latter to prepare a scheme of settlement. To have Dunn involved was the last thing Barber wanted; but the outbreak of war in September 1939 evidently engaged Dunn's attention elsewhere, and when he did not present his proposals by Hepburn's appointed time—October 1939—the railway management, briefing a lawyer of high reputation, opened direct negotiations with the government. A settlement was secured, on the terms set out in the second appendix at the end of this chapter.

This was really the end of Sir James Dunn's attempts to secure control of the railway. While some of the tactics he employed were at times a little unorthodox, he was fighting for the interests of the Steel Company as surely as Barber was defending the interests of the railway; and no one in the Soo would deny that Dunn did a massive job in building the efficiency and prosperity of Algoma Steel toward the very high position it holds in Canadian industry today. An account of the modern plant, now undoubtedly the best customer of the Algoma Central Railway, is contained in Chapter 15 of this book. Personal relations between Barber and Sir James improved, though there was an amusing contretemps at Wawa in post-war years when Earl Alexander of Tunis, as Governor-General of Canada, visited Sir James and Lady Dunn, to see the Mine and Sinter Plants at Wawa. The special train was stopped at Franz, and Barber relates the story thus:

> I met Lord and Lady Alexander and delivered a letter from Lady Dunn to them, apparently containing an invitation to stay the night as their guests at 'Eagle's Nest' at the Mine. There had been heavy rains, and as one section of track was partly flooded I wanted a definite time, namely 9 am, for leaving Wawa for the Soo. Asking for my view regarding the invitation, I suggested it might be advisable to return to their own car for the night or the departure might be delayed, which they did. During the trip from Franz to Wawa, Sir James had telephoned the Agent to have the train stopped at the Sinter Plant gates where motor cars were assembled to convey the guests and aides to the Mine. Upon hearing this I ordered the train to stop at the Station where many people had come to see the Governor-General and not at the gates, which resulted in Sir James and his party driving to the Station after the train passed the Sinter Plant gate. As he walked passed the Railway business car he was very angry and called out to say 'Don't you know how to run your —— Railway' to which I waved my hand and smiled.
>
> On the trip to the Soo we also hauled the Canadian Pacific Railway special car Sir James had rented and relations continued quite pleasant. Sir James explained to the party the reason for his getting control of Canada Steamship Lines and I mentioned my concern as to the effect this would have on the Railway fleet, his answer being 'none'. From Hawk Junction through the Canyon Lord Alexander was locomotive engineer, saying I need not worry as it was not the first time he had handled locomotives.

At various places in this book I have endeavored to pay tribute to men who have rendered long and loyal service to the Algoma Central and the present is a good moment to mention Walter Hugill. He began in circumstances as humble as those of E B Barber, as a car checker, in 1903. From that he was promoted step by step to train dispatcher and then to Train Master. He enlisted in the Canadian Army in 1914 and was gazetted as Lieutenant, but was sent back to Canada because of bad eyesight. After the war he was promoted to Superintendent of Car Service, and for many years was Chairman of The Car Service Division of the Railway Association of Canada. He was appointed Assistant to the President in July 1945, and later became General Superintendent. In August 1952 he was promoted to Vice President of Rail Operations, in which office he continued until his retirement in December 1959. He was one of those dedicated railwaymen who, over the years, acquire a vast and intimate knowledge of all phases of operation, and his experience and advice were invaluable when the time came to introduce diesel traction, as related in Chapter 12.

After all the strained relations that had persisted between the railway and Steel Company, arising from the expansionist tactics of Sir James Dunn, it is pleasant to be able to recall the very much more cordial situation that developed later, to a very large extent on account of the statesmanship of E B Barber. He himself relates:

> Late in 1948 Mr J A Goudge, Chairman of the Bondholders Committee, asked me to come to London for a conference at which he informed me of his intention to resign from the Committee as he was now eighty-five years of age, and that he would like to see some interest paid to the Railway Bondholders who had received nothing since the new 'Scheme of Arrangement' was made in 1931. There were still some Terminals Bonds outstanding but as great progress had been made in the rehabilitation of the properties it was decided to call the balance which would leave sufficient funds available to make an initial token payment of one per cent interest on Railway Bonds in 1950.

Relations with Sir James and officials of the Steel Corporation were good, and Barber suggested that Robert W Adeane, a son-in-law of Sir James, might be added to the London Committee, with the view of succeeding Goudge as Chairman. Barber quite rightly felt that such a move would please Sir James, and still further cement the good relations that then existed. Barber asked Goudge to defer his resignation for another year and this he did, to be succeeded as planned by Robert Adeane.

In the early 1950s a representative of an investment company from London, England, called upon E B Barber, at the Soo, and in discussing the affairs of the railway suggested it was about time the ordinary shareholders should be represented on the London Committee. He mentioned that Sir Denys Lowson, Bart, a well-known international investment banker, controlled a very large block of shares and thought he should be made a member of the Committee. This, of course, as Barber pointed out, was a matter for the Committee itself and not for the Railway Management at the Soo; but he also felt that as the maturity date of the bonds was getting closer, representation of the shareholders on the Committee would be desirable. He therefore wrote London to that effect, and Sir Denys Lowson was elected a member in 1954. The financial position of the company was becoming ever more favorable, and during the years 1946 to 1959 not only had large sums been expended for rehabilitation of its line and equipment, but funds to a total value of more than $57 million had been provided for capital expenditure; the original cost of the vessel *E B Barber*, redemption of Central Terminal Bonds (1941–50), redemption of the 1910 preferred shares; interest payments on Railway Bonds (including arrears) 1950–9 and work orders.

Following a meeting in London, in 1958, Sir Denys Lowson prepared a scheme for new capitalization to provide for redemption at maturity of the railway bonds and the arrears of interest on them that remained. The new capitalization was approved by a special Act of the Federal Parliament and the 1910 issue of Railway Bonds, and also the original preferred shares of 1910, were redeemed in full on

31 March 1959. The London Committee which had functioned for 43 years was then dissolved, and control passed back to the Common Shareholders. Sir Denys Lowson was elected Chairman of the Board, and E B Barber, who had labored so unceasingly for the benefit of the company, was created Honorary President, with a seat on the new Board. So the company passed back into the status of an ordinary railway company controlled by its shareholders. It was a triumph of long sustained endeavour, resolution and skilful financing.

APPENDIX 1

SCHEME OF ARRANGEMENT—1930

The gist of the Scheme approved by both parties is as follows:

1 A new Holding Company to be incorporated, named Algoma Consolidated Corporation, to take over all the assets of Lake Superior, whose shareholders would receive 400,000 shares, and the Committee 200,000 shares, (one-third) for distribution to the Bondholders

2 The Consolidated would issue $3,000,000 5% Cumulative Income Debenture Stock or Bonds to be given to the Committee for delivery to its Railway Bondholders

3 The Railway would create a new issue of $10,380,000 5% First Mortgage Income Debenture Stock or Bonds of which the new Holding Company would receive $4,123,400 and the Railway Bondholders would receive $6,256,600 replacing the $10,080,000 Bonds now held which were to be turned in and cancelled

4 Lake Superior agreed to deliver to the Committee for its Bondholders 206,170 Railway shares and transfer the balance of 214,585 shares to the Holding Company with voting rights in the Committee

5 The Central Terminals Company to redeem 40% of its outstanding bonds with funds received from the sale of Algoma Eastern Terminals bonds and stock amounting to $900,000 and other funds available, plus $100,000 received from Algoma Central

6 The Central Terminals agree to transfer all its terminal property at Michipicoten to the Railway Company upon the receipt of the $100,000 payment

7   The Michipicoten property to be excluded from the Railway Trust Deed securing its bonds

8   Upon the receipt of 200,000 shares of the Holding Company and other considerations, the Railway Bondholders agree to the cancellation of interest unpaid as of 31 December 1930 amounting to $8,013, 600 and the Terminals Bondholders agree to cancellation of $1,739,031 unpaid interest as of 1 February 1931

9   The Committee to receive the right to have two representatives on the Boards of Directors of the Holding Company, Lake Superior, and Algoma Steel Company, and the Holding Company to receive the right to appoint two directors on the Board of the Railway Company

10   The $3,000,000 Terminals Bonds outstanding to receive as a fixed charge the full 5% per annum as against the provisions in the 1916 'Scheme of Arrangement'

11   The preferred shares (125,000) of the Railway to be reduced to $4 per share

12   The Guarantee of Lake Superior as to principal and interest of the Railway and Terminals Bonds to be cancelled

APPENDIX 2

The agreement provided that the claim for $2,276,010·54 would be settled by:

1   A cash payment in March by the Railway of $121,812·22

2   Transfer of Land Grant acreage south of the Canadian Pacific Railway to the Province of approximately thirty-eight Townships containing 850,150·23 acres, being carried on the books of the Railway at $589,589, the actual value being much greater

3   The waiving of a claim by the Railway for dues paid on Jack Pine cut on its Townships amounting to $208,934. (The Grant specified 'pine' which the Province contended did not include 'Jack Pine')

4   Retention by the Railway of its interest in the contract between the Railway under the 1912 agreement with the Paper Company on the lands to be transferred to the Government

5　Retention of all lands sold under agreements for farms; and on all lands sold or leased or staked as mining lands; existing rights-of-way and Station Grounds, etc. The lease to Algoma Steel Company of the Goulais magnetite claims were part of the lands retained by the Railway

On its part the Province agreed:

1　No further charge would be made for Fire Taxes on Railway lands as from 1 January 1940

2　Land Grant Lands south of the Canadian Pacific Railway would be exempt from the Land Tax Act from 1 January 1940

3　That the Mileage Tax for the five years from 1940 to 1944 would be at the rate of $6·25 per main line mile and there afterat the rate imposed by the Act. (This tax was paid only for 1940 as the Tax agreement between the Federal and Provincial Government in respect of Provincial Corporation Taxes was included in the Federal Income Tax on Corporations)

CHAPTER NINE

The Changing Pattern of Business: 1950–66

This is no more than a short chapter; a kind of halfway house between the old and the modern Algoma Central. While the financial affairs of the company were moving steadily out of the long period of difficulty and stress, the changes in the pattern of traffic, in the type of business, and in the methods of operation began to undergo changes so eventually complete, as to make the company as a whole a strikingly different one from that which existed up to 1950. In that year two major developments in Canadian railway operation generally had just begun, and the one was undoubtedly assisted by the other. First of all the diesel electric locomotive was rapidly coming to the fore as the most important form of motive power on Canadian railways, and secondly the practice of making major movements of iron ore was under way. The sources of supply of iron ore were changing. The great resources of the United States had been much depleted by the enormous demands of World War II; prospectors had found and were developing rich supplies in Canada, but in many cases located where railway transport was essential. The terrain was invariably difficult, and involved steep gradients; and it was in such conditions that the inherent performance characteristics of the diesel electric locomotive showed a marked superiority over steam. The technical considerations involved are discussed in Chapter 12 of this book.

Conditions favorable to the introduction of diesels existed in full measure on the Algoma Central. In Chapter 7 I described how the substantial movement of sintered ore from Wawa to the Soo, as an all-rail operation, originated. This was only the beginning of a gradual switch from lake to rail transport for the output of the Wawa plant. Between 1950 when it began, and the year 1966 the annual tonnage conveyed by rail increased from 310,000 to 1,623,000 while in the same span of years the tonnage moved through Michipicoten Harbor declined from 811,000 to no more than 370,000. The increase in total tonnage over this period was of course indicative of the increased productivity of the Wawa plant, from 1,121,000 tons to 1,993,000, but the transfer to rail was impressive, and it was greatly assisted by the introduction of diesel electric locomotives, and the complete superseding of steam by the end of 1952. By then 21 road switchers, of the General Motors Standard 'GP7' type, were doing the work formerly needing 38 steam locomotives. Two yard switchers had replaced two steam o–6–o locomotives. Moreover the diesels were able to handle the steadily increasing tonnage of freight that was a feature of this expanding period.

A less welcome change arising from the general dieselization of railway motive power in Canada, was the decline in coal imports through Michipicoten Harbor. Much of this had been locomotive fuel for the Canadian National Railways, while the coal imports declined still further after the opening of the Trans-Canada oil pipe line in 1958. A further major change came in 1960. Until that year the Algoma Central Railway had been virtually the only form of inland transport in the area, but in that year the Trans-Canada Highway was opened north of the Soo, and exposed the busiest part of the ACR operation to highway competition. This change was undoubtedly the cause of a serious drop in revenue from petroleum products from $668,000 in 1960 to no more than $269,000 in 1966. The opening of the highway also had its effects on the company's receipts from passenger and express business. There were also signs of a decline in revenue from the conveyance of ore. It must be noted that in the year 1959 the tonnage of freight carried had reached what was then an all-time high level of 4,913,076, but for the reasons just mentioned there was a subsequent decline.

The decline would have been much more serious to the company had there not been a strong increase in the movement of forest products. The principal contributory factor in this was the switch of the Abitibi Paper Company in the Soo from delivery by water of its requirements of pulpwood, to delivery by rail, an interesting instance of the policy of a former member firm of this Clergue 'empire' assisting another. The modern activities of the Abitibi Paper Company some eight years later than the period now under discussion are described in Chapter 16. Mainly as a result of this change in policy earlier on, the tonnage of forestry carried on the Algoma Central Railway increased by 102 per cent between 1950 and 1966—349,391 tons to 707,553. Nevertheless, in view of the overall decline in freight tonnage of some 10 per cent between 1960 and 1966 the railway made strong efforts to stimulate additional mineral traffic.

A very important feature of this period of change has been the virtual metamorphosis of the steamship activity. The Algoma Central justly prides itself on being the oldest Canadian operator in continuous service on the Great Lakes; but long establishment can sometimes be a disadvantage in the harboring of old traditions and stereotyped ways. In no part of the Algoma Central organization however has

108

the flexibility of outlook been more marked or more successful than on the Great Lakes and the St Lawrence Seaway; and the way in which the fleet has been modernized to meet changing conditions and new opportunities has been very striking. Since 1963 no fewer than eight ships built between 1901 and 1908 have been sold out of service, and replaced by the fine modern fleet, the activities of which are described in Chapters 13 and 14. The record of these disposals is of interest as showing how, up to 1963, reliance had been placed on old ships, all purchased second-hand, and not ideally adapted to the traffic that the Algoma Central desired to stimulate.

VESSEL DISPOSAL 1963–72

Ship	Originally built		Purchased Date	Sold Date
	Builder	Date		
Algorail	Lorain	1901	1917	1963
Algosoo	Lorain	1901	1913	1965
Algosteel	Wyandotte	1902	1935	1966
Algocen	Lorain	1909	1935	1968
Agawa	Cleveland	1908	1963	1968
Algoway	Bay City	1903	1940	1964
Michipicoten	Bay City	1905	1964	1972
Goudreau	USA	1906	1966	1969

Three instances only of increases in traffic, as a result of developments that needed heavy capital investment, may be quoted.

Traffic	Period	From Tons	To Tons
Grain	1962–6	202,000	725,000
Coal	1963–6	708,000	1,583,000
Stone, sand, salt	1963–6	5,000	905,000

This is, therefore, by way of an interim report on the position at the moment of major changes in activity, and from this we can pass on to the modern company in all its manifold activities.

CHAPTER TEN

The Railway Today: Its Track, Bridges, Communications and People

After the stories of early days, and of the chequered career of this company through so many trials and tribulations, it is time to turn to the present and to see the Algoma Central Railway, in all its manifold activities, as a going concern. Dealing with rail operations first I will begin with the road itself; for it is the very foundation of all railway working. Nothing can make up for deficiencies there, and a thoroughgoing modernization began in 1960, soon after the control of the company had passed back to the ordinary shareholders. First of all we can look at the route itself, in all its rather remarkable physical characteristics of heavy gradients and severe curvature. On pages 112 and 113 is shown a gradient diagram of the line between the Soo and Hawk Junction. North of the latter point, except for a severe initial climb the gradients and curves are easier. The nature of the line between the Soo and Hawk Junction, and particularly that part of it south of Canyon station, is a legacy from the days of penury. A traveler over the line will perhaps be surprised to find that despite the rocky, tumbled nature of terrain there is not a single tunnel.

Donald Burns, the present Chief Engineer, remarked to me that he wished there were some, because by going through outstanding bluffs and hillsides instead of wriggling a way round them them a much better alignment could have been obtained. But tunnels are expensive things to construct at the best of times, and where they would have had to be blasted from the intensely hard rock of the Canadian Shield, in the Algoma country the cost would have been completely beyond the resources of the ACR in its early days. Even now, when the railway is a sound revenue-earner, the traffic would not warrant extensive realignment schemes in this most difficult mountain country. There is no case for such colossal projects as the spiral tunnels on Field Hill in British Columbia that the Canadian Pacific built to improve their operation. But within the remit of existing conditions of gradients and curvature a remarkably fine job of modernization has been done on the Algoma Central.

In the much more favorable financial circumstances of the railway a number of moderns tools for mechanized track maintenance were purchased, and the introduction of these not only greatly improved the road but effected a marked reduction in track maintenance costs over the whole line. Four machines in particular may be mentioned. The 'tie-spacer' ensures uniform spacing of the ties, and has resulted in a reduction of the total number required, by avoiding sections where the ties were spaced unnecessarily close together. Then there is the 'track-liner' utilizing geometrical principles to secure distortion-free straight or curved track. Two other machines, the 'ballast-regulator' and the 'electromatic auto jack tamper' are concerned with the laying and packing of the ballast, and before describing their operation I must refer to the positive revolution that has taken place in the nature of the roadbed. As mentioned earlier in this book the Algoma Central was veritably a contractors' road. It was not the only one in the early days of Canadian railroading! I am writing this chapter at a time when the television serial 'The National Dream' is being shown in Canada, and certain episodes depict most vividly how, in the race to get the Canadian Pacific Railway built across the prairies, the ties were just laid on the ground and the rails spiked down to them there and then. There was no ballasting. On the Algoma Central, prior to modernization, things were little better, though the presence of so much solid rock beneath the line on the section south of the Canyon made it necessary to have some kind of packing, mostly no better than dirt, or gravel.

At the same time railways in Canada have one characteristic that is not found in warmer countries. For a period extending over nearly half the year heavy frost is continuous, and unless there are heavy snowfalls as well the frost can penetrate to 3 feet or 4 feet below the surface. The ties are literally frozen in place, and unless conditions of frost 'heave' are experienced the track keeps its line and level remarkably well. It is when the thaw comes that the engineering department expects, and usually gets, serious trouble. It is then that such trouble is aggravated many times with a track having no more than dirt or gravel packing, because it holds the moisture and drainage deteriorates. But quite apart from the time of the spring thaw there is every advantage in having a substantially ballasted track, and on the Algoma Central, fortunately, one of the finest materials for providing this is readily available at the Soo, in blast furnace slag from The Algoma Steel Corporation.

The program of upgrading was spread over five years—none too long, when some 325 miles of route had to be covered. The first task was to make a survey of the line and note all the ties that needed replacing, and section by section new ties were distributed along the track at the places where they were to be inserted. Then a hydraulic pulling machine lifted the spikes from the ties that were to be replaced. The next stage was to bring up a power jack by which the rail was lifted sufficiently

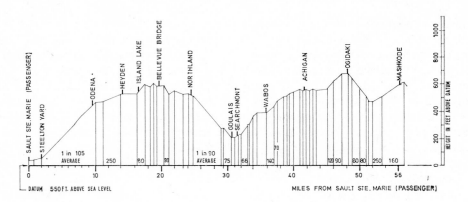

7   Gradient profile of the railway—Sault Ste Marie to Mashkode

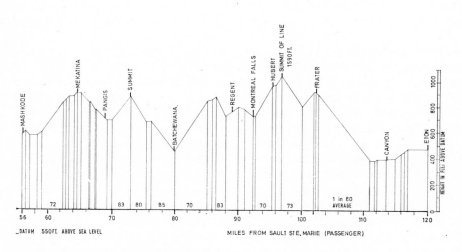

8   Gradient profile—Mashkode to Eton

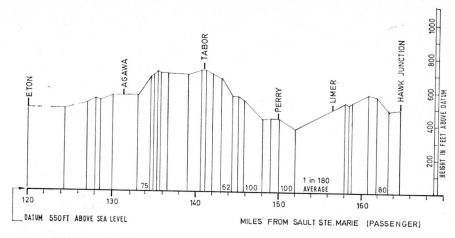

9 Gradient profile—Eton to Hawk Junction

to take the weight off the tie and allow the renewal gang to pull out the old tie. While the tie was out and while the rail was lifted, shovel crews levelled out the old ballast and then inserted the new tie. This was followed by the tie-spacer, which spaced the new tie correctly. In some places many more than one had to be inserted adjacently. After the ties had been correctly spaced the spikes were positioned ready for driving home by a compressed-air operated hammer. Then the ballast train was brought up, and clean, blast furnace slag dumped from bottom-discharging hopper cars. In the improvement programme the road bed was raised between 6 and 9 inches, by the insertion of this layer of ballast. The slag provides excellent drainage as well as having good maintaining qualities.

This extensive program was rounded off first by checking the line, for geometrical accuracy on tangent track and curves—not that there is much tangent on the Algoma Central! Then the ballast is checked, which has to be securely packed beneath the ties to maintain what is sometimes called a 'good top'. For this the electromatic auto-jack tamper is used. AC railway engineering men today take pride in the appearance of their track and the ballast regulator is brought into operation to shape the outer flanks of the roadbed to achieve proper drainage. I first traveled over the Algoma Central toward the end of the summer season, and the neat, well-shaped edges of the ballast were a pleasure to see. The ballast regulator is used both in major renewals and on routine maintenance and has proved invaluable. More recently an important program of relaying, with heavier rails, has been in progress. Previously the line was laid with rails weighing 85 lb to the yard, but these are now being replaced with 100 lb rails.

113

Traveling over the line in the depths of winter, with the whole countryside deep in snow, and no more than the upper surface visible, one could indeed wonder how the track was kept in good condition. There is no cessation of heavy traffic, and very often the siding tracks at the passing loops are completely invisible after a heavy fall of snow, and the main-line rails lie in a channel perhaps 3 or 4 inches deep. The answer is that for the most part the frost holds the track securely—it is more securely held indeed than at any other time of the year. The more the lines are plowed, removing the top covering of snow, the deeper the frost can penetrate. Sometimes one does experience the phenomenon of 'heave', previously referred to. In the summer, when the top level of the rails is affected, from one of many reasons, it is corrected by packing additional ballast under the ties; but that, of course, cannot be done in conditions of heavy frost, and the level is then corrected by inserting shims—thin wood plates—between the rails and the ties to correct the level. I have traveled over the Algoma Central in both summer and winter conditions and can testify to the excellence of its modern track, particularly in the smoothness with which the diesel locomotives and rolling stock negotiate the almost incessant curvature.

In Chapter 7 I have referred to some of the reconstruction work carried out on the older bridges during the days of the Bondholders' Committee control. The line today still includes a number of timber trestles, and some of these are of great interest. They are to be found on the northern part of the line, where there are no deep valleys or ravines to be crossed. North of the intersection with the Canadian Pacific, at Franz, the line enters the muskeg country. It is relatively flat, and it was possible to build a fairly straight line. But in crossing the numerous creeks and larger lakes a problem was experienced in finding a solid foundation for the timber piling. Mr Burns very kindly turned up for me drawings of some of these trestles, as they are today, and from a careful study of these drawings I could appreciate that there is some uncertainty as to where the bottom really is. For this reason they are often referred to as 'floating bridges'. The more northerly part of the line makes up for its lack of dramatic mountain and canyon scenery by the beauty of the lakes set amid the forests of spruce. When I made my more extensive explorations of the line in April 1974 the lakes had a deep covering of snow over the 2 ft thick ice; but although losing a little in scenic attraction by the absence of reflection in the water, they still had a charm and fascination that I find difficult to put into words. One certainly did not find so much 'movement' when crossing the floating bridges.

Near Eton, in which name, I may add for British readers, the accent is on the second syllable, there is a bridge unlike any other on the Algoma Central Railway—a Warren girder 'through' bridge carrying the line across the Agawa River. At the time the original timber trestle at this location was due for replacement the engineer of the Company learned that the Canadian Bridge Company of Walkerville, Ontario, had on their hands a bridge ordered by the Chinese Government Railways that was after all not required. It so happened that in span and carrying capacity it met the requirements at the Agawa River crossing almost exactly, and no more than slight adjustment to the position of the abutments was necessary for the 'Chinese Bridge' to be used exactly as it was. The drawings as now preserved in the ACR drawing office at Steelton still bear the inscription 'Chinese Government Railways'!

A one-time characteristic form of structure not only on the Algoma Central but on most Canadian railways in the days of steam traction was the octagonal timber framed water tank. On Plate 19 are reproduced photographs of a fine example at Brient just inland from Michipicoten Harbor, where locomotives working on the branch were based. This particular water tank was built in the summer of 1917, and from the photograph it is evident that whatever financial distractions might be prevailing at the time there was no cheese-paring in the quality of workmanship put into that tank. Today all the old water tanks on the Algoma Central have been removed, but a fine example still remains at Franz, on the CPR line immediately east of the ACR crossing. Mention of Michipicoten Harbor leads me to the equipment installed there for the import and export activities in connection with the mines at Wawa.

The photographs reproduced on Plates 7, 15 and 40 show perhaps more clearly than much description the process of development that has taken place at Michipicoten Harbor: how the coal dock was built on reclaimed land to replace the old jetty and how the introduction of self-unloading ships in the Algoma Central fleet rendered unnecessary the 'coal bridge'. As described in the following chapter, ore traffic through Michipicoten Harbor is very much less than in former days, though it continues to form an important adjunct to the mining and sintering operations at Wawa.

On a railway like the Algoma Central communications play a most vital part and from my own connection with signalling in so many countries for much of my working lifetime, I was most interested to talk to W G Brittain, Superintendent Communications and Signals of the ACR. Of course with no more than three regular freight trains, and one passenger train in each direction between the Soo and Hawk Junction signalling, as understood on busier lines, is not necessary; but communication is all important. This is done entirely by telephone. Train orders are telephoned to those stations where delivery to the trains is made; they are taken down by hand and then read back to the dispatcher as a cross-check. Then all the trains are equipped with VHF radio telephones between the locomotive and the caboose, and the range of this radio telephone system is such that at places where 'meets' of opposing trains are ordered the crews of these trains can communicate with each other.

At places where there are grade, or level crossings with highways, the standard type of color light warning signals are installed, consisting of the flashing red lights and warning crossed bars. The lights are actuated by an approaching train by means of track circuits. These latter extend to a distance of 1800 ft on each side of the crossing and are normally of the battery-fed direct current type. There are certain instances where adjacent crossings are nearer than 3600 ft to each other, and rather than have one long track circuit covering two crossings, and thereby set the warning in operation prematurely for the second crossing—to the annoyance of road users—the track circuit providing the warning for the second crossing is of the alternating current, overlaid as necessary on the first. Power for this latter is also derived in the first place from a battery, but feeding through a transistor-fed oscillator.

There are two places on the line where trains of the Algoma Central come under the control of full color light signalling of the standard Canadian type. These are at the intersections with the Canadian Pacific at Franz, and with the Canadian National at Oba. Both these lines are equipped with Centralized Traffic Control, and the panels from which the respective dispatchers regulate the train movements are at White River (CP) and at Hornepayne (CN). At the intersections priority of movement is usually arranged on the basis of 'first come first served'. The approach of a train on the Algoma Central line would be shown up on the illuminated track diagram at White River, or Hornepayne, as the case might be, though the 'first come first served' philosophy might not apply if a heavy ACR freight approached shortly before one of the big transcontinental passenger trains on one of the other routes.

Traveling through Algoma Central country, which is little less remote than when the line was first driven north from the Soo, one naturally thinks of the men who keep the line in such splendid order. Few roads lead to the lineside and there are precious few of the amenities of modern life. Each section foreman and his men live right on the job, the men in a bunkhouse. I was told that in earlier days the foremen usually had their wives with them and raised their families there, tending a vegetable garden and perhaps keeping a cow. Today, however, there are not many married men taking these jobs. Not many years ago however in the magazine *Scotiabanker*, a writer who made a trip up the line did meet a section foreman's wife who apparently enjoyed living on the job. She said she did not find it lonely, with the trains going through all the time and appreciated the convenience of having mail, daily newspaper and groceries delivered at the front door—by train! Her four children received their schooling through Government correspondence courses.

There was however another family whose biennial journeys on the railway caused a bit of a problem. They were Indians, living a somewhat nomadic existence and each year they used to pack up 'house' and home and move to another part of the line. Their household effects were not very extensive but mother was so large in diameter that she could not get through the ordinary carriage door. So they had to hoist her up and stow her in the baggage van.

Inspections are often carried out by an automobile with flanges attached to the wheels so that it can be run on the rails. When out on the line it is run under the regulation of the train dispatcher. The operator must be a qualified supervisor familiar with all the rules of the road, as well as holding a highway driver's license. The section men and train crews are of course familiar with this vehicle; but there was an amusing incident one day on a section of line near to one of the ordinary highways. The car carrying some railwaymen on an inspection was spotted by a member of the Provincial Police who was new to the district, and he stopped them at a crossing yelling: 'Hey, what do you guys think you're doing riding along the track in an automobile?'!

CHAPTER ELEVEN

Modern Freight Operation

Freight is the life blood of the Algoma Central, and unlike the characteristics of several other Canadian railways it is not by any means a one-way traffic. From the revenue earning point of view some of the heaviest carriers spend almost half their train mileage hauling empty cars; but over the years the Algoma Central has built up a valuable balancing traffic to the heavy hauls of ore and timber coming southward to the Soo. Much of this is connected with the operations of Algoma Steel, because in return for the southbound loads of ore from Wawa there are sent large tonnages of finished steel products, such as plate, rails, and so on, transferred to one or another of the great transcontinental lines. The regularly scheduled service provides for three freight trains a day in each direction between Sault Ste Marie and Hawk Junction, and one in each direction between Hawk Junction and Hearst. On the branch line between Hawk Junction, Wawa, and Michipicoten Harbor trains are run as required. The statistics of operation are impressive enough, but there is nothing like going out on the actual trains and seeing the problems of working at first hand.

I was able to make a four-day tour of the line, in the pleasance and comfort of the business car *Michipicoten*, and it proved indeed to be the railway experience of a lifetime. When my friends of the ACR collected me at my hotel they remarked upon the mildness of the morning, after a night that promised a hard frost, and I wondered if I should not see a great deal left of the winter snow, as we made our way northward. We went by road to Steelton Yard where the business car was marshalled at the leading end of Train No 7, immediately behind the four locomotives, ready for departure at 10 am. Our party in the car consisted of Russell Rankin, General Superintendent, Don Burns, Chief Engineer, and Hugh Paul, Traffic Manager.

118

Rankin explained to me that on this particular day the train would be serving the function of a 'way-freight'. The normal running time of the northbound freights over the 165 miles from the Soo to Hawk Junction is roughly 7 hours; but once a month during the winter the morning train, which conveys a high proportion of empty ore cars, acts as a 'way-freight' making stops as required to deliver supplies to the various stations en route. These supplies are loaded in a box-car at the rear end of the train, and one could appreciate the value of radio-communication between the engineer at the head end, and the conductor in the caboose. By means of this the conductor could advise the engineer of the exact place to 'spot' the box-car for unloading. On a train of more than 60 cars one can rarely *see* the tail end, on a line of such incessant curvature as the Algoma Central.

On my trip, although we had a train of 63 cars, it was, by ACR standards, quite a light one, not amounting to more than 1800 tons, and although we had four loco-motives—three of the latest 'SD40' type of 3000 horsepower, and one 'GP7' of 1500 horsepower this was a case of 'balancing' locomotive requirements, that is getting the power back to Hawk Junction ready for maximum tonnage trains on the south-bound run. We pulled out of Steelton Yard at 10.8 am and within ten minutes we were climbing hard. With a total of 10,500 horsepower, the heavy gradients pre-sented no problems with our lightly loaded train. Russell Rankin took me through to the leading unit, and passing from a car to the head end while running was, for me, reminscent of the London–Edinburgh non-stops in Great Britain, except that on the ACR we were walking along the *outside* of the locomotives for most of the time. No more than 9 miles on our way, at Odena, we had an order to meet Train No 8, a maximum tonnage job, and we had not been standing long on the passing siding when she came through, with, to me, an enormous load. We were under way again at 10.50, running very slowly until we received a radio message that the tail was clear of the siding and the switch there had been reset for the main line.

I must not dwell upon the scenic beauties of the route at this stage, for this is primarily a chapter about freight operation; but already the snow was lying deeply. At Heyden, 14 miles out, I saw the first of many frozen lakes, thickly covered with snow over ice that the trainmen estimated would be about 2 ft thick. Then we came to the lofty Bellevue trestle—one of the highest steel viaducts in Canada; it was quite an experience to cross this delicate looking structure, 1510 ft long and 169 ft high, outlined against the snow. The locomotive rode well on this severely curved stretch of line, gliding smoothly through iced-up rock cuttings, on a track where no more than the top surface of the rails was visible, and there was ample evidence of how the snow had earlier been plowed clear. The rough notes I took at the time are full of exclamations of wonder at the wintry conditions I saw, and of how delighted I was not to be too late to see something of the winter wonderland in the Algoma country; but in view of what happened on the following day I must write of this first day's experience in a minor key—weather-wise at any rate. Nevertheless I cannot resist mentioning the great frozen 'waterfalls' to be seen on the sides of some of the rock cuttings. Here successive cataracts had frozen, one on top of the other, until they had the appearance of some finely moulded ice shape, semi-transparent, and having a wonderful greenish-blue color.

Thirty-two miles out from the Soo, just beyond the crossing of the Goulais River, is Searchmont. This is the largest centre of population until Hawk Junction is reached. We had some way-freight business to do, and as we approached the train order signal on the station building was in the diagonal-upward position, and we picked up an order as we passed. The leading locomotive had to run a long way ahead in order to bring the box-car with the supplies opposite to the unloading point, and as we drew ahead the conductor radioed to the engineer: '7 car lengths', '3 car lengths' and so on, as we drew very slowly to the stopping point. The time was then 11.35 am—32 miles in 87 minutes—and as Stan Chapman, the incomparable steward of the *Michipicoten*, had previously announced that lunch would be at 12 noon I made my way back to the car. The next 32 miles on to a 'way-freight' stop at Mekatina took another 1½ hours, through some of the most beautiful country on the south end of the line. There the snow was 6 inches above the level of the rails, and there was no doubt I was not to be disappointed in my 'winter wonderland' sight-seeing, even though it was now the first week in April. We had an order to meet southbound No 10 at Regent, and here I went back to the leading locomotive. It was extraordinary to look ahead, and see the passing track to be quite invisible. However, as I wrote earlier, this was nothing to what I was to experience later.

At 2.53 pm we started away to pass through some of the most dramatic railway scenery I have ever experienced. First came the descent, on very sharp curves, to the famous viaduct at the Montreal Falls. There were immense snow drifts at the line-side, 'frozen' waterfalls on the rock sides, and then as we pulled away on the heavy gradient from the viaduct we neared the summit level of the whole line, just beyond Hubert, at Mile 97—1589 ft above sea level. As we were soon to come in sight of Lake Superior however, the altitude would not appear to be so great, because the level of the lake itself is 602 ft above sea level. The depth of earlier snowfalls was evident from the profile athwart the line on embankments, where the track ran in a 'cutting' about 2 ft deep formed on the top of the embankment, by successive plow-ing operations. At Frater, 102 miles from the Soo, reached at 3.31 pm, we picked up further orders, and after some way-freight business began the long and severe descent toward the Agawa Canyon. If the winter-wonderland snow-train passenger excursion had been running on this day I felt that those making the trip would certainly have had their money's worth in the way of snow, and icy conditions. Soon after begin-ning the descent there was a glimpse of Lake Superior away to the west, its surface alternating with ice and open water. Frater is at an altitude of 1462 ft but in 12 miles the line descends over 500 ft. The heaviest gradient is 1·8 per cent, or 1 in 55.

Down in the Canyon, with snow piled up almost to the eaves of the roof of the station building, I thought of my earlier visit when the passenger train brought some 800 excursionists to climb, picnic, and enjoy to the full the beauty of this gem of

Canadian mountain country. Today one could see the odd pool of open water on the Agawa River, but it was mostly frozen over. Most remarkable among the sights at the Canyon were the waterfalls at the southern end—immense cataracts frozen into solid, gleaming bluish-green ice. We had a way-freight stop at Canyon, and there were several more stops to be made in the last 45 miles to Hawk Junction. Eventually we arrived there at 6.45 pm—just over 8½ hours from the Soo. Although this had involved an average speed of barely 19 mph I thought it was a very good performance in view of the number of stops we had to make, and the very slow draw-ins, in order to place that far-away box-car in the correct position. The *Michipicoten* was berthed on a siding near the station, and there we stayed for the night.

Next morning we were ordered to go out attached to Train No 5, not a maximum tonnage train, but heavy enough for all that. The load was given as 4038 tons, and it was originally intended that it would also perform way-freight business. But when daylight came it was evident not only that fresh snow had fallen in the night, but that weather conditions were very bad. Rankin called me at 7 am to see a freight with three locomotives arrive from the south fairly plastered with snow, and at Hawk itself the storm was quickly reaching blizzard intensity. Already snow had piled up to a height of 4 or 5 inches on the railings at the back platform of our car, and Newell Mills, the dynamic Trainmaster at Hawk Junction, called in to say that loose snow around the station was lying to a depth of 2 ft. There is a heavy gradient for about 5 miles north of Hawk Junction, and the snowplow propelled by four 'GP7' units left at 9.45 am to clear the way for us up the grade. Mills came in again to ask Mr. Rankin's authority to reduce the load of No 10, because in the prevailing conditions he was afraid of stalling in the snow. It was agreed to reduce by 300 tons, still leaving the mighty total of 5200 tons to be taken south.

Apart from the immediate start out of Hawk Junction the gradients on the northern part of the line are not so severe, and for our load of 4038 tons we had two 'GP7s'. On this section these locomotives are rated to haul a load of 2950 tons, so that ordinarily our train would have been comfortably within the capacity of a pair of them. But to say that the conditions were 'not ordinary' would be the wildest understatement. Without any doubt the first hour after leaving Hawk Junction was the most terrific experience I have ever had in the tens of thousands of miles I have ridden on locomotives, all over the world. Our engineer, Kuyek by name, got this big train away skilfully, without any wheel slip, and although the plow had been up the hill ahead of us the rails were invisible. Snow was driving level, and building into huge drifts, and so the speed gradually rose, to 12 mph then to 14, and after the worst part of the grade had been mounted we ran at a speed varying between 18 and 27 mph until we came to Alden. This was as far as the plow had gone. From now onward we were doing the plowing ourselves—and how! Snow came in a torrent over the front of the locomotive, so thickly at times that the look-out was completely obscured, and it was dark in the cab. The windscreen wipers were going flat-out, but they could barely clear it, and soon the rear cab windows were plastered too!

Far from seeing any rails ahead there were times when we could not see anything at all, such was the avalanche of snow thrown up by the pilot. We went pounding through Goudreau at 20 mph and on easier gradients beyond got up to nearly 40 mph and it was only then that Engineer Kuyek eased back a little from full throttle. But at Mile 186 one of the warning bells began to ring to tell us that an engine was over-heating, and judging from his knowledge of the road, at a favorable point Kuyek stopped. From long experience he and the leading brakeman guessed that the most likely cause of trouble was the clogging up of the air vents on the sides of the loco-motive, so preventing the normal circulation of air; but next there came the job of getting out of that cab. The door leading backward was snowed up to a height of about *four feet*. Hefty bucking on the door from inside managed to wedge it open sufficiently to get to work with a shovel, and then they proceeded to dig themselves out. All along the open platform snow was about two feet thick. This had to be shoveled away before they could get to the vents, and break away the accumulation of ice and snow. All this had to be repeated on the second locomotive, and although this had collected almost as much the door into the cab could be freed from the out-side. By the time they had gone that far the warning bell had stopped ringing, and my own spell in the cab was ended. I had intended to ride through to Franz, but it was now past noon, and once the gangways were clear I went back to the car.

The episode was reported laconically in the daily operation report on April 5:

'No 5 yesterday was delayed 25 mins at Mile 187 cleaning snow off Unit 157, also delayed 15 mins at Mile 217 for the same reason'.

It was however when we got to Franz and the two units uncoupled and set back to the rear of the train that the truly spectacular part of the episode became fully apparent; for as the photograph reproduced on Plate 30 shows a mountain of snow was piled 2 feet high on the top of the leading unit. Severe though the conditions were however I gathered it was something of a freak storm. It was reported raining 30 miles east of Franz, and friends in Thunder Bay told me afterward that they had nothing of the storm.

Freak or not, blizzard conditions continued along the line of the Algoma Central north of Franz. We left at 1.43 pm having set off some cars for the Canadian Pacific, and in the car *Michipicoten* it was evident that our leading unit was still bucking snow almost continuously. In the car it was like riding behind a steam locomotive with the exhaust beating down. For much of the distance we could see little outside. There were occasional glimpses of spruce heavily weighed down by the snow, and whole trees broken. At the beautiful Oba Lake, seen at 2.23 pm, there was 2 ft of snow on top of the ice. The *back* platform of the car became completely snowed up to a depth of more than a foot, and the rear windows entirely obscured. At Mosher, 217 miles from the Soo, another stop was necessary to clear snow from the locomotives, and so nearing 4 pm we came toward Oba, and the intersection with the transcontinental main line of Canadian National. There was a good deal of activity here, and we were held outside for a little time. The CN main line is now under CTC control of the train dispatcher at Hornepayne 40 miles to the west of Oba, and Algoma Central trains come briefly under CN regulation.

While we waited, short of the diamond crossing, a heavy CN westbound freight went through, and that was followed by a passenger train, consisting only of a single car and a baggage van. Then we were able to proceed to the exchange sidings, for we had much traffic to hand over here to the CNR. The operation was made all the more interesting for me because the *Michipicoten* was detached from the train and I could see the working across two or more tracks. Certain citizens of Hearst, including the inimitable Mayor, Rene Fontaine, had been invited to come to the car on our arrival, and because of the late running of No 5 Russell Rankin decided to have the car transferred to the passenger train from the Soo, which was following at no great distance behind. As the snow-plastered locomotives of No 5 set about the transfer work I saw some of the loads we had brought up from the Soo, including large tonnages of rails, steel tubes, plates, and one fully-fabricated girder. Most of this came from the Algoma Steel works—today the ACR's best customer.

Although from now onward the business car was being attached to No 1, the northbound passenger, my friends of the ACR had one final 'thrill' to round off a memorable day's railroading. While we were attached to the rear of the passenger train, behind us was the snow flanger. This is a vehicle the size and form of a caboose, but exactly at its mid point there is a diamond-shaped wedge that can be lowered to a depth of 2 inches below the surface of the rails. It forms a kind of double-ended wedge plow, and when lowered clears the snow from between the rails. The plow points are raised and lowered by compressed air, and are operated by a crew in the car. These men must have the most intimate knowledge of the road, because the points must be raised when passing over switches, road crossings, and anything else that extends up to rail level. When we got going and the flanger was in action the effect, as seen from the rear end of the business car, was spectacular, to say the least of it. The snow was thrown out to a distance of 30 to 40 ft on either side, and with the locomotive at the head end bucking the snow ahead of it the track was very efficiently cleared. It was surprising however that there was so much more to be cleared when we returned south on the following morning. The storm may have been freakish, and altogether exceptional for the time of year, but on the Algoma Central it was certainly a case of 'business as usual', freight and passenger alike.

That evening over dinner in the business car I had the pleasure of meeting some of the men whose organizations provide much valuable traffic for the Algoma Central. They were mainly concerned with the trade in timber and its products. At this point I must explain the difference in terms, which I for one did not previously appreciate. For transport by rail, trees cut to specified lengths are classified as timber, and freightage rates are charged by the 'cord'. A 'cord' is a volume of 128 cubic ft, including the air space between the round sections of the trees. As a rough guide a cord would contain about 85 cubic ft of solid wood. Now although the men who cut the trees are known as lumberjacks the timber itself does not become 'lumber' until it is sawn. Then rates are charged by the 'board foot', which is a section 12 inches wide, 1 inch thick, and 1 ft long. From the Hearst area the Algoma Central conveys a variety of wood traffics: large trees, smaller sections destined for pulping and sawing into lumber. At Mead, 20 miles to the south, a fine new plant has recently been put into operation, which will add the conveyance of wood chips to the Algoma Central traffics from this area. Much of this wood is destined for the Abitibi Paper Company at the Soo, once a unit of the Clergue 'empire', but large quantities are also forwarded to places in the United States. To me it was interesting to see the close integration of activities that exist between the Algoma Central Railway, and the industrial enterprises along its line. They are widely spread, and attuned to the great expanses of Northern Ontario; but the co-ordination is as close as in the original set-up of the Clergue empire at the Soo, only that it is now founded on an altogether sounder basis.

Next morning, in weather that proved an astonishing contrast to that of the previous day, we returned from Hearst as far as Hawk Junction. By 7 am when we left attached to the rear of the southbound passenger train the sun was up in a cloudless sky, and it remained brilliant until nightfall. The sunshine on the crisp, freshly-fallen snow was indeed dazzling, and made the journey memorable for me in yet another way. The conductor of the passenger train, Johnny Bain, joined us for breakfast in the *Michipicoten*, and I soon appreciated I was meeting another great 'character'. He is not merely a long established servant of the company but another of those sturdy souls whose very being is bound up with the Algoma country. His father was a locomotive engineer in the steam days, but long before the railway penetrated north of the 'Pangis Turn' he was in the transport business running the mails by dog team from Missinabie to Moose Factory. Our breakfast that morning was gay and sometimes hilarious, but one felt that a passenger train on the Algoma Central would be in good hands with such a big hearty soul as Johnny Bain as conductor.

Once again there was much activity when No 2 arrived at Oba. A lengthy east-bound two-unit CN freight was waiting at the west end, and that great train, the 'Super-Continental', was just leaving for the west, with the usual three passenger-type diesels at the head end. The day was Friday, and its respective sections would have left Montreal and Toronto about noon on the previous day. It was due to arrive at Vancouver in the early afternoon of Sunday. The eastbound CN freight got under way as soon as the 'Super-Continental' was clear, and then when that freight was clear of the crossing, we headed south. We reached Hawk Junction on time, at 10.50 am, and after an early snack lunch were ready to go down to Michipicoten Harbor and Wawa. It had originally been intended to make this journey of about 26 miles on a rail-borne motor car, but because of the severity of the storm on the previous day it was thought advisable to go by car on the ordinary highway.

Mineral traffic through Michipicoten Harbor is much less than it was at one time. Reference has been made in Chapter 7 to the switch of the sinter traffic from Wawa to the Algoma Steel plant in the Soo to an all-rail operation. The wisdom of this, in view of the need for continuity of supply, was amply evident when I visited Michipicoten in mid-April, and the whole place was frozen solid, in at least two feet thickness of ice, covered with deep snow. During the 'open' season about 100,000 tons of ore is exported through Michipicoten to Port Colborne, while to supplement production about 100,000 tons of ore fines and 250,000 tons of limestone is imported and taken up to Wawa by train. But the main business of the branch line now is the conveyance of sintered ore from Wawa to the Soo, to the amount of two million tons a year—roughly 5000 tons a day.

Next morning the car *Michipicoten* was to be attached to train number 8, a heavy tonnage freight which was ordered out of Hawk Junction at 4.30 am: 68 cars, 5000 tons, and I was to ride the leading unit for at least the first three hours. Stan Chapman brought me a cup of coffee—very welcome at 4.00 am when the temperature was about 20 below zero; and so, well wrapped up, carrying a lantern, and helped by the light of the moon I climbed along four 'GP7s', in succession number 153, 158, 154, and 151, and so came to the head end where I met the engineer Lorne Strum on locomotive 161. It was a new experience for me to make a night run in such conditions. The headlight shone upon the frozen track ahead, lighting the trees so heavily laden with snow after the storm of two days earlier, and then at 4.34 am those five locomotives with a combined horsepower of 7500 fairly walked that big load away from Hawk Junction. There are one or two steep, if short grades in the first 30 miles, and between Perry and Tabor, for example, on a section of 1·8 per cent, or 1 in 55, the speed came down to $12\frac{1}{4}$ mph. The locomotives were certainly working, and in the low roar of their engines one had a sense of power something akin to the blasting exhausts of hard slogging 'steamers'.

By the time we passed Tabor, $23\frac{1}{4}$ miles out of Hawk Junction in 59 minutes' traveling, the dawn was coming up, exquisitely beautiful in this snow and ice covered landscape. The ice was glittering in the locomotive headlight, and at the stations the siding tracks were still invisible beneath the snow. We had a meet with train No 11 at Agawa, and opportunity was taken of this meet to have inspection of one train carried out while running. The rules require that 'all freight trains must stop and make complete train inspection within 40 miles of initial terminal and at intervals not exceeding 80 miles thereafter'. The dispatcher had contrived the meet at Agawa very efficiently, so that both trains were approaching the place simultaneously. We, as the southbound train, had priority, and in the half light just before full daylight we saw the headlight of the other train coming. Pulling in to the siding track to stop it cleared the entrance switch in time for us to run very slowly through without stopping, and its crew carried out the inspection and then gave us the highball. While such an inspection did not relieve our own crew of the responsibility of assuring themselves that all was well, it will be appreciated that a running inspection is really better than one made when the train is stationary, because it would reveal any irregularities in running that would not otherwise be apparent.

Getting into speed again we were now approaching the most picturesque part of the line, where the mountains close in on either side at the northern entrance to the Agawa Canyon. Running practically at the maximum speed of 30 mph permitted to freight trains on this part of the line, we rounded the curve at the Goudreau gorge and, snaking our way beneath the ice-clad rock walls, with the frozen river beneath us on the left, I was at last able to catch a glimpse of the rear end of our long train— some two-thirds of a mile away! We ran through Canyon station, where the snow was drifted practically up to the roofs of the little houses, past the spectacular frozen waterfalls, and so across the iced-up river to begin the longest and most severe ascent on the route. In climbing from the level of the Agawa River to the summit level of the whole line at Mile 97 there is a really toilsome 7 miles between Miles 110 and 103. The worst pitch is around 1 in 75, 1·3 per cent, and in climbing this 7 miles we took $39\frac{1}{4}$ minutes—an average of no more than $11\frac{1}{4}$ mph. Those diesels were certainly working! The motors were taking 725 amperes, which at the voltage of 600 shows a horsepower of 580. The total output from the five locomotives would have been about 6000 horsepower. This is not so much less than the rated horse-power of the locomotives.

Technicalities apart however it was a marvellous ride. We were climbing higher and higher above the level of the river and toward that place where there is a distant view over Lake Superior; and, as two days earlier, I could see on the surface of the lake the alternate patches of ice and open water. For more details of ice on Lake Superior I would refer my readers to Chapter 14! So, at 7.20 am we came to Frater, 1462 feet above sea level, having covered $62\frac{1}{2}$ miles from the start at Hawk Junction in just over $2\frac{3}{4}$ hours. Although we had another five miles of climbing to reach the summit of the line, just before Hubert, the slow running through Frater gave a good opportunity for me to climb back along those five locomotives for breakfast in the business car. There was much to talk about over the excellent meal that Stan Chapman had prepared, and afterward, from the lounge of the car, continuing to clock the miles, I could appreciate all the better the work necessary to operate one of these massive trains, having seen the artistry of Lorne Strum at the throttle, and no less importantly on the brake valve.

Crossing the ever-fascinating Montreal Falls viaduct, at 7.57 am we saw, briefly, the tail end of the train, brightly marked by the characteristic orange-yellow caboose of the Algoma Central Railway, and after some good speed on the high ground beyond we came to one of the most difficult parts of the railway, when handling a train of this weight and length. From Montreal Falls, for the next 30 miles, it is an alternation of sharp adverse grades, equally sharp descents and constant curvature. It is very dramatic and picturesque from the scenic point of view, passing beneath high frozen crags, sweeping round snow covered lakes, with the speed falling to 12, and sometimes no more than 10 mph on the hardest pitches, and running up to the maximum permitted of 35 mph elsewhere. It was interesting to me that so far we had not made any stop since leaving Hawk Junction, and we had now been on our

126

way for more than five hours—with a 5000 ton freight train in such a terrain as this. But we had an order to meet the northbound passenger train at Ogidaki, and as we were approaching this station several minutes before No 1 was due it was unlikely that we should get a non-stop meet this time, even though we, as the southbound train, had the priority. We drew slowly into Ogidaki, in a beautiful situation beside the frozen snow covered lake, at 10.3 am, 5 hours and 28 minutes after leaving Hawk Junction, 117 miles away, a start-to-stop average speed of $21\frac{1}{2}$ mph. Seeing that everywhere we were limited to a maximum speed of 35 mph and still more severely to 30, over 56 miles of the run, this was a very excellent performance.

While we were waiting for No 1 it was good to climb down for a moment, and enjoy the crisp mountain air in this brilliant sunshine; but the passenger train was not long in coming—five cars altogether, hauled by a 'GP7'—and after a total wait of 12 minutes we started again. Our next run was of no more than 39 miles, for we had a meet at Odena, with No 7 northbound freight, the same train and the same meet that I had experienced two days earlier. There is a heavy climb uphill from Searchmont, 16 miles from Ogidaki, passed in $21\frac{1}{2}$ minutes, and we had a toilsome spell at 12 mph, up to Northland. But after passing this point we were only 25 miles from the Soo, and the rest is all downhill. We met No 7 as ordered, but apparently it was too long for the siding at Odena and we had to stop while he drew ahead once our tail end was clear. Northbound trains, which contain a considerable proportion of empties, are often made up of many more cars than the fully-loaded southbound trains. We covered the 39 miles from Ogidaki to Odena in 89 minutes, start to stop, and after a wait of $4\frac{1}{2}$ minutes we ran gently down the final descent and turned from the main line into Steelton Yard at 12.10 pm—7 hours and 36 minutes from the start at Hawk Junction. We spent another 9 minutes in drawing that long train to the furthest end of the yard; and so ended, for me, a round trip of nothing but the most vivid and enthralling memories.

CHAPTER TWELVE

Diesel Locomotive Power and Rolling Stock

In the years just after World War II, the diesel electric locomotive, so assiduously developed and standardized by General Motors at the La Grange plant, Illinois, and using the highly developed '567' engine designed by C W Kettering, was enjoying a vogue of great popularity in the United States. In Canada at first there was some scepticism as to whether these new locomotives would be equally suitable in the severe climatic conditions experienced during the Canadian winter; but in 1949 and 1950 General Motors sent on loan some units of their standard 'passenger' type, with nosecab and fully enclosed body. They made a tour across Canada in the depths of winter, and in addition to running on the Canadian Pacific and Canadian National Lines, including the sections through the Rockies, one of them was tested over the most heavily graded section of the Algoma Central, between Franz and the Soo. Their performance was studied very carefully by Walter Hugill, then General Superintendent, and he had no hesitation in recommending their adoption.

A performance characteristic of the diesel electric locomotive in comparison to that of steam must at this stage be emphasized. Both may have the same tractive power at normal running speed, but the diesel develops maximum power at much lower speed, and is therefore superior in performance when toiling up a heavy gradient with a maximum load train. It is also much less liable to wheel-slip, particularly the road-switcher type in which the entire weight of the locomotive is available for adhesion. It is significant that in the programme of dieselization undertaken by the Canadian Pacific which involved several thousand locomotives, the first divisions changed over were those including the very severe gradients west of Calgary. On the Algoma Central which then had only 38 steam locomotives in service the problem was studied very carefully.

6 Southbound freight train hauled by four 'GP7' locomotives crossing the Montreal River bridge

The factors considered were the possibilities of securing much higher utilization, because diesels could be turned round from one duty to the next without the lengthy servicing involved in fire and tube cleaning, re-coaling and such like; while the duty of re-coaling on the road, as instanced at Frater in Chapter 5, would be eliminated. Furthermore if units of the General Motors 'GP7' type were purchased there was little doubt that heavier loads could be taken, by a single unit, and still longer and heavier trains handled by a single crew, with locomotives coupled in multiple. The outcome of these studies was a finding that the work of the existing steam locomotive fleet could be satisfactorily done by nineteen road switchers of the 'GP7' type and two 800 horsepower SW-8 type switchers. These latter would take the place of the unpopular 2–8–2s 70 and 71, which had been acquired from the Virginian Railway during World War II.

Delivery of the new road switchers from General Motors began in January 1951, and five of them numbers 150 to 154 were in service by the end of March that year. In view of the hard work that was expected from them on the heaviest gradients of the Algoma Central, and the fact that the nature of the road elsewhere positively precluded any really fast running, they were geared to provide a maximum speed of no more than 55 mph. These first five locomotives fulfilled all expectations; they were able to handle, but with greater ease and certainty, the maximum tonnages previously worked by the two 'Santa Fe' class 2–10–2s, and excelled in climbing the heavy gradients. An order for a further 14 was placed and locomotives 155 to 168 were delivered between September 1951 and March 1952. A month later the Algoma Central Railway was completely dieselized, with 21 new locomotives—two switchers and 19 road switchers—replacing 38 steam locomotives. The company was the first in Canada to be completely dieselized. Two more 'GP7s' were added in January 1953, numbers 169 and 170, and with these 23 units the Algoma Central was well provided. No further additions took place for another 10 years. I should add that all these locomotives were built in Canada, at the newly established plant of General Motors, at London, Ontario. For those who are interested, the builder's numbers of ACR locomotives 150 to 170 were A170–173, A231, A262–275, A441 and 442, thus showing that they were amongst the earliest built at the new plant.

Whatever affection one may have for the steam locomotive one has got to 'hand it' to these 'geeps'! Before I came to the Soo in April 1974 I had seen many of them at work in different parts of Canada, doing a great job; but it was not until I experienced the runs with freight trains described in the foregoing chapter and saw them bucking volumes of snow and pulling masterfully up gradients of 1 in 55, with loads up to 5000 tons, that my earlier warm appraisal of them changed to the greatest admiration. When traffic was further on the increase following the re-assumption of control of the railway by the Common Shareholders in 1959, two of the larger 'GP9' type with 1750 engine horsepower were acquired, though these did not have the special low gearing fitted on the 'GP7s'. These new locomotives, numbers 171 and 172, were delivered in August and September 1963.

The tonnage ratings fixed for the 'GP7' and 'GP9' locomotives is as follows in which the rating 'A' is the maximum in ideal conditions, but not often worked to; 'B' is the normal, while 'C' represents a further reduction of 10 per cent used when rail conditions are bad.

CLASS	GP—1500 HP			GP9—1750 HP		
	A	B	C	A	B	C
NORTHWARD						
Steelton–Goulais	1600	1490	1440	1865	1740	1680
Goulais–Frater	1250	1160	1125	1460	1350	1310
Frater–Hawk Junction	1500	1395	1350	1750	1625	1575
Hawk Junction–Hearst	2950	2745	2655	3440	3200	3100
SOUTHWARD						
Hearst–Hawk Junction	3100	2890	2790	3615	3370	3255
Hawk–Mekatina	1400	1300	1260	1630	1515	1470
Mekatina–Goulais	1550	1440	1395	1810	1680	1625
Goulais–Steelton	1650	1535	1485	1925	1790	1730
WESTWARD						
Hawk–Siderite Jct	1350	1255	1215	1575	1465	1415
Siderite Jct–Brient	1800	1675	1620	2100	1955	1890
EASTWARD						
Brient–Helen	1000	930	900	1165	1085	1050
Helen–Hawk Junction	1430	1330	1285	1670	1550	1500
Siderite Jct–Siderite	1000	930	900	1165	1085	1050

In September of 1971 I paid a visit to the General Motors plant at London, Ontario and I saw coming brand new from the assembly lines three of the standard 'SD40' diesel electric locomotives of 3000 horsepower capacity, destined for the Algoma Central Railway, numbers 180, 181 and 182. These again were of a type already in extensive use in Canada, and well proved in heavy load haulage on severe gradients. Their increased tractive capacity made them ideal units for the conditions prevailing on the Algoma Central, but it should not be assumed that because their engine horsepower is double that of a 'GP7' that they can be allocated tonnage ratings that are double as well. Generally speaking the ratings have been fixed at about 50 per cent greater making allowance for the greater locomotive weight that has to be hauled up the steep inclines. They are essentially heavy freight haulers, not general purpose units like the 'GP7s', which are used on the passenger trains as well. Because of their increased weight certain speed restrictions below the line maxima are imposed, particularly where there is much curvature.

During my visit to the Algoma Central in 1974 I saw two interesting examples of the use of 'GP7' and 'SD40' locomotives on the heavy southbound freight No 8. On the first occasion five 'GP7s' were provided, and multiplying the maximum tonnage rating of 1260 for 'C' class conditions by five would give 6120 tons. On the second, three 'SD40s' were on the job, with a total tonnage rating—three times 1955—of 5865. The first train was the one on which I rode on the leading unit, from Hawk Junction to Frater; the load was originally given as 5600 tons, but because of the very severe weather conditions this was further reduced to 5000. With the second train on a day when the rails were dry and weather conditions well nigh perfect the three 'SD40s' had practically the maximum rated load, 5750 tons, against 5865. Although it was still wintry with much snow on the ground 'B' conditions might well have been operated, giving these three locomotives a load of 6060 tons. The success of the three original 'SD40' class locomotives 180, 181 and 182 has led to the leasing of six more numbers 183–8 which were delivered to the Algoma Central at the end of September and the beginning of October 1973. Since the original purchase of the 21 road switchers 150–70 having a total engine horsepower of 31,500, the nominal power of the Algoma Central locomotive stud has been practically doubled by the addition of the two 'GPs' totalling 3500 hp and the nine 'SD40s', 27,000 hp, an addition since 1963 of 30,500 hp. But for reasons previously explained the total haulage capacity of the stud has been increased by about 55 per cent rather than the 92 per cent represented by the nominal engine horsepower. Even with this very large increase in haulage capacity however the total number of road switcher units is only 32, compared to the 36 steam locomotives hauling a vastly less ton mileage per year in 1951.

The 'SD40s' are beautiful machines. They are the completely standard products, without the special low gearing used on the 'GP7s'. With their maximum rated loads they are able to climb the hills at higher speeds, and avoid the punishing treatment sometimes meted out to the 'GP7s' when speed might fall as low as 4 or 5 mph. That these latter units could take it, albeit with something of a strain on their engines, is a resounding tribute to the robustness and dependability of the locomotive design as a whole. The 'SD40s' have a more generous look-out with additional windows in the centre looking out over the 'bonnet'. The 'GP7s' have front windows only at the sides, though this of course was not felt in any way restrictive by men used to working steam locomotives. I mentioned earlier that the latest units of the 'SD40' type are leased. This the company is finding more economical than outright purchase, not only with locomotives but also with freight cars.

The freight car stock of the Company is geared to the major products conveyed. There has been an interesting development in the design of ore hopper cars used. The older cars, with transverse opening bottom hoppers, are now being rapidly phased out, though naturally there are still many to be seen in service on the line. A later design, of larger capacity, have ship-hull shaped bodies, and longitudinal-opening hoppers. These are of distinctive appearance, painted black with the Algoma

TONNAGE RATINGS FOR 'SD40' LOCOMOTIVES

CLASS	A	B	C
NORTHWARD			
Steelton–Goulais	2510	2330	2260
Goulais–Frater	1960	1825	1765
Frater–Hawk Junction	2350	2185	2115
Hawk Junction–Hearst	4620	4300	4160
SOUTHWARD			
Hearst–Hawk Junction	4800	4460	4320
Hawk Junction–Mekatina	2170	2020	1955
Mekatina–Goulais	2400	2230	2160
Goulais–Steelton	2560	2380	2305
WESTWARD			
Hawk Junction–Siderite Jct	2120	1970	1910
Siderite Jct–Brient	2820	2620	2540
EASTWARD			
Brient–Helen	1550	1440	1395
Helen–Hawk Junction	2220	2065	2000

Central logo, including the black bear on their sides. The latest design, of which many were already in service when I was on the line in April 1974, are very large modern cars, specially designed for the movement of sintered ore. They have a capacity of 100 tons and are equipped with rapid discharge hoppers. They are easily recognizable by their greater height than previous ore-hopper cars of the Algoma Central and by their distinctive dark green colour. No fewer than 300 of these fine cars are being added to the stock in 1974–5.

The gondola cars in use are of conventional North American pattern and are loaded with miscellaneous manufactured products, such as rails, steel plate, and special items of fabricated steel, although rails are also loaded on to flat cars. A typical design of gondola cars of which a number were built by the National Steel Car Corporation of Hamilton, Ontario in 1947 have a cubic capacity of 1843 cubic feet. The unloaded weight is $22\frac{1}{2}$ tons (Imperial) and the load limit 67 tons. Like all freight cars of the Algoma Central they have an overall length of around 50 feet. The company has not a great deal of traffic that requires ownership of the ordinary box-car. Most of the traffic so conveyed is loaded into cars of Canadian National ownership, originating outside ACR territory, or similarly beyond the southern end of the system in Soo line cars.

The forestry products are carried both in gondolas and on flat cars. Trees cut into 8 foot lengths are loaded transversely, and the rough surface of the bark keeps them from shifting, even when loaded high above the sides of a gondola. A number of foot lengths are however stacked vertically across each end of the car to prevent end movement of the loaded trees. The need to do this is avoided by the use of flat cars with end bulkheads. The photograph reproduced on Plate 27, showing the modern situation at Steelton yards, shows also, very clearly, the methods of loading timber on to the various types of car. Gondola and bulkhead flat cars are prominent in the picture. The older type of ore hopper cars can also be seen attached to the switching locomotive. Further reference to the loading of Algoma Central freight cars is made in Chapters 15 and 16, dealing with the business allies of the company in the Soo.

Although it is taking the story back nearly 50 years, I cannot conclude this chapter without mention of an interesting item of freight stock purchased in 1924. In Chapter 7 I referred to the many trestles on the original section of the line that were filled in and on Plate 21 are reproduced photographs showing the operation in progress. For this duty a special kind of gondola car was introduced. The sides were hinged at the top and could be swung outward by a small amount. Inside, the floor was above what would be the normal bottom level, but it terminated about 1 foot from the side. From this edge there was a sloping surface leading down to the true bottom of the car. This slope was provided on both sides. When a train of such cars were on a trestle the side doors would be swung open a small amount allowing the filling material piled inside the car to slide down the slope and through the narrow opening. The ends of the cars were also hinged, but at the bottom and these were lowered outward to make a continuous platform inside from end to end of the train. Loading from the spoil bank at the line side, by steam shovel was continuous all along the train. There was a steam winch-operated pusher, that was dragged along inside the cars to clear such filling material as had not trimmed down the slopes and through the side doors by itself.

CHAPTER THIRTEEN

Traffic on the Great Lakes, and the Ships That Run It

I have referred earlier in this book to the unrivalled position of the Soo, as a veritable 'grand junction' of the Great Lakes. The map on page 82 shows how the Algoma Central Railway has exploited this remarkable situation. As an Englishman, I have clear memories of the way the old private railway companies of England and Scotland advertised their services by dramatically contrived maps, that suggested even the smallest company served at least half the whole country—whereas its actual geographical extent was really very small. But a map of the activities of the Algoma Central needs no such stretches of the imagination. Its ships ply from Duluth, at the far western end of Lake Superior, to Sept Iles on Atlantic tide water far down the estuary of the St Lawrence. These two ports alone are 1250 miles apart as the crow flies—if any bird would fly such a distance in a straight line!—but the run from the Soo to Sept Iles through Lakes Huron and Erie, the Welland Canal and its locks, Lake Ontario, and then down the great St Lawrence River is around 1400 miles.

The routes covered by the nine great ships of the modern fleet, and the cargoes conveyed, make a fascinating study. In commenting upon them in must always be borne in mind that the lakes are closed to navigation for at least three months in the year, and that continuity of supply to the numerous industries involved has to be maintained by massive stockpiling in the open season, to provide adequate supplies for the months when the lakes are frozen. This applies as much at the points of export as in the receiving areas. In view of this fundamental difficulty, and equally bearing in mind the comparative slowness of transport by water a visitor to the area might wonder why, in this modern age, transport by water is used at all. It is however incomparably the most economical way, and the map alone is enough to show the geographical extent of the Algoma Central marine activities. At the outset it is

134

nevertheless important to emphasize that there is a great difference between these services and those of the great majority of other railways that operate, or used to operate, ships as well. In Great Britain, for example, ships of the old railways like the London and North-Western, the Great Western, and the Caledonian were run in direct connection with the trains, providing an extension of land-based passenger, mail and freight services; but as I have told in Chapter 6 of this book, in the Clergue build-up at the Soo, shipping actually preceded the railway, if not under the same name. The railway was built to serve the ships.

In studying the map of present day ship services of the ACR an important point of principle must be mentioned. In supplementing the basic traffics, while every endeavor is made to secure return loads, as a Canadian company the ACR ships cannot ply between one United States port and another. Traffic from Canada can be taken to a US port, and a return load collected for a Canadian one; but of course the ships can carry freely between any number of Canadian ports. Some of the longest runs are made by the bulk vessels, continuing the notable tradition of being the oldest Canadian continuous operator on the Great Lakes. Some of the huge wheat crop of the prairie provinces is stored in grain elevators at Thunder Bay and from there the Algoma Central bulkers set out on the journey—some 1750 miles when carrying American grain from Duluth—to ports on the estuary of the St Lawrence. Montreal is the first port of discharge, then Quebec, Baie Comeau and Port Cartier. Then the ACR ships proceed a short distance further down the estuary to Point Noire and Sept Iles. These two latter ports are the rail-heads of the recently constructed railways bringing ore from the immense deposits in Labrador. When I was in Canada in 1971 I had the opportunity of traveling over the Quebec North Shore and Labrador Railway, and seeing something of its traffic in ore. It is interesting to know that some of it is conveyed in ACR bulkers to points on Lake Erie. This is an exceptionally interesting example of a profitable return load. The only stage of this operation on which the ships are in ballast is westward from Lake Erie, when they are proceeding either to Thunder Bay or Duluth to pick up more grain.

Another interesting traffic is in salt. There are large underground salt mines at Goderich, on the eastern shore of Lake Huron, and at Windsor, and this is taken to both Canadian and USA points. The country to the west of Lake Michigan is a very heavy snow belt, and the ACR ships take large quantities of salt into Chicago, Green Bay and Milwaukee, and elsewhere on Lake Michigan for ice control in the winter. In return they load coal and bentonite, a form of clay, which is brought into Chicago by rail from the State of Wyoming. The clay is conveyed to Point Noire. From Chicago this balancing run is nearly as long as the grain haul from Duluth; but the form of clay conveyed has been found very effective for binding the pellets in which form iron ore is exported both from Point Noire and Sept Iles. Iron ore is taken into Indiana Harbor, and a return load of sand is obtained at Grand Haven some way up the eastern shore of Lake Michigan. This sand is conveyed to Windsor and Hamilton, for use in the large foundries in those areas. And so a fascinating and profitable

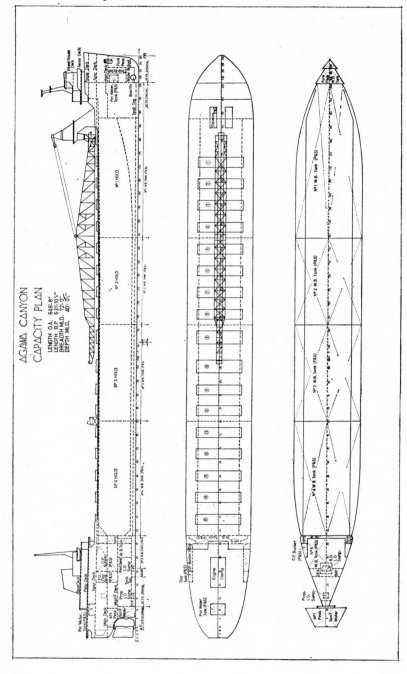

AGAWA CANYON
CAPACITY PLAN

LENGTH O.A.   646'-8"
LENGTH B.P.   631'-10½"
BREADTH MLD.   72'-0"
DEPTH MLD.   40'-0"

10   Diagram of the *Agawa Canyon*, sister ship to the *Algoway*

jig-saw of traffic is built up from an intimate knowledge of the Great Lakes area, and with a finger surely and continuously on the pulse of innumerable industries in both Canada and the USA in this very busy area.

I have referred several times earlier to the way in which the original Clergue foundations at the Soo were established and developed at a geographical location that could well be called the 'grand junction' of the Great Lakes; but today, while the headquarters of the Marine Division of the ACR remains at the Soo, a very important branch office has been established at Port Colborne on Lake Erie, conveniently adjacent to the strategic Welland Canal area, and favorably situated for easy contact with the numerous United States ports along the southern shores of the Lake, ranging from Toledo and Cleveland, to Buffalo. A great deal of the coal needed for the steel and the hydro-electric companies in the Soo and Thunder Bay is collected from this area. Coal for the Algoma Steel Corporation is conveyed from Toledo, while at Conneault and Ashtabula coal is stockpiled ready to be shipped to the various hydro-electric plants in Toronto and Sarnia and to a lesser extent to Thunder Bay. One of the shorter hauls is the traffic in crushed limestone from Calcite and Stoneport—very appropriately named cities—to Sarnia and Windsor, mainly for the manufacture of concrete. The ships on this run then proceed to Toledo to pick up coal for the Soo.

Looking at the map again and seeing the very large number of ports where the ships of the ACR do business, many of them with names that are not very familiar except to people with direct shipping interests, it might well be wondered how it is possible to berth ships of such size as those of the Algoma Central fleet to load and unload cargoes that often approach some 20,000 tons. None of them are less than 575 feet long and three of the 'bulkers' measure no less than 730 feet. It is in respect of the conditions prevailing at many ports in the Great Lakes area that the development of the self-unloading type of vessel has proved so invaluable. The comparatively shallow draught and completely flat bottoms of all these ships, bulkers and self-unloaders alike, enable them to get inshore to a degree quite impossible with an ocean-going vessel. Providing one can get within the 250-foot span of the unloading boom the cargo can be dumped on shore ready for the customer to collect. At some places there is no dock, as such, at all; not even jetties, to which members of the crew can be swung overboard, as I was to see at the ore dock in the Mission River, at Thunder Bay. It is then necessary to put men ashore in small boats, carrying the ropes attached to the hawsers with which to make the vessel fast during the unloading operation. There are times when the depth of water is so shallow that when a ship is first tied up, and prior to unloading, it is actually on the bottom! All this may sound a little primitive; but elaborate dock facilities cost money and if a carrier such as those of the Algoma Central can 'deliver the goods' without requiring its customers to have any sophisticated equipment to receive it, the operation is one that can attract additional and profitable business.

I have referred earlier to the complete cessation of traffic on the lakes during the winter months, and it may well be questioned as to where these big ships are berthed during that time. The Marine Division of the Algoma Central has no 'home port'. The yard at which all the more modern ships have been built is at Collingwood on Georgian Bay, but this in no way constitutes a base. The ships winter where they happened to be at the conclusion of their last voyage before the season closed, and their distribution during the winter of 1973-4 was as follows: The bulkers *Algocen*, *Glossbrenner* and *Scully* were at Midland and Port McNicol, loaded with storage grain. The *Scully*, I should mention, is powered by steam turbines, and is one of the few vessels in the present fleet not built at Collingwood Yard. The ship in which I made my own trip, described in Chapter 14, the *Algoway*, was also at one of the Georgian Bay ports, and also Owen Sound, together with the first of the modern bulkers, the *Sir Denys Lowson*. Both were loaded with grain. In the case of the *Algoway* this was unloaded at the beginning of the 1974 season before she took up her first trip on the Soo–Thunder Bay ore run, on the second of which I traveled. During the winter of 1973-4 the *Agawa Canyon* was at Sarnia, light, while the *Roy A Jodrey* and the *E B Barber* were at Port Colborne. Lastly there was the *Algorail* at Toronto, loaded with grain for the ports down the St Lawrence. So far as the *Algoway* is concerned, she is not normally operated on the ore run from Thunder Bay to the Soo. She is the newest of the fleet, and is fitted with a vibratory mechanism in her bunkers. This would not be needed with a cargo like pellets of iron ore, which trims readily; but there are other bulk cargoes that are more 'tacky', and the vibrator device gives them some necessary 'encouragement' to trim down on to the longitudinal belt conveyors when unloading is in progress.

In the next Chapter I have given an hour-by-hour account of a run by one of the self-unloaders, because it was a trip very full of incident; and it is interesting at the same time to have an overall survey of the positions and destinations of all the other members of the fleet. The dispositions following refer to Friday, 12 April 1974.

Agawa Canyon	arrived Sarnia 2 pm with stone
Algocen	still in winter quarters at Port McNicol, awaiting the ice breakers to make a path for her to get out
Algorail	passed through the Soo locks upbound for Thunder Bay
Algoway	heading down Lake Superior with ore, Thunder Bay to the Soo
E B Barber	departed from Port Colborne 2·45 pm with the first load of stone of the season for Fairport
A S Glossbrenner	still in winter berth at Port McNicol awaiting ice breaker to make a path for her to get out
Roy A Jodrey	left winter berth at Port Colborne, 1·30 am for Goderich, to load salt
V W Scully	fitting out in winter berth at Midland
Sir Denys Lowson	at Thunder Bay loading grain for the St Lawrence ports

Finally, to complete this picture, the following are details of the ships of the present fleet.

E B Barber	constructed by Port Arthur Shipbuilding Company, and began operation in June 1953. She has a carrying capacity of 14,000 net tons, and is powered by an oil-fired steam turbine. In the winter of 1963, when the great advantages of the self-unloading type of vessel were appreciated she was converted from a 'bulker' at Collingwood Shipyards and re-entered service on 19 July 1964. This conversion, which provided the first example of a ship of this type in the Algoma Central fleet was very successful and led to the purchase of four more between 1965 and 1973, of a greatly improved type
Sir Denys Lowson	built by Collingwood Shipyards and delivered to Algoma Central on 31 March 1964. Powered by four Fairbanks-Morse diesel engines it was the first of this type to be operated by the Company. The *Sir Denys Lowson* was also the largest vessel to enter the fleet up to that time, with a length of 605 feet and developing 5332 shaft-horsepower. The ship was also then the most modern, with pilot house control and bow steering propeller
*Roy A Jodrey	A new 639 ft self-unloading type vessel: was delivered by Collingwood Shipyards on 11 November 1965. Its four diesel engines develop 6664 BHP and include a power assist arrangement from two 500 KWL diesel generator sets. This vessel has a bow steering propeller and pilot house control
Algorail	On 5 April 1968 the Company took delivery of the new *Algorail* at Collingwood. This vessel with a few modifications was a sister ship of the *Roy A Jodrey*
Algocen	The new *Algocen* was delivered by Collingwood Shipyards on 21 September 1968. This was the Company's first maximum size vessel with a 730 ft length and 75 ft beam and four diesel engines combined with the power assist from two diesel generating sets developing a total BHP of 9400. It is complete with pilot house control and bow steering propeller
Agawa Canyon	On 20 November 1970 the Company received an additional self-unloading, multi-diesel ship. It was similar in most respects to the *Algorail* and *Roy A Jodrey* but has certain changes in hull design to provide a greater carrying capacity
A S Glossbrenner	Maximum size bulk vessel similar to *Algocen* but with single diesel engine purchased from Diamond Shamrock Co. in April 1971

Vessel	Type	Built	Dimensions (Feet)			Capacity at Seaway
			Length ft in	Breadth ft in	Depth ft in	26 Ft—Gross Tons
*Hull 206	Self-Unloader (Boom 252 ft)	Collingwood 1974	730 0	75 0	44 6	27,640
MV *Algoway*	Self-Unloader (Boom 250 ft)	Collingwood 1972	648 6	72 0	40 2	20,905
MV *Agawa Canyon*	Self-Unloader (Boom 250 ft)	Collingwood 1970	646 8	72 0	40 0½	20,850
MV *Algorail*	Self-Unloader (Boom 250 ft)	Collingwood 1968	640 5	72 0	40 0	20,475
MV *Roy A Jodrey*	Self-Unloader (Boom 250 ft)	Collingwood 1965	640 6	72 4	39 11	20,450
SS *E B Barber*	Self-Unloader (Boom 225 ft)	Thunder Bay 1953 Converted to Self-Unloader Collingwood 1964	574 5	59 0	31 0	13,730
MV *Algocen*	Bulk Vessel	Collingwood 1968	730 0	75 0	39 8	26,355
MV *A S Glossbrenner*	Bulk Vessel	Lauzon 1966	730 0	75 0	39 8	25,745
SS *V W Scully*	Bulk Vessel	Montreal 1965	730 0	75 0	39 0	25,365
MV *Sir Denys Lowson*	Bulk Vessel	Collingwood 1964	604 9	62 0	33 10½	16,250

* Not in service at the opening of the 1974 season.   Name not yet decided.

V W Scully	Maximum size vessel powered by steam turbine purchased with *Glossbrenner* from Diamond Shamrock—entered service with this Company in April 1971
Algoway	New *Algoway* built at Collingwood Shipyards. A multi-diesel, self-unloading vessel similar to *Agawa Canyon* but with certain improvements in detail. Entered service in April 1973

To summarize the details of the present fleet the table on page 140 is appended. The ships all carry the black bear insignia of the Algoma Central Railway. The funnels are black, with a red-white-red band near the top.

*The MV *Roy A Jodrey* was lost on 20 November 1974, whilst the ship was proceeding westbound in the St Lawrence Seaway with a cargo of iron ore pellets. These had been loaded at Sept Iles, Quebec and were bound for Detroit, Michigan. Near Alexandria Bay, New York, in the American Narrows, the ship struck Pullman Shoal and was run aground on Wellesley Island. The severity of the damage and the nature of the shoreline meant that the ship could not be kept afloat. Four hours after the striking, and after all the crew members had been taken ashore, the vessel sank in 150 ft of water. Investigation has indicated that salvage is not possible.

141

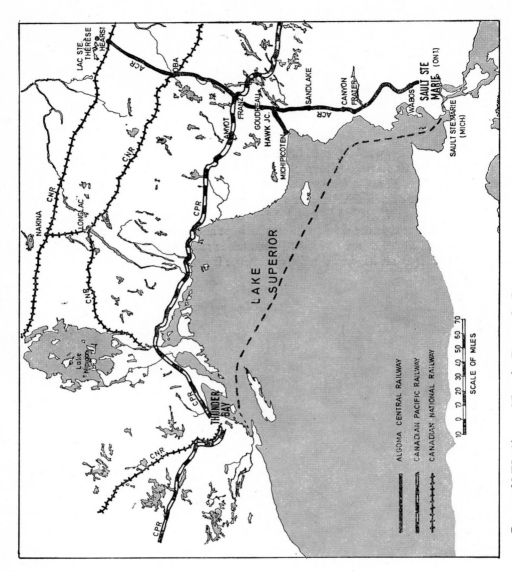

11   Route of MV *Algoway*, Thunder Bay to the Soo

CHAPTER FOURTEEN

The Soo to Thunder Bay and Back by MV *Algoway*

To further my appreciation of the modern fleet of special purpose vessels I was accorded the privilege of making a trip on what was then the latest unit of the fleet, the MV *Algoway*, and the equipment and operation of these splendid ships will be perhaps better appreciated by an account of what I saw than by so much factual recitation of details of machinery. In company with Peter Cresswell, Manager of the Marine Division of the Algoma Central Railway, we went by car from downtown Sault Ste Marie to the ore dock of the Algoma Steel Corporation. Dusk was falling, at the end of a cloudless day, and making our way through the complicated purlieus of the steel works we came to the dock where the *Algoway* was unloading a cargo of iron ore she had brought from Thunder Bay, 16,000 tons of it; and as soon as the unloading was finished she would be off again for another load. Climbing on deck we met Captain Bruce Shepherd, who told us he expected to leave about 10 pm. The intervening two hours gave an excellent opportunity to see the operation in progress and later, with the Chief Engineer, Bill Dance, to visit the engine room of the ship. So with such 'effects' as I had brought stowed in the luxurious state room so kindly put at my disposal, I was able to drink in all the fascination of the scene spread around.

Ranged alongside the ore dock, their chimneys silhouetted against the darkening sky, were the blast furnaces of the steel plant. The 250-foot unloading boom of the *Algoway* was swung round at right angles to the length of the ship, and a continuous torrent of ore was being discharged, forming a tall cone on the dock side. In the vessel the ore is carried in hopper-bottomed bunkers that discharge on to belt conveyors running longitudinally. In the fore part of the ship there is a bucket-elevator which lifts the ore to the level of the unloading boom, and discharges it on to the conveyor of the boom itself. The whole operation is entirely mechanized and works rapidly and very cleanly. Ahead, in the channel of the St Mary's River I could see much ice floating down, and across the channel on the United States side were the lights of Soo, Michigan. Every now and then a big ship passed, bound for some US port on the Great Lakes, carrying cargo from one of the American ports at the western end of Lake Superior. To right of us were stockpiles of limestone, brought from the ports of Calcite and Stoneport, Michigan, on Lake Huron. All the time the boom-unloader of the *Algoway* was discharging ore on to that ever-increasing pile at the rate of 4200 tons per hour.

This had been only the first round trip of the season, and earlier in the day a traditional ceremony had been enacted at the dock side when the ship arrived with its load. Each year the captain of the first ship to bring in a cargo from outside, and thus to open the port, is presented with a silk hat and a $20 bill to spend at local stores. Our skipper, Bruce Shepherd, had that honour in 1974, and had been duly featured on television that same evening, before he set out again. The turn-round at Thunder Bay had been much delayed by ice; for although it was now breaking up there was still a great deal of it floating, and the east-bound trip had been slowed up considerably by much thick ice floating in Whitefish Bay, off the western shores of the Algoma country. Captain Shepherd expected something of a rough start to our journey westward.

In the meantime there was a good hour before departure time, and Bill Dance took us down to the engine room. The ship is powered by four diesel engines having between them a shaft horsepower of 6664. This might not seem very great for a ship of such carrying capacity, and where the horsepower of ship engines is concerned I always recall the remarkable case of the Irish Mail steamers on the Holyhead–Kingstown run. The British Post Office contract stipulated a very strict schedule of 2 hrs 55 mins for the crossing, and this entailed a speed of 25 knots. To do this meant building no less than 16,000 horsepower into those mail steamers, so much so that a marine engineer of another British steamship line once remarked to me that they were 'All engine; there's no room for anything else'! At breakfast next morning when we were at full speed on Lake Superior, in conversation with Bill Dance I said I judged the speed to be about 15 knots. He laughed, and said 'Oh yes, about 17 mph—we don't use many nautical terms on these jobs'. On the *Algoway* the diesel engines are not reversed for navigating astern. Reversal is effected by the modern practice of the variable-pitch propeller.

In referring to breakfast time on the following morning however I have rather jumped ahead of the story; for it was now nearly 10 pm and as anticipated the unloading was completed. The boom was very gradually swung across until it lay along the length of the ship, and then Peter Cresswell and I went forward to the wheelhouse. I have always felt that for a visitor to be invited on to the bridge of a ship is as great a privilege as to ride the head end of a railway train, and in recalling the many trips I was able to make in the years before World War II on ships plying

144

the narrow seas round Great Britain, I soon sensed that there had never been one remotely like this before. We nosed our way gently out of the dock, with blocks of floating ice spotlighted in the powerful searchlights, and so out into the channel. In the narrow waterway, marked by numerous winking lights, we were soon meeting much floating ice. At first this took the form of closely grouped blocks, but soon there were solid masses of it, and we were crunching through with the blunt bow of the ship making a most curious noise. It was interesting to see the ice cracking apart in places, as we plowed through. Progress was naturally slow and cautious, and we met several United States vessels heavily loaded and passing toward the Soo. One of these was a positive giant, more than 800 ft long. This would be confined to the upper lakes, because it would be too long to pass through the locks of the Welland Canal. It was nearly midnight before we were passing clear of the channel leading to the Soo, and out into the open water of Lake Superior; and this seemed a good moment to turn in for the night.

Dawn came with cloudless skies once again and the ship plowing the open sea of Lake Superior, with not a sight either of land or ice; but I learned later from Captain Shepherd that he had to make a considerable detour in the early part of the night to avoid ice. He explained that before we left the Soo he had discharged some of the water from the forward cargo compartment, needed as ballast, so that the ship was very slightly tilted upward toward the front, and the flat bottom of her hull was slightly above water level, and tended to crush or depress any ice in our path. The fine morning passed pleasantly, and after an early lunch Peter Cresswell and I went forward to the wheelhouse. Ice was expected on the western part of the journey, and the forward horizon was anxiously scanned.

By 12.30 pm land was sighted ahead. We could see ice away on the starboard side, and by 1 pm we were nearing Passage Island. Snow was still lying deep, and ice was packed around its shores. Isle Royale now lay to port, but rather ominously a broad band of ice was stretched across the horizon ahead of us. At first we were able to skirt it, making a course for Thunder Cape. We crunched our way through ice floes, and then into open water again; but then we came to more ice that could not be avoided. It now became really hard going. Our captain reckoned the ice was 2 ft thick, and it slowed us down; he said that he thought we should not have made it if we had been loaded. The second mate was searching the ice ahead, with binoculars, for a track; we made for one that had been made by an ice-breaker, but the mass of ice seemed to have closed in since it went through. There was another ship off Thunder Cape coming very slowly toward us. It was an old vessel, the *Goderich*, built as long ago as 1906, and carrying grain. We passed her at 2.50 pm just off Thunder Cape and she immediately took the track that we had plowed through the ice. Half an hour later however we learned that she had become completely stuck, and had called for assistance from the ice-breaker. In the meantime we were going steadily in the track of chopped up ice; but it was pretty solid on both sides of us.

The sky had now become entirely overcast, and the fine crags of Pie Island

145

showed up as little more than colorless silhouettes, and by 3.40 pm the industrial complex of Thunder Bay was looming out of the mist. The track through the ice was continuous and made things easier, after our earlier spell of ice breaking on our own account. Apart from this one track however, the whole expanse of Thunder Bay was covered with thick ice. The snow had melted a good deal but there was still much of it on top of the ice. We saw the ice-breaker *Norman McLeod Rogers* going out to the assistance of the *Goderich*. This is a relatively small but very powerfully engined vessel, with a crew of no less than 65, against no more than 29 on the *Algoway*. The ice-breakers are designed to have their fore part just above water level, as we had been on the outward journey. On the return run, loaded with 16,000 tons of iron ore we should be much deeper in the water and not so ideally equipped to crush or depress the ice.

We were now approaching Thunder Bay, through a track in the ice that Captain Shepherd described as just a 'highway', and shortly after 4 pm we were passing the light at the entrance to the channel that leads into the Mission River. The accompanying sketch plan shows the layout here. There were large ice floes in the river, and in slowly making our way upstream we pushed them aside and sent them swimming toward the banks. On the starboard side as we went up was a huge coal dump that Algoma Central ships had brought in the previous summer at 25,000 tons a time, from Ashtabula and Conneault on Lake Erie, for the Thunder Bay power station of the Hydro Electric Power Commission of Ontario. The ore dock, where we were to load for the return journey, is on the port side going up the river; but the ship had to be taken upstream to the confluence of the Mission and Kaministikwia Rivers to be swung round until facing down stream. It was then that I had an interesting exposition of the value of the side-thrusting propellers at the bow, which assisted in the swinging operation, and enabled this big ship to be turned end for end in a very small space without any need for tugs. The place where this took place had an additional interest for me, in that the yards of the Canadian Pacific Railway are adjacent to the left bank of the Kaministikwia River, and there was much activity to be seen. The view upstream was backed by the majestic outline of Mount McKay.

We then made our way gently down stream to the ore dock, and I then saw members of the crew preparing for an operation that was unusual to me. There are no shore staff on the dock, and deckhands from the *Algoway* were launched overboard by cradle from a derrick, and received the ropes thrown from the ship to make it fast against the dock piers. At 5.5 pm we were at rest, alongside. The ore we were to take to the Soo, for the Algoma Steel Corporation, is brought into Thunder Bay by the Canadian National Railways, from the Steep Rock iron mines at Atikokan. It was very tidily stockpiled inshore from the loading dock, and two loading booms were available to convey it into the ship's bunkers, at 5000 tons per hour. Before loading could start, however, certain preparations had to be made on the ship itself. The self-unloading boom which I had seen in operation at the Soo had to be lifted clear; but before it was swung completely out of the way it was moved slightly outward to

146

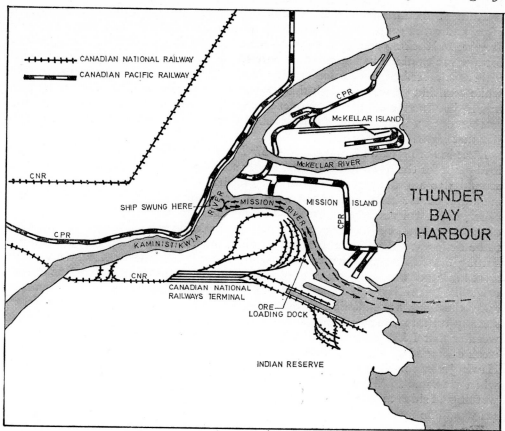

12   Large scale map of harbor area at Thunder Bay

balance the loadings of ore into the bunkers, which of course would be tipped only on one side at the start of the operation. With these preliminaries completed, loading began shortly after 6.30 pm.

From the observation lounge I had an excellent view of the operation, with the two loading booms moving from one hopper to another, and in the strong wind the red dust was flying thick at times. The booms were not continuously in operation, but about 11 pm we had taken our full complement of ore, 16,000 tons, and were preparing to start away for the Soo. Captain Shepherd was anxious about that ice. The easterly wind which had freshened during the westbound journey was tending to pile up ice in the bay, and there was a definite risk that the channel we had followed going in might have closed up. With the searchlights on each side of the wheelhouse there would be no difficulty in locating where it was, and as things happened the situation at one time grew distinctly grim. The huge ice floes were being turned on edge, and coming up the ship's sides to within 2 ft of the deck. Worse than this, they began blocking up the sea cocks to the engine cooling system. This was another form of the trouble I had seen on the railway, north of Hawk Junction, only a week earlier, as described in Chapter 11. The last thing Captain Shepherd wanted to do while crunching a way through this ice was to stop. But around 1 am he had to, briefly, because the engines were overheating. However we made it eventually, and reached open water; but there is no doubt we were fortunate to get out of Thunder Bay that night!

Later in the night we had passed the *Sir Denys Lowson* bound for Thunder Bay to load grain for the St Lawrence ports. I slept soundly enough and when dawn came, around 5.30 am, the promised wind and rain had come too, and the *Algoway* was making a course head on into the wind. Apart from some slight pitching she was riding the storm very smoothly. Most of this chapter was written in the beautiful observation lounge of the ship, and it was a remarkable experience on this morning to be sitting at a desk looking ahead to the fore part of the ship, seeing the bows cutting through waters covered with 'white horses', while just below, deck hands were hosing down the covers of the hatches to remove the remaining pellets of iron ore spilled from last night's loading at Thunder Bay. The heavy rain had washed away the thick accumulation of dust, but not the pellets. So the fine ship drove steadily on into the storm and I thought again of the extraordinary diversity of weather that I had encountered during this visit to the Algoma country. Only a week earlier I had been watching that amazing snow plowing on the railway up at Hawk Junction. Today Captain Shepherd was expecting more trouble with ice when we came to Whitefish Bay. He told me also that the coastguards had been warning all ships to keep clear of the ice back in Thunder Bay. The strong wind and sea would be driving it in, and causing it to pack up.

Watching the *Algoway* as she forged her way eastward I could see how her hull was flexing under the action of the waves. Provision for this to happen on a long vessel of this kind is an interesting feature of modern marine engineering design. As we progressed eastward, although the rain continued very heavy and continuous from dawn, the sea itself was not quite so rough by the time it was 1 pm. In anticipation of drifting ice, propelled by the strong wind from the accumulation in Whitefish Bay, Captain Shepherd was making somewhat of a detour to the east in order to avoid it, as far as possible. So far there had been no sign of any, and we expected to be off Whitefish Point, at the entrance to the St Mary's River on the American side, about 4.30 pm. Nevertheless, Peter Cresswell, Captain Shepherd, and all members of the crew with whom I talked were agreed that the conditions were quite exceptional for mid-April; but while the journey was not so pleasant scenically or weatherwise as the long summer runs of the bulkers, through the lakes and down the St Lawrence, I was fortunate in being able to witness at first hand the resolution and skill with which the conditions of severe icing were surmounted.

At 1.10 pm there was ice on the starboard bow, and we turned a little to port, to keep clear. But these first patches were no more than isolated 'streaks' and we were able to keep going at full speed in open water. The afternoon passed almost without incident. There were some patches of ice, with large floes, greenish white in the centre and ringed with a frill such as might have been made by a fancy cake decorator; and then around 3.30 pm we struck a belt of heavy packed ice. Speed was reduced, and we entered the belt. One could feel the ship shouldering her way through, and things were made worse by the high wind driving the ice toward us. Our speed became dead slow, and although we could see open water not far ahead it was a thoroughly nasty place. Around 4.30 pm with the weather clearing a little I made my way forward to the wheelhouse; but although far ahead the flashes of the lighthouse on Whitefish Point could be seen that detour had put us somewhat behind our anticipated timing. Nevertheless Captain Shepherd's maneuver proved fortunate beyond measure, as things turned out. We ran through another ice belt off the western shore of Ile Parisienne, but we were soon in open water again. Peter Cresswell and I went back to the after part for a quick dinner, but when we got back to the wheel-house, there was some anxiety. We were approaching the lighthouse at the south end of Ile Parisienne, cutting through hard ice floes. Bruce Shepherd estimated that some of them were 3 ft thick, with most of this thickness below water. It was mighty hard going. In these calm waters the surface looked like some vast crazy-pavement, made up of giant ice blocks. They had been broken up, but had partially re-frozen together. As we forced our way through they cracked open again, some turned on edge, while others were driven down under their neighbors.

However, by Captain Shepherd's navigation we kept clear of the worst of the ice in the Whitefish Bay area. On the radio we heard of other ships that were well and truly stuck, and preparing to anchor for the night just where they were. On the other hand by 6.50 pm we were passing out of the ice into stormy open water, to meet that most unwelcome hazard of all traveling—fog! It was not the still motionless smog that can grip everything, but very low cloud bringing torrents of rain, and blinding the sight of everything ahead. Visibility was so bad for a time that there was talk of our stopping, and anchoring for the night. We saw the red flashes of the lighthouse at Gros Cap, but were approaching the narrower navigation channels leading into the St Mary's River, and it was a question whether we should be able to see the ranging lights that are such a valuable marker for making a course. It was ironical after all the earlier struggles with ice, and now less than 10 miles from journey's end and in open water, that we might not be able to make it, on account of fog. However another ship of the fleet, the *Algorail*, was coming out, loaded with coal for Thunder Bay, and talking to her on the radio we got better news of the visibility nearer to the Soo. We were also just glimpsing the ranging lights at the end of the first reach of the channel, and now it seemed a case of patiently feeling our way in.

It was a good commentary upon the conditions, and those of navigating a big ship in confined waters that it took us roughly 3 hours more, until the *Algoway* was alongside the ore dock in the steel plant. By the time we had turned into the inner reach and were steering toward the green ranging lights the visibility had much improved, and soon the full array of the Soo's lights were spread out ahead. The rain had ceased and the clouds had lifted, and far ahead against the night sky could be seen the outline of the International Bridge. We made our way slowly toward the channel leading to the Canadian locks, and then eventually turned slightly to port to head for the ore dock. I could write pages of the skill and precision with which Captain Shepherd swung the ship completely round, and then inched her stern first up to the dockside; but these are maritime technicalities. We were alongside shortly after 10.15 pm, having taken roughly 22½ hours for the run from Thunder Bay. As soon as the ship was unloaded they were going straight back. One last point concerns fuel consumption. The *Algoway* has a capacity of 525 tons of fuel oil; this is enough to last 20 days, including both the times of loading and unloading and when under way. When I clambered down the ladder on to the dock side I felt I could not have had a more interesting or incident-packed trip, nor pleasanter shipboard companions.

CHAPTER FIFTEEN

Business Allies in the Soo:
Algoma Steel

When running a railway it is good to be assured of a steady annual work-load; and in sending sintered ore from Wawa to the Soo, the Algoma Steel Corporation loads about two million tons every year on to the ACR. Algoma Steel is indeed the third largest steel producing plant in Canada and at the Soo it is most favorably situated for receipt of the raw materials this great plant needs. It is interesting to look first at those sources of supply, because taking the land and water operations together they make the Corporation the Algoma Central Railway's best customer.

This is primarily a book about the railway; but from earlier chapters it will be gathered how closely the railway and the steel corporation were financially linked in the earliest days, and more than a passing reference is needed to the history and eventual climb to eminence of a concern that is now, at one and the same time, business ally, friend, and best customer of the Algoma Central Railway. The steel company was not one of the earliest developments of the Clergue 'empire', which it is important to emphasize was based in both the Soos—Soo, Ontario and Soo, Michigan. It did not figure in the impressive family trees of the Clergue companies that had been incorporated by the year 1900, as shown on page 152. It was actually incorporated on 10 May 1901, and was immediately acquired by the Consolidated Lake Superior Company.

It must be pointed out at this stage that a steel company had been contemplated for some time, though not originally as a subsidiary of the Consolidated Lake Superior Company. It had been part of Clergue's well-established technique of founding new companies to provide markets for the products of the older ones. In the case of steel it was to provide for sales of ore, wood for charcoal, and so on and to ensure regular business for the Algoma Central Railway. By the end of 1901 the

Bessemer steel plant and a 28-inch blooming mill had been installed; but even before the rail mill had been completed, in 1902, Clergue had taken substantial orders for rails, for delivery in 1901! One was for no less than 15,000 tons, for the Intercolonial Railway, which was then relaying its main line with 80 lb rails. In

THE CLERGUE COMPANIES IN 1900

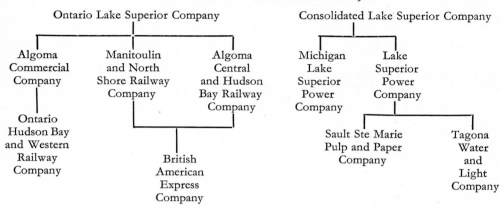

September 1901 *The Sault Star* commented upon the difficulties in which Clergue found himself, especially when by way of extrication he advised the Federal Government to obtain the rails from England, at $36 a ton. Other Canadian firms and the Government opposition in Parliament were furious because they could have been obtained in Canada for considerably less.

The prime object of the steel works was to produce rails, and although the blooming mill got into production in May 1902 its first efforts were not satisfactory, and in December of that year it closed, for lack of orders. This setback however was nothing to the financial crisis that developed at the same time, which led to the 'crash' in September of the following year and eventually to the bankrupting of the whole Clergue 'empire'. The Consolidated Lake Superior Company has been aptly called the 'Colossus of Algoma': it is interesting to see the extent of its make-up at the time of its catastrophic fall.

After the crash the steel plant began operations once again in 1904, with orders for rails from the Intercolonial, and by the end of the year production was up to between 400 and 500 tons a day. In March 1905 the second blast furnace was brought into operation and orders flowed in liberally at first from the Canadian Pacific, the Grand Trunk and the Algoma Central. By 1906 however the trend everywhere in the steel industry was to change to the Siemens-Martin open hearth process, instead of the Bessemer, and two new furnaces were added in 1907. But this high productivity was short lived; orders became scarce once again, largely due to a financial panic in that year, and in the spring of 1908 the plant was once again closed down.

CONSOLIDATED LAKE SUPERIOR COMPANY—1903

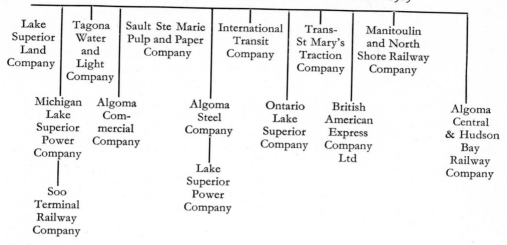

Lake Superior Land Company	Tagona Water and Light Company	Sault Ste Marie Pulp and Paper Company	International Transit Company	Trans-St Mary's Traction Company	Manitoulin and North Shore Railway Company
Michigan Lake Superior Power Company	Algoma Commercial Company	Algoma Steel Company	Ontario Lake Superior Company	British American Express Company Ltd	Algoma Central & Hudson Bay Railway Company
Soo Terminal Railway Company		Lake Superior Power Company			

Also two inactive railway companies:
1 Ontario, Hudson Bay and Western Railway Company
2 Pacific and Atlantic Railway Company

In the meantime however arising from the financial arrangements that had followed the crash of 1903, there had been a continual struggle between rival United States interests for control of the entire Lake Superior Corporation. The eventual outcome was that neither succeeded and that in 1908–9 control passed to English interests. It was then that James Dunn first came upon the scene. It cannot be said that his activities brought him 'into the picture', because for many years they were entirely covert. But in association with the English financier Robert Fleming, he introduced new financing that proved a powerful 'shot in the arm' for the steel company. Nevertheless, nearly a quarter of a century was to pass of further ups and downs, and closure for the third time in 1930, before Sir James, as he had become in 1921, began to build the company steadily up to its present stature and prosperity. Of the rivalry that developed between him and E B Barber, of the Algoma Central Railway, I have told something in Chapter 8 of this book. There also I was able to record the eventual rapprochement that came about between these two giants of the Algoma scene—a situation that is symbolized today in that J B Barber, a nephew of 'E B', is now Senior Vice-President of the steel company, while 'E B's' son, James, also holds high executive office in the company. It was through their interest and courtesy that I was enabled to see and hear much about the present activities of this great corporation.

Dealing first with the sources of supply, in the previous chapter I described how the ore is brought from Thunder Bay. This comes from mines at Steep Rock, near

Geraldton, and is hauled into Thunder Bay by the Canadian National Railways. It is stockpiled at the Soo during the time when the Great Lakes are open for shipping; but in 1974 the prolongation of severe winter weather, that I have amply described in earlier chapters of this book, led to the supply from Steep Rock getting near to exhaustion, before the ships could begin operating. Emergency arrangements were being set up to get about 100,000 tons of ore to the Soo by an all-rail route, via the Canadian National Transcontinental main line from Longlac to Oba and thence down the Algoma Central. It would have been an expensive alternative, and fortunately the ships were able to get going just in time to make it unnecessary.

It is however with the great operation at Wawa that I am more particularly concerned now, being right in the territory of the Algoma Central Railway; and as a prelude to a visit to the steel works itself, I had the pleasure of meeting James E Barber, General Manager, Exploration and Project Development of the Corporation. For a little time, I fear, we talked railways rather than mining. It was my fault; but I must admit that Jim Barber did not need much encouragement from me to yarn about the days when his father was President of the Algoma Central and some of his anecdotes have been interpolated at various places in this book. Then he also brought into our talk the veteran mining engineer, George W MacLeod, now 82 years 'young'. He, a second generation Canadian, whose ancestors had emigrated from that veritable *alma mater* of the Clan MacLeod, the Isle of Skye, Scotland, was with the railway from 1922 to 1943, and then had joined the formidable Sir James Dunn, in the steel company. MacLeod laughingly suggested that in working with a man so adept at 'hiring and firing' his own service of 13 years continuously must constitute, as he put it, a 'world record'!

But while Sir James's immense drive, energy and financial acumen was the mainspring behind the building up of the plant at the Soo from a derelict, boarded up wreck, peopled only by a few watchmen and some accountants, toward the mighty organization it is today, MacLeod was responsible for the highly successful geological work and mining prospecting that confirmed the existence of a vast reservoir of iron ore, compared to which the winnings from the old and new Helen Mines were a mere scratching on the surface. The iron ore deposits in the Michipicoten range could well be likened to an iceberg in which only the merest fractions of the whole are near the surface. At Sir James Dunn's instigation MacLeod drove a shaft down to a depth of one mile from the surface, with the result that the existence of iron ore was proved, sufficient to maintain the supply of two million tons of sinter a year to the Soo at least until the year 2000! The accompanying cross sectional diagram shows the situation at the present time, and how operations are not merely well below the level of Lake Superior, which is only a few miles away, but that the present workings are 646 ft below *sea* level. When the Helen Mine was being worked the ore, as mined, was brought down to the sintering plant at Wawa by train, as so vividly depicted in the aerial photographs reproduced on Plate 43. But from the present mine ore is brought to the surface by the inclined rope way shown in the diagram

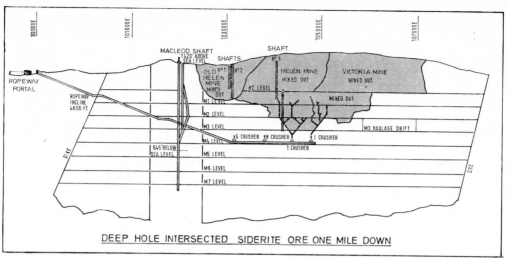

13   Cross section: Macleod Mine, at Wawa

—another of George MacLeod's innovations in the area. In appreciation of his work the present workings have been named the 'George W MacLeod Mine'—though as he wittily explained: 'I do not own it!' So, every day of the year, winter and summer alike, a train carrying about 5000 tons of sintered ore thunders down the line from Wawa to the Soo.

Then Jim Barber took me down to the steel plant. I had already seen this from the dock side, when we had brought in our load of pelletized ore from Thunder Bay in the MV *Algoway*. But although the array of blast furnaces ranged along parallel to the dock is most impressive this gives really no impression of the size and productive capacity of this great works. It was however the logical starting point for a tour, being the fountain head of the entire activity. Our guide explained that steel production at the Soo now is by the basic oxygen process. This could be broadly described as a modern development of the Bessemer process, which in turn was superseded in most plants, as at the Soo, by the open hearth process. There is still one open hearth shop in operation in this plant however. The benefit of the basic oxygen process is that it increases, by very many times, the speed of production of steel, of outstanding quality. The phasing out of the old open-hearth furnaces in the Algoma plant began in 1957 with the installation of two new basic oxygen furnaces, each capable of producing 100 tons of steel an hour. The rate of production became some 6 to 8 times faster than with the old equipment.

The process may be briefly described as follows: steel-making is a refining process, in which impurity elements in iron, and steel scrap, are oxydized out; it is conducted in an egg-shaped vessel, open at the top, and charged with a mixture containing about

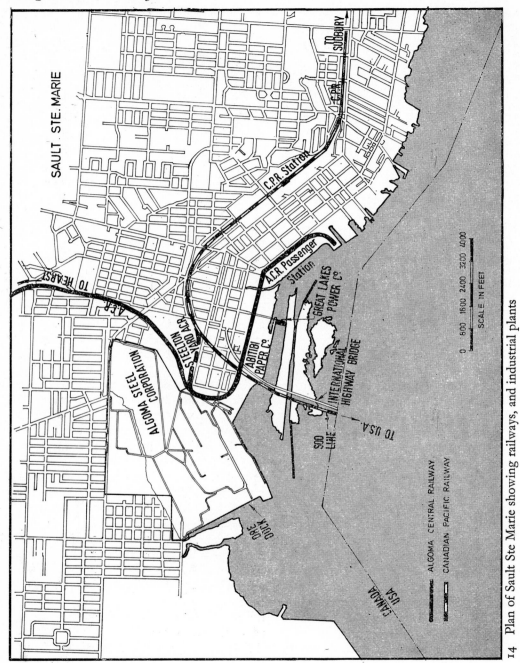

SAULT STE. MARIE

TO SUDBURY

C.P.R.

C.P.R. Station

A.C.R. Passenger Station

TO HEARST

ACR

STEELTON S. YARD A.C.R.

ABITIBI PAPER CO.

GREAT LAKES & POWER CO.

INTERNATIONAL HIGHWAY BRIDGE

SOO LINE

TO USA

ALGOMA STEEL CORPORATION

ORE DOCK

CANADA

USA

0 800 1600 2400 3200 4000

SCALE IN FEET

—————— ALGOMA CENTRAL RAILWAY.
□□□□□□ CANADIAN PACIFIC RAILWAY

14   Plan of Sault Ste Marie showing railways, and industrial plants

70 per cent of molten iron, from sinter, and about 30 per cent steel scrap. A water-cooled lance is lowered into the molten mass and pure oxygen is blown into the metal. The impurities are removed in the waste gases, or they combine with the fluxes charged to form a liquid slag. The molten, purified steel is then poured off, either to be cast into ingots—large blocks, that will be reheated for rolling into plates or bars, or into a continuous casting machine to produce primary shapes the purpose of which I will mention later. I have been round many large works, in many countries all over the world, but I must say I found the basic oxygen steel process, as used at Algoma, one of the most impressive ever. When I visited the plant another giant new blast furnace was in course of erection, and while it was 'cold', its details of construction could be studied. There is no opportunity to do this once a plant like this gets going!

It goes, I suppose, almost without saying in this day and age, that the operation of the basic oxygen furnace at the Soo is controlled by computer, in respect of the amount of scrap loaded, the timing of the process and the checking of the chemical composition. The computer does not actually *check* the latter, which is done by skilled metallurgists; but it could be used to halt the process if a chemical analysis did not show the correct results. Different customers can require different percentages of alloys added, such as manganese or nickel; and these have to be added to the vessel in which the 'blow' takes place. All the necessary data concerning each particular batch are fed into the computer, and it keeps track of, and controls the use of the raw materials. It responds to the varying stages, controlling the oxygen flow, and reacts to test results, either automatically, or by the intervention of the operating personnel. The basic oxygen furnaces at the Soo are the largest in Canada.

Having obtained steel in the form of ingots or cast primary shapes by the most modern and efficient process in operation anywhere today, it is processed into commercial forms by equally fine and up-to-date machinery. I saw the Bloom and plate mill in action, taking the ingots straight from the blast furnaces and rolling them into heavy plate. I was shown the parallel flange beam mill, the first of its kind ever to be installed in Canada, and outside, examples of many finished basic sections, used in building construction. The variety of products now turned out from the Algoma steel works is very large. For many years in the earlier days rails were the staple product, and as I have told earlier the fortunes of the plant tended to rise and fall with the demand for rails, and the success or otherwise with which export orders were obtained to supplement the fairly regular demands of the Canadian railways. But today the products of the plant are greatly diversified, and although the actual tonnage of rails rolled is probably not greatly different from that of earlier days it now represents no more than about 21 per cent of the total output.

Today there is a heavy demand for all kinds of steel sections for the building industry, and Algoma supplies these in great variety. There are beams ranging from the large parallel flanged type, rolled from a primary shape, to the older standard, and various sections for car-building and ship-building. In the yard I saw large quantities of hot-rolled sheet, and strip, made up into coils, up to 8 ft in width, and steel in tubular form; but knowing from past experience what a dirty business steelmaking can be I was very interested in the numerous ways in which the Algoma Steel Corporation is dealing with the very important matter of pollution control, both as regard the air and the water. Without going into fine detail Algoma Steel is constantly engaged upon a comprehensive pollution abatement program, employing skilled specialists for every facet of their multifarious operations, not excluding solid waste disposal. There used to be an old saying in the industrial north of England: 'Where there's muck there's money'. Today the 'muck' must be eliminated, and this Algoma Steel are very successfully doing.

CHAPTER SIXTEEN

Business Allies in the Soo: Abitibi Paper and Lake Superior Power

In the introduction to this book I commented at some length upon the beautiful aerial photograph which so vividly reveals the geography of the industrial activities beside the Canadian Lock, and the power canal. The concentration of plants in this western area of the Soo, with the Abitibi, and the Power Company's generating station both relatively near to Algoma Steel, and all three adjacent to the Algoma Central Railway yards at Steelton, could be seen as a modern embodiment of Francis H Clergue's original conception, were it not for the fact that these four neat complexes do not by any means represent the full total of the companies' activities. Just as the Algoma Central has extended far beyond the business of running trains, so both the Abitibi Paper Company and the Great Lakes Power Company have widespread ramifications, even beyond the District of Algoma, to back up their original functions. Both are on historic ground, beside the Canadian Lock, and overlooked by the towering new structure of the International Bridge.

Perhaps I may begin with a little history. I have mentioned the old canoe routes at a number of places in this book, and how the Indians had become expert in the downward negotiation of rapids—and how the laborious job of manhandling the canoes up the rapids was a way of life for the early inhabitants of Western Ontario, as of many other regions of Canada south of Hudson Bay. But while rapids on rivers in country traversed by the northern part of the Algoma Central Railway were one thing the drop of nearly 20 ft between the levels of Lakes Superior and Huron was quite another, and on the land now occupied by the Abitibi Paper Company there is preserved a small lock, just big enough to accommodate one of the old canoes. It stands now on land that has been reclaimed, but at one time it must have been in the line of the waterway. It is indeed a fascinating piece of local history.

I enjoyed a most instructive tour of the paper mills with Alf Askin, the Mill Manager. We went out to see the very start of the operation, where many Algoma Central flat cars loaded to capacity with the 8 ft logs were standing ready in line. To my unaccustomed eye it seemed that there was a tremendous amount of timber on hand, but I learned that 12,000 cords represent about one month's supply. The 8 ft length is the maximum that is convenient for transport by rail, as I could appreciate in seeing the neat and economical space stacking on the railway flat cars; but this length is also interlinked with the first operation in the mill, which consists of cutting them into 4 ft lengths. I must not digress upon the intricacies of modern paper-making machinery, which is a highly specialized branch of mechanical engineering, but only to comment on certain points that impressed me very much in the fine plant at the Soo. Paper-making can be a 'messy' business, in stripping the logs of their bark, and then grinding them into pulp, in all of which large quantities of water are involved. The 'trimmings', as it were, have to go somewhere, and with a fast flowing river just outside, passing downstream to some very large inland 'seas' like Lake Michigan and Lake Huron, there would be a natural tendency just to discharge the rubbish 'overboard' as it were. But with everyone now pollution-conscious, and rightly so, this one-time easy way out is just the thing one cannot do; and so careful arrangements are made for collection and disposal, by approved methods, of all the trash.

I saw the raw logs coming in on the belt conveyor on which they are placed by the 'grab' cranes that lift them from the railway cars; then massive handling machinery positions them ready to be cut in half, and then they are passed to the mill in which they are violently agitated in water to remove all the bark. But it was the actual paper-making machines that were the most impressive, from the point of introduction of the pulped wood to the eventual delivery, about 200 yards away down the lengthy shop, of the finished paper. In noting many of the features of these gigantic machines and their specialized design one was conscious of an immense bank of experience, extending over many decades. Finally there were baled up stocks of paper, of various grades, size and colour, stacked ready for transhipment by rail, to many different destinations.

In the tranship shed were many box-cars of the Soo Line being loaded. The destination of practically all the paper made at the Abitibi plant in the Soo is the middle-west cities of the USA. Alf Askin mentioned Chicago, Milwaukee, St Louis, Memphis, Louisville (Kentucky) and Minneapolis as among the largest customers. The demands of the USA for newsprint do indeed seem insatiable, and I recall hearing the same story of high demand when I was visiting the British Columbia Railway some years previously and witnessed their large traffic in forest products. I should add that the Abitibi Paper Company has, in its long history, passed through as many changes of ownership, and of rising and falling prosperity, as any member of the original Clergue 'empire'. In the various arrangements following the crash of 1903, then as the 'Sault Ste Marie Pulp and Power Company', was its sale to American

8 In the land of lakes and forests north of Hawk Junction, the diesels make their way

9　A four-locomotive freight, loaded to maximum tonnage in the lake country south of Ogidaki

Plate 33   MAINTAINING A FAMOUS NAME

a   The first *Algorail*, purchased in 1917 as the *William S Mack*, and renamed. She was sold out of service in 1963

b   The new *Algorail*, a self-unloading type vessel, that entered service in 1968

Plate 34   ALGOMA SHIPS, WINTER AND SUMMER

a   Maiden voyage through the Soo of the *Sir Denys Lowson* in April 1965 with the ship dividing the two different ice conditions

b   The *E B Barber*, loading stone. This remarkable picture shows how closely the huge flat-bottomed ships can get inshore. The self-unloading boom is swung clear while loading is in progress

Plate 35   ON THE *ALGOWAY*

a   Looking forward toward the wheel house, while full speed ahead on Lake Superior

b   Looking aft from the wheel house, showing the cables by which the unloading boom is raised

a Close up view of the unloading boom looking toward the wheel house

Plate 36   THE MV *ALGOWAY*

b Mounting of the unloading boom

Plate 37   THE MV *ALGOWAY*

a   The ship arriving alongside the ore dock of the Algoma Steel Corporation at the Soo

b   Unloading coal at the Soo

a   Snow plow propelled by four 'GP7' diesel loco-motives leaving Hawk Junction

Plate 38   WORKING IN THE SNOW

b   Clearing points at Oba

c   The snow flanger in action

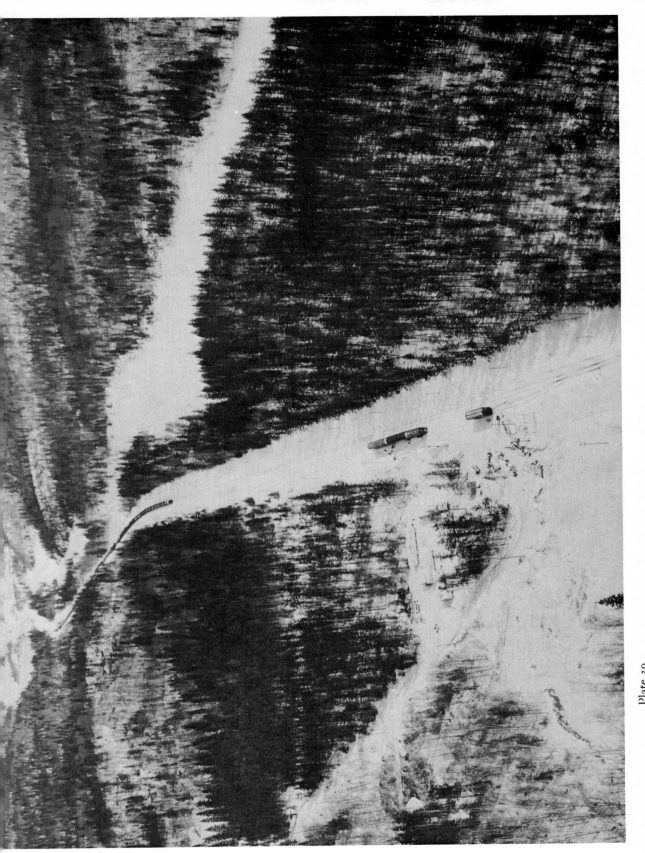

Plate 39
Algoma Country in mid-winter: train operation normal, as usual

Plate 40   MICHIPICOTEN HARBOR

a   April 1974—completely ice-bound; view looking to the old jetty

b   Aerial view showing the coal bridge and a bulk-vessel alongside the old jetty

Plate 41   ALLIES IN THE SOO

a   Generating station of the Great Lakes Power Company

b   The Abitibi Paper Company plant seen across the waterway leading to the Power Company's 'bridge'

Plate 42   BUSINESS ALLIES

a   Aerial view of the great sintered ore plant of 'Algoma Steel' at Wawa

b   A train of ore cars, with longitudinal opening hoppers, awaiting loading at Wawa

Plate 43
MINING AT WAWA

a   An aerial view over the Helen Mine area, showing a train of loaded cars descending to Wawa

b   An aerial panoramic view showing the sintered ore plant, and in the middle distance the town and Wawa Lake

Plate 44 RAILWAYS IN THE SOO—THEN AND NOW

a   Steelton, in steam days

b   The head office building on Bay Street

c   The new passenger station. The head office building can be
     seen in the right background

Plate 45   MONTREAL RIVER TODAY

a   A northbound passenger train crossing, as seen from the upstream reservoir side

b   A view looking south showing how the dam has been built to integrate with the position of the railway viaduct

Plate 46   PASSENGER TRAIN CARS

a   Steam generating unit

b   Baggage van, formerly used
    on the California Zephyr

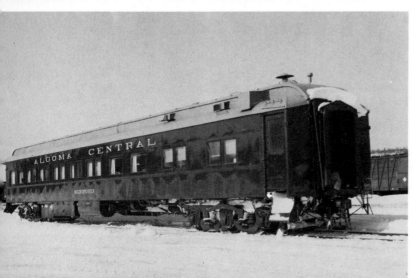

c   Business car *Michipicoten*,
    formerly on the New York
    Central RR

Plate 47 PASSENGER TRAIN CARS

a Business car *Agawa*

b Express and baggage car

c Observation car—*Canyon View*

Plate 48 THE CANYON TOUR
A day when the train had to be run in two sections: the cars in the siding track alongside the Canyon park, while passen-

interests in 1911. It was in fact the first company to be detached from the 'Lake Superior' group. The name Abitibi was introduced during subsequent financial operations, and by the year 1930 it was in receivership. The American ownership was ended in 1944 by order of the United States Government, and the company then passed back into Canadian hands.

The history of Great Lakes Power Company extends back, through its various predecessors, to pre-Clergue days in the Soo. The possibilities of power generation at the falls in the St Mary's River had attracted the attention of John Laird and Jonathan Henderson as far back as 1877; but in the same year a private corporation known as the Sault Ste Marie Water, Gas, and Light Company acquired both the Laird and Henderson, and also the Hudson's Bay Company properties adjacent to the falls. In this new undertaking W H Plummer, H C Hamilton and J J Kehoe were leaders, and I have told in Chapter 1 how an almost chance conversation in a train, in which Kehoe and Hamilton were involved, led to Francis H Clergue's introduction to the Soo. In March 1889 an Act was passed by the Legislative Assembly of Ontario defining the powers of the company, and changing its name to the Ontario Sault Ste Marie Light and Power Company. In 1894 Clergue took it over. At this stage its name was changed and later it was divided into two parts: The Lake Superior Power Company, which operated the generating station, and the Tagona Water and Light Company, which distributed water and electrical energy to the domestic consumers in the community.

I need not go into all the financial and other difficulties in which these two companies became involved when the collapse of the Clergue 'empire' came about in 1903, except to mention that in 1916 The Great Lakes Power Company was incorporated, and took over the power plant, and certain other activities. We can move ahead to the year 1926, when another company, The Algoma District Power Company, was formed to generate power on the Michipicoten River and transmit it to the Soo. During these years of uncertainty and financial stress the demands for electrical power had been unceasing, and several increases in capacity had been made at the generating plant beside the Canadian Lock. Then in October 1931 The Great Lakes Power Company and the Algoma District Power Company were amalgamated to form Great Lakes Power Company—a slight difference from the title of the first of the two constituents, made by omission of the initial 'The'. It was controlled by Middle West Utilities of Canada, a Canadian holding company of Middle West Utilities Company (Delaware).

Throughout the 1930s, whatever difficulties might beset other industries in the district the demands for power continued to rise, and a very interesting and important development was the construction of a new dam and generating station at Upper Falls on the Montreal River, crossed in such spectacular fashion by the viaduct of the Algoma Central Railway. This took place in 1936 and it is remarkable to record that in the 20 years since The Great Lakes Power Company was formed in 1916

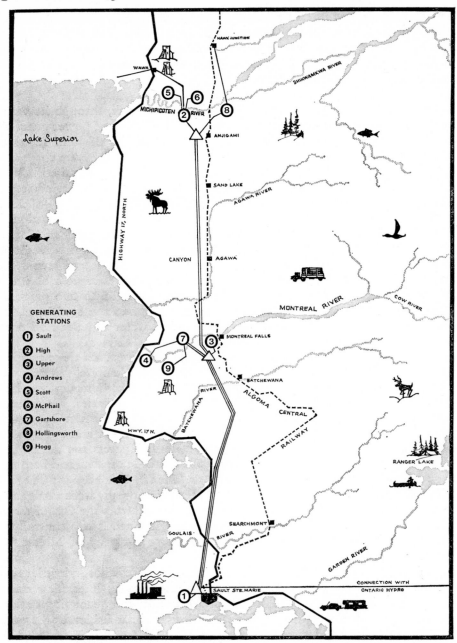

GENERATING STATIONS

1 Sault
2 High
3 Upper
4 Andrews
5 Scott
6 McPhail
7 Gartshore
8 Hollingsworth
9 Hogg

15   Great Lakes Power Company: diagram of generating stations and power lines

generating capacity had increased from 4700 KW to 47,750 KW—just over *ten times*. Despite the difficulty of financing and obtaining materials during the war such was the demand for power that Government authority was obtained for further augmenting of the generating capacity at the Montreal Falls; but in 1944 a change in structure of the company itself was involved when the Government of the United States directed the Middle West Utilities Company of Delaware to divest itself of certain properties, including Middle West Utilities of Canada Ltd. In consequence of this a new, all-Canadian organization, Great Lakes Power Corporation, was incorporated in 1949, and all the more recent developments have taken place under this company.

I had the pleasure of seeing the generating plant at the Soo, but to indicate the enormous expansion of generating capacity and supply in the District of Algoma the accompanying map has been prepared from information supplied by the Corporation. From this it will be seen that the plant at the Soo is now one of *nine*, the other eight being divided between four on the Michipicoten River and four at or near the Montreal Falls. This map also shows the distribution of the power lines, and it will be noted that in addition to these there is a fourth line into the Soo, forming a connection with Ontario Hydro. At the Soo the huge turbine rotors are mounted on vertical shafts, which are continued upward to carry the rotors of the generators. There are 24 of these generators, having a combined capacity of 21,000 KW. The voltage as generated is 2300 and this is boosted to 11,000 for distribution.

The building of the power lines to the north of the Soo, in the late 1920s and the early 1930s, involved great difficulties, from the extremely rugged nature of the country; yet they were difficulties of a kind different from those experienced some 15 years earlier in building the railway. Naturally an endeavor was made to secure the shortest possible route, and this involved cutting through forest-laden country, and clearing a right-of-way so as to salvage as much of the timber as possible. Government regulations required that a fire permit had to be obtained where burning was necessary, but in such a way as to minimize the risk of a forest fire. Most of the pole holes had to be drilled in solid rock, and as much of the route was away from the railway, the poles and line material had to be hauled in over logging trails or tote roads. A difficulty not mentioned in any contemporary accounts of railway construction, but which no doubt existed in full measure, was the pest of black-fly and mosquito. During construction of the pole line in summer reports were made of black-fly settling on and biting sweating work horses, and causing their deaths.

In earlier days the 112-mile transmission line between the Soo and the generating stations on the Michipicoten River was patrolled by no more than two men. One started at one end, and the second at the other, and they kept going until they met. There were huts spaced out along the line at which the patrolmen stayed overnight and cooked their meals, and there were telephones in these huts by which reports could be sent to headquarters. But it was tough going in the winter. The average snowfall along this route totals 7 to 8 ft per season, with a bad winter amounting to as much as 12 ft with high drifts. In the winter the patrolmen worked in snow shoes. Every five years the right-of-way had to be cleared of the growing bush, so that the patrolmen could walk through. Today things are very different. Depending upon the kind of weather snowmobiles, jeeps and muskeg tractors are now used for patrolling, and a light aeroplane is available, so that the line can be patrolled by air in case of emergency.

CHAPTER SEVENTEEN

In the Track of the Black Bear: Passenger Business and Mail

In recent years the Algoma Central has pulled off one of the most astounding feats of expansion in passenger business ever seen on the world's railways. At a time when countless services have been withdrawn, never to be reinstated, and many others were struggling to keep fairly level far less than showing an increase, the Algoma Central has a train on which the number of passengers per year has increased from 3019 in 1960, the year, it will be recalled, after the Common Shareholders had resumed control of the company, to a phenomenal 95,612 in 1973. This is no freak performance, but the development of a sweeping upward trend that began to gain momentum in 1965. Why, one may well ask? Why indeed! This is the Agawa Canyon Tour Train, operated throughout the summer months and through the fall, and run on a slightly different basis during the months of deep snow and ice as a 'Winter Wonderland Tour'.

From its very inception, more than 70 years ago, the Algoma Central was not unmindful of the tourist attractions of its territory; and a brochure issued in the difficult days of 1909, the cover of which is reproduced, includes these alluring words:

> The time has come when tired humanity seeks surcease from heat, smoke, toil and trouble, and the exodus begins, to the waters, where blow cool breezes, and to the woods, where there is rest and shade

The modern literature of the railways puts the situation in different words, but essentially the same theme:

> North of Sault Ste Marie, Ontario, stretches a vast expanse of forest and mountains interlaced with countless clear lakes and brawling rivers, a

land virtually unspoiled. Through this immense land, around lake and mountain, over gorges and into the river valleys, the Algoma Central Railway winds its way . . .

No reader of this book will be under any misapprehensions as to what it cost the ACR in toil and sweat to build this railway, or to keep it going through long years of great financial stress. But that fortunately is now a matter of history, and there now exists a magnificent, if hilly and sinuous road, and fine modern equipment to provide a day excursion service without parallel. Several times previously in this book I have mentioned the strategic position of the Soo. So far as the Agawa Canyon Tour Train is concerned it is strategic in another way, lying at the very front door, as it were, of the great American State of Michigan. Visitors from the United States have only to drive their cars across the International Bridge over the St Mary's River and park just beside the station from which the tour train starts. And every year from 1965 they have been coming in ever increasing *thousands*. In the height of the summer season, and in the glorious coloring of the fall it is not unusual for 1000 people to make the trip in a single day. But before coming to a detailed account of the operations that make this service such a success it is fascinating to look back to the days when the Algoma Central possessed no more than twelve passenger vehicles. That was in 1925, when the consist was eight coaches, one combined passenger and baggage, one buffet and two baggage cars. The total had at one time been up to 18, in 1915, from the eight with which the company opened for business in 1900; but there had been something of a recession in passenger business after World War I.

In the early 1920s there was, as now, only one regular passenger train in each direction and I was able to study several sheets from the working table of 1923. At that time Franz was a major divisional point, and any passenger who wished to travel right through from the Soo to Hearst had to spend from 7.45 at night till 11.20 next morning at Franz. On both stages of the route the daily trains were 'mixed', calling at every station. One of the terms of the Railway Subsidy Act of 1912 was that the company was required to run four trains a day calling at all stations. This the Algoma Central did by numbering its trains 1, 2, 3 and 4 even though they ran on different sections of the line. They were also required to provide for the conveyance of mails, and letters carried by train were postmarked by the train conductor. It is interesting to find that in 1923 there were refreshment rooms— euphemistically described as 'restaurants'—at Frater and Hawk Junction. The mixed trains shown in the timetable paused for 15 minutes at Frater. As mentioned in Chapter 5 this was a station where locomotives were re-coaled and fires cleaned, and the stop gave the passengers a chance to freshen up too! The mixed trains stopped no more than briefly at Hawk Junction; but the refreshment room there was presumably for the benefit of branch-line passengers awaiting connections. Actually no regularly scheduled trains at all were shown on the branch in the 1923 timetable.

Coming now to the present time, during the winter months the northbound passenger train number 1, leaving Sault Ste Marie at 8.30 am, runs on Thursdays, Fridays, Saturdays and Sundays; and the southbound number 2, on Fridays, Saturdays, Sundays and Mondays. The 'Snow Train', as it is now called, providing the winter wonderland tour operates on those days when there is a regular train in both directions. Coaches and a dining car are conveyed to Eton, 120 miles up the line, and there transfered to the southbound train. So, as the company's literature aptly puts it, passengers ride in a warm picture-window coach, through temperatures sometimes as low as 40 degrees below zero, skirting the frozen shores of Algoma's many lakes, and through the Agawa Canyon. Because of the weather conditions often prevailing passengers are not allowed to get out during the switch of the tour cars from the northbound to the southbound train at Eton. I made this winter journey myself just a fortnight after the exciting snow-plowing run on northbound number 5 freight, described in Chapter 11.

At various stages in this book reference has been made to the business cars. In my first journeys over the line my wife and I had the pleasure of traveling in the *Agawa*, a beautiful car built by Barney and Smith in 1913, at Dayton, Ohio. Unnamed at first it worked on the Longview, Portland and Northern, but in 1930 it was sold to the Wabash, on which it ran for 23 years. It was bought by the Algoma Central in 1953 and named *Agawa*. It is in every way a sumptuous vehicle, including two staterooms, with a washroom between, the usual dining and observation lounges found on such cars and four berths for staff. A specially enjoyed feature on our trip was the open platform at the rear, with just enough side partition to protect against cross draughts but not to interrupt the view. On our trips in July 1972 the weather was genial enough for us to spend much of our journeys sitting out on that back platform. A much admired feature of the car are the curved windows, and the inlaid panelling. The *Michipicoten* in which I traveled on the freight train journeys described in Chapter 11, is an enormously heavy 12-wheeler from the New York Central. It differs from the *Agawa* in having four bedrooms, instead of the two luxurious state rooms, and not so extensive a back platform. The *Michipicoten* weighs no less than 94 tons.

When I went up the line for the second time during my visit to Canada in April 1974, I had the experience once again of traveling in the business car *Agawa*, with the pleasant company of Len Savoie, President of the Railway, Jack Thompson, and Ed Moore, the Manager—Passenger Sales. We were attached to the rear of the passenger train, number 1, and on a day of the most glorious unbroken sunshine saw the line to the very best advantage. The more genial weather that had intervened since my last trip, described in Chapter 11, had melted a good deal of the snow; but as we made our way north there was still plenty of it about, and I saw lakes and waterfalls in the process of thawing out. Having seen something of the freight operation on my previous trip it was now interesting to hear from my friends in the car the many facets of the passenger business, and how it is being fostered. Freight topics were not entirely out either, because the meets we had with other trains gave me a further insight into this tremendous operation.

Out of the Soo our train consisted of six cars; from the locomotives, rearward in succession, these were heating van, baggage and coach, going through to Hearst, then coach and dining car going to Eton and returning thence on number 2, and the business car *Agawa* on the rear end. The train was hauled by two 'GP7' diesel electric locomotives though one of these was working only to Hawk Junction for balancing purposes. It was certainly not needed for traction. On this beautiful day quite a number of passengers were going to Eton and back, for the ride, while several 'flag stops' were made en route to set down parties, bound for isolated dwelling houses beside, or near to the line. Those who had come for a sightseeing ride were richly rewarded. The lakes were still frozen over, but the snow on their surfaces was melting, and the rivers though still having large areas of ice were flowing fast, and in places turbulently. In the wonderfully clear air the absence of foliage in the forests enabled us to see much farther than is possible in the summer and at times the sun was warm enough for Len Savoie and I to sit out on the rear platform of the *Agawa*, albeit well wrapped up in coats!

We received an order to meet southbound freight number 8, the train I rode on my previous trip, at Frater. The meet was an excellent one. As we approached we could see the freight was already there, detaching some cars from the front, and it was only a matter of minutes before she was under way again, with a load of 5750 tons hauled by three 'SD40' locomotives. We then set out on what is always the most beautiful stretch of the northbound journey—down the hill into the Agawa Canyon. The scenic gem on this particular day was the Bridal Veil Falls, just before reaching the Canyon Park. When I traveled this way a fortnight earlier they were frozen solid, but now the lake near the mountain top was evidently thawing, for amid the great mass of ice a torrent of water was surging down in the utmost splendor. On this trip I could not help feeling that those who make the winter tour, to Eton, have one advantage not enjoyed by those participating in the summer tour; the continuation north of Canyon station is made through the narrowest and most dramatic part of the run, where the line works its way on a ledge at the foot of a vertical rock wall, with the river just below on the opposite side.

Fascinating though the winter tour can be, especially if made in such beautiful weather as we enjoyed on my second trip in April 1974, it is, of course, the summer Canyon Tour, operated every day, including Sundays, that provides the main test of the Algoma passenger organization. As in the winter months the tour coaches and dining car are attached to the regular train; but while we had no more than a single coach and the dining car to be transfered from one train to the other on my April trip, when I traveled nearly two years earlier, on a Sunday in late July no fewer than ten cars were put off at Canyon, leaving the hundreds of passengers nearly two hours to explore, picnic, and enjoy the scenery before train number 2 arrived from the north to collect those ten cars and bring them back to the Soo. The northbound departure time is earlier, and departure from Hearst later during the summer months to provide a pleasant interval at the Canyon. Then although the coaches remain in the passing track passengers are at liberty to leave the train as they wish.

This tour train is really 'something'! It is equipped throughout with modern coaches, all having large picture windows through which the beautiful scenery can be enjoyed in comfort. In the twists and turns of the track there are many times when looking forward one can see the locomotives, and looking backward the rear of the train. In the height of the season the consist is often of as many as 20 cars, because in addition to those providing the Canyon Tour there will be at least three going forward to the northern end of the line, at Hearst: one heater van, one baggage car and one coach. To keep schedule time with this heavy load, weighing something between 1500 and 2000 tons, at least four of the smaller diesel locomotives of the 'GP7' type will be required, and although the train will be so very much reduced from Canyon all the locomotives usually continue to Hawk Junction. On a quiet day one could, therefore, have more locomotives than cars between Canyon and Hawk Junction. The Algoma Central Railway does everything possible to add to the interest and enjoyment of the trip, and a leaflet is issued free to all passengers explaining what can be seen at the various stages of the journey, and the times to look out for these scenic points. The times are given in Eastern Standard, which is worked to by all railways in Canada; but when summer time is in operation the actual times are one hour later than those quoted.

The coaches used, built to the finest North American standards, have come from many railways further south. The serious recession in passenger traffic in the USA has made much first class equipment superfluous to requirements and the Algoma Central, with its own unique passenger business booming so remarkably, has been able to purchase a number of fine cars, and to retire some that have done long duty on the line. Visiting the car shops at Steelton I saw coaches from the Central of Georgia, Illinois Central, Gulf, Mobile and Ohio, together with some interesting four-car sets from the Southern Pacific, each consisting of two articulated 'twins', having only three trucks for the equivalent of two cars. I greatly admired some stainless steel Budd cars from the 'California Zephyr' train of the Denver and Rio Grande Western, and a dining car from the Santa Fe. All these additions to the stock of the Algoma Central are being very thoroughly refurbished in the Steelton shops. I was very impressed with the excellence of the work performed there, and one of the former Rio Grande vehicles repainted, with the panels in the standard ACR red in particular looked truly splendid. For the benefit of European readers I may add that Algoma Central 'red' is almost identical to the red of the British London Midland and Scottish Railway.

The Algoma Central is doing its best to encourage patrons to make a complete tour of the line, by continuing to Hearst and returning on the following day. Having enjoyed the scenic glories of the route between the Soo and the Agawa Canyon there is certainly ample inducement to go a second time, and see what lies to the north.

It is certainly an education. The scenery continues very fine as far as Hawk Junction, although the hills are becoming noticeably less in height. One should really travel this northern part of the line with a map, so that the full extent and unique character of this remarkable countryside can be appreciated. This was the country of the canoe routes used by the fur traders, in which one could travel for 50 miles or more at a stretch, without having to resort to portage. Today one can travel from near Hawk Junction almost to Oba, where the Algoma Central line intersects the principal transcontinental route of Canadian National entirely by water. It was here that the tentative explorations for the proposed continuation of the line to Hudson Bay took place, as described in Chapters 2 and 4 of this book.

Rail buffs, or 'ferroequinologists'—as an enthusiast in Winnipeg likes to call his particular cult—will be interested in the intersections with the Canadian Pacific at Franz, and with the Canadian National at Oba. As described in Chapter 12 there is frequently some activity to be seen on these great trunk routes. There is however not a great deal else save railway interest at these stations; but on leaving Oba the Algoma Central line cuts through an interesting country including long stretches of muskeg before reaching the clay belt, where there is more evidence of farming, lumbering, and other human activity than at any point on the whole route—save of course at the Agawa Canyon, when the tour train disgorges its passengers. Hearst, the northern end of the line, is a thriving little town dependent almost entirely upon forest products, and providing a useful exchange point with that section of the Canadian National system, that was inaugurated as the National Transcontinental, running on a course little removed from a straight line, throughout from Quebec to Winnipeg.

During the summer months when the Agawa Canyon Tour train is operated and number 1 leaves the Soo at 8 am (summer time) the arrival at Hearst is at 6 pm; train number 2 leaves Hearst at 8.00 in the morning, and the long summer evening gives a pleasant opportunity for a walk round the town, and a chance to absorb something of its 'frontier' character. Today, however, situated on the route of a major east-west highway the atmosphere is becoming rather more sophisticated. Nothing succeeds like success, and the astonishing growth in patronage for the Canyon Tour train is in no small measure due to the fact of delighted excursionists telling their friends, and coming again themselves. Advance bookings and seat reservations are not made, except for a limited number of block bookings for party organizations. Prospective passengers arriving overnight at the Soo can book their tickets this one day in advance, and this gives them the privilege of free car parking at the station.

At the height of the summer tourist season it has sometimes happened that the regular Canyon Tour train has become completely sold out before departure time. Every passenger booking is given a note attached to his ticket showing the number of the car to which he is assigned, and no overcrowding or standing is permitted. So as not to disappoint any patrons who might arrive after the regular train is fully booked the Algoma Central has in readiness a special train, to take the 'overflow'. Tickets for this, which are printed in a different color from those of the regular train, are not issued until the latter has actually departed. The special 'relief' train is timed so as to arrive at Canyon station after the regular train has left on its return journey, thus avoiding the detraining at the Canyon of an excessive number of visitors at the same time. In the shops at Steelton I was shown a very fine dining car, formerly owned by the Atchison, Topeka and Santa Fe Railway, which was being refurbished in readiness for use on the second Canyon train.

From the emphasis I have laid in this chapter to the Agawa Canyon Tour I may, up to now, have given the impression that other passenger business on the Algoma Central was small, and not very significant. This is far from being the case. It is true that this one train, this one activity, provides more than three-quarters of the total number of passengers carried by the whole railway, but there are times when the regular passenger trains are busy north of Hawk Junction, where all ordinary highways end. There are some tracks that are negotiable in dry weather, but these are unconnected with the main highways to the south and west. Hunters, fishermen, and others who have interests in the wild untamed regions to the north drive their automobiles to Hawk Junction, where at times it is difficult to find space in the station parking area; and so the passenger trains, which are apt to be thinly patronized north of the Canyon can become busy north of Hawk Junction, and they provide a much appreciated service.

An analysis of the total passenger journeys made on the railway makes interesting reading, and I am indebted to Ed Moore for the following details for the year 1973. Here a return ticket such as the Canyon Tour, counts as two, because actually two passenger journeys are involved.

Number of Passenger Journeys, 1973:

Canyon Tour (summer service)	190,000
Snow Train (winter season)	18,200
Tour of the line (Soo to Hearst and back)	5000
Ordinary passenger journeys, booked principally at Soo, Searchmont and Hawk Junction	29,300
Total passenger journeys	242,500

Until recently there was no passenger station, as such, at the Soo. Trains started from the tracks just outside the headquarter offices. But in 1973 a new station of modern design was brought into service, about a quarter of a mile to the west of headquarters. This has a most attractive waiting room, with souvenir shop, where every manner of souvenir can be bought, from toys for the children to stylish glass and chinaware. In the waiting room are various railway relics, but in the station area as expressed by a great friend of the Algoma Central—there is one thing missing— a preserved steam locomotive. Nevertheless the Algoma Central Railway of modern times has not done things by halves, and as told in Chapter 12 its changeover from steam to diesel traction, in 1952, was so swift and thoroughgoing that no one thought of preserving one of the 'old faithfuls'. By the time the vogue of preserving steam locomotives had really caught on in Canada the remains of the old Algoma Central stud had long since passed beyond the stage of being merely scrap metal. The atmosphere of early steam days on the railway is however revived in the 'Pufferbelly' snack-bar in the Station Mall, described in Chapter 18, though not to the stage of becoming three-dimensional.

One last point to be mentioned about the passenger business is one on which the Algoma Central may be justly proud. Never in its 73 years of operation has it caused the death of a single passenger. In the old days of indifferent track there were one or two cases of derailment on the 'mixed' trains, not of the passenger coaches but of freight stock, which became unsteady through a shifted cargo; but not even in the days of the 'Pangis Turn', when operating methods were haphazard, to say the least, was there any loss of life among passengers. Stories of one or two accidents with freight trains have been told to me, but these form no part of the present story.

CHAPTER EIGHTEEN

Natural Resource Developments on Lands Owned by the ACR

Travelers by the Algoma Central Railway winter and summer alike are enthralled by the passing scene, especially on that part of the line south of Hawk Junction. But while enthralling it can also be a bewildering ride in the way the train twists and turns in its tracks. On a fine day the sunshine is sometimes streaming in through one window, and sometimes through the other. There are frequent glimpses of the head end of the train, and almost from the point of leaving the Soo the countryside has little signs of industry or habitation. It has been said that if the modern business techniques of market research or feasibility studies had been initially applied the railway would never have been built! That however was not the way in anything with which Francis H Clergue was concerned. He had enterprised a paper mill at the Soo; pulpwood was needed, and a railway was projected to carry the logs down from the interior. All this has been told in considerable detail in earlier chapters of this book; but before a railway could be built authorization, in the form of an Act of Parliament, was necessary, and the one concerning the Algoma Central was complicated, to say the least of it.

The part that concerns the present theme is that relating to the land grants. When Clergue came to the Soo there was literally no development, no 'nothing' in the rocky, forest-clad track of virgin country extending north to the single-tracked main line of the Canadian Pacific Railway, some 200 miles away, and there was still less in the wilderness of stunted forest and muskeg stretching far to the shores of Hudson Bay. Apart from haulage of forest products, I have told earlier how Clergue had ideas of running nightly fish trains from Hudson Bay to Chicago; but the main point now was that as an inducement to build the railway and to investors to put capital into it, the Government of Ontario made a land grant of 7400 acres for every mile of track that was built. The original proposal extended to no more than a connection with the Canadian Pacific, somewhere in the neighborhood of Hobon Lake, together with a branch to link up with the mining activities near the valley of the Michipicoten River; and in the light of these proposals, and of the preliminary surveys of the route it was then expected the railway would take, the original Act provided for Land Grants as shown on the accompanying map.

In more recent times it has become the fashion to denigrate the wisdom and indeed the social justice of those who made these early provisions, suggesting that the railways of Canada which received these grants had unearned riches thrown unheedingly into their laps. Whatever may have transpired elsewhere in Canada this was certainly not the case with the Algoma Central. The 'townships', as the 36-square-mile sections are called, were out in the wilderness. To many of them the railway was a long time in coming, and with no means of transport other than by canoe and portage there was not much incentive for immigrants to settle there. The Act of Incorporation of the railway required the development of a colonizing activity amounting to 1000 settlers a year; but it was not altogether surprising that this did not materialize. And with the financial crash at the Soo in 1903, construction of the railway came to a grinding halt at less than 60 miles north. For a time the collateral construction efforts from the Soo and from Michipicoten Harbor remained unconnected. Because of the delay in completing the line provided for in the Act fee-simple patents for the land, totalling 1,600,000 acres, were not issued to the Algoma Central Railway until the period 1913–17.

It is most interesting to study on the map just where those land grants were, particularly in relation to the old Indian Trails, and to the fur trade canoe routes, on the Michipicoten and Missinaibi Rivers. These were the only ways of communication that existed in the District of Algoma before the building of the Canadian Pacific Railway and the projecting of the Algoma Central. It will be seen at once that the greatest known source of mineral wealth in the district, the iron ore deposits around Wawa Lake, were not included in the land grants received by the Algoma Central Railway. These were already in the hands of the Algoma Steel company and its associates. But an interesting feature of the land grants in the north of the original territory, extending to 36 miles west of the present line of the railway north of Hawk Junction, is their possible connection, initially, with a proposal to build a connecting line from the Algoma Central in the Magpie River area to join the Canadian Pacific at White River.

As will be recalled from my accounts of the original surveys, when extension of the line to Hudson Bay was an immediate and active issue, the earliest proposals were to strike north-eastward from Hawk Lake, cross the CPR at Missanabie, and head for Moose Factory, on James Bay. In the ambitious but ill-directed early efforts in development, a second outlet to the Canadian Pacific in the north seemed desirable. It can be seen how the original land grants in this area, which are still owned by the

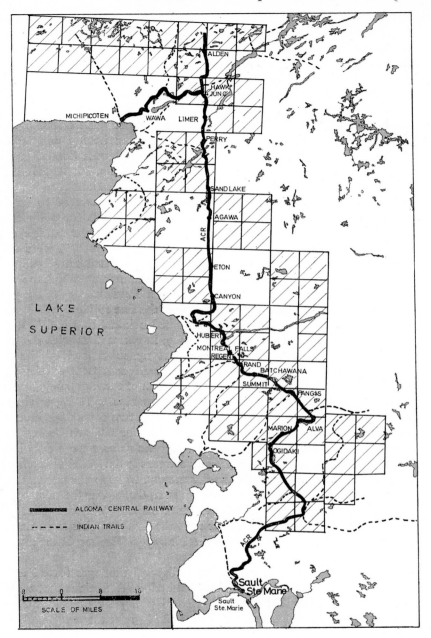

16   The Southern Land Grants, shown crosshatched: also the Indian trails

Algoma Central, tie in with this project. There was also a trail from Michipicoten Harbor northward into this territory. The line of this one-time proposed railway is now followed closely by the Trans-Canada Highway, and the area is becoming rather less remote.

The land grants represented a potential source of revenue to the railway, but at first the 1,600,000 acres were virtually useless without a completed railway, and because of the financial disaster in the Soo in 1903 no funds were available at first to build the line beyond the 70th mile, apart from the short isolated section from the Helen Mine down to Michipicoten Harbor. So far from having unearned riches heaped upon it by an 'over-generous' Government the Algoma Central Railway at first had nothing with which to reward its luckless investors. I have told earlier in this book how the original proposal, in fulfilment of the '. . . and Hudson Bay . . .' part of the railway's title, to make for Moose Factory was altered to head for a terminal farther on the western shore of Hudson Bay. Funds for completing the original part of the line, extending it to a connection with the National Transcontinental Railway at Hearst, which was then under construction were obtained from a financial maneuver in 1911, when the Algoma Central transfered all their buildings and real estate properties to a subsidiary company called the Algoma Central Terminals Company. The latter then floated a bond issue, with the property as security, and those funds were used to complete the line to Hearst.

Because this extension from the much attenuated original line had been undertaken as a result of a Government request in 1909, in connection with the building of the National Transcontinental, which was heavily subsidized by the Federal Government, a further land grant was made to the Algoma Central of 5000 acres for every mile constructed north of Franz. The location of these grants is shown on a further map. In this northern area most of the townships were larger than those south of Franz, being 9 miles square, instead of 6. The two townships immediately north of the CPR main line were an exception to this. The Algoma Central thus became possessed of an additional 500,000 acres, and the patents were duly issued in the period 1914 to 1916. Far from bringing any rewards to the shareholders however, the company was in such desperate straits for money, to keep the railway running and carry some of the additional traffic thrust upon it, that it was forced to sell some of the lands almost as soon as it received title to them. Disposal of those in the Northern Grant began almost at once and by the year 1924 the surface rights to some 350,000 acres were sold. They are held today by the Newaygo Timber Company, which places much traffic upon the railway.

This unfortunately was not the end of land disposal that was forced upon the Algoma Central Railway. In Chapter 8 I have told of the difficulties that arose over tax demands, through successive changes in fiscal policy by the Government of Ontario, and particularly in respect of Land Tax; and in 1925 there was added to the difficulties that of Railway Fire Charges, an extraordinary tax borne by railway land grant lands that no other private landowner had to pay. While it probably

10　The MV *Algoway* forcing a way through an ice field en route to Thunder Bay during the author's trip

11 The Canyon Tour train, headed by four 'GP7' diesel electric locomotives at the southern end of the Canyon, beginning the climb to Frater

12 Nearing 'Journey's End': the Canyon Tour train, nearing the outskirts of Sault Ste Marie after its daily trip into the 'wilderness'

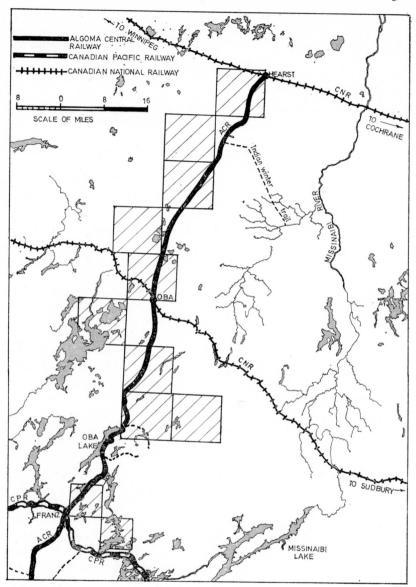

17   The Northern Land Grants

originated through the risk of land being set on fire by red hot cinders ejected by steam locomotives, it was mainly due to the need for providing forest fire protection to any large block of forested land, such as existed over much of the land grant areas owned by the Algoma Central Railway. There is a similar charge made upon Crown timber licensees for 'Forest Protection'. In 1940 however the Algoma Central Railway was in no position to pay these charges, which were made heavily retroactive. An agreement was reached whereby the company paid half of the taxes demanded, and half of the remaining lands, amounting to 850,000 acres, were transfered back to the Crown.

Even then the difficulties of land ownership by the Algoma Central were not over. A change in Government annulled the 1941 agreement just described, reimposed the Land Tax and the Railway Fire Charges, and introduced legislation that prevented the company—or indeed the owners of any railway lands—from controlling their use for fishing and hunting purposes. An agreement, which at the time of writing still stands, was however reached in 1969 transferring all pine rights on the company's land to the Algoma Central, in exchange for the surrender of the fauna rights to the Crown. With the various disposals made earlier the Algoma Central now owns 39 townships, all south of Franz, a total of about 850,000 acres. This land is owned in fee-simple, with all rights, including mining rights, but excluding fauna rights. These latter cover all matters concerning the management and harvesting of the fish and wildlife on the Algoma Central lands.

Today forestry is a very important activity on ACR lands. It includes the logging operations themselves, and transportation by train to a varied number of uses. In Chapter 16 I referred to the traffic in pulpwood to the Abitibi Paper Company, the present development of one of the original purposes for which the railway was built. While actual statistics may vary a little according to business fluctuations the railway delivers about 12,000 cords of pulpwood a month into the works of the Paper Company at the Soo. This would be equivalent to around 12 flat cars or gondolas every day. Some of this would come from direct logging by the railway, but most of it from contractors of the Paper Company. It is nevertheless a traffic that has marked fluctuations, and management has its fingers on the pulse of the industry, and has been ready to switch to other forest product activities, and to encourage developments elsewhere. Among the most important of these are the sawmills of the Dubreuil Brothers, now established in the very fine plant at Dubreuilville, and those in the Hearst area. The railway is encouraging a northward flow of spruce to these, so providing a balancing traffic to what is a predominating southward flow elsewhere.

When traveling over the line one can become aware of the vast extent of the forests, and equally of the apparently small area in which the trees are being cut. There is much variety in the trees, and their value for industrial purposes differs considerably. Even in such an area however the cutting must be carefully regulated, and the Algoma Central now has in Len Oliphant, a scientist trained and highly skilled in forestry, in charge of the Lands and Forests Division. From him I learned

178

of the many other kinds of timber that are cut on ACR lands, and of the direct revenue and subsequent traffics arising from them. It is not only the major customers like Abitibi and Dubreuil that receive careful attention; useful agreements have been concluded with smaller logging contractors, dealing with scattered hardwood and pine, while Dubreuil are installing a new mill for dealing with low grade hardwood fiber which it is hoped will bring additional business to the railway, both as landowner and haulage contractor.

For many years the Algoma Central has been involved in prospecting and mining exploration on its lands. Having regard to the great size of the iron ore deposits in the Wawa area it would seem likely that others might exist at no great distance away. On a small scale there have been finds of gold, and other valuable minerals. Since the early 1920s indeed the Algoma Central has printed a booklet of prospecting and mining regulations, which provides for the sale of prospecting permits, for the staking and recording of claims and the taking up of claims to the extent of mining lease. In recent years the company has greatly extended this activity by encouraging the participation of larger exploration companies, and entering into agreements that call for considerable capital expenditure to provide for modern, highly sophisticated geophysical equipment.

The conditions under which Prospecting Agreements are made require that the company making the agreement with the Algoma Central Railway shall undertake prospecting in the area stipulated to the extent of a minimum expenditure over a period, usually of three years, with named sums for each successive year. If in the course of explorations a worthwhile mineral deposit should be found then a lease is drawn up, which involves the Railway Company as 'Joint Venturers', with an entitlement to 25 per cent of the profits. In addition to this program of mineral exploration, which is being very actively pursued, the Company has also developed a policy of issuing recreational leases, of which there are now about 340. Some little time ago an article in the *Detroit Free Press* put this proposition in picturesque language:

Want to be a pioneer? Want to homestead your own piece of wilderness? Build a log cabin from timber cleared on your homesite?

It's possible. And in a rugged, beautiful wilderness area a few hours' drive from Detroit.

The province of Ontario, Canada, is several times as large as Michigan. Most of it is still inaccessible by road. While city sprawl has affected southern Ontario, millions of acres, from Lake Superior north to Hudson Bay, are still nearly virgin. Brook trout are spawned, grow up and die without ever seeing a fisherman in some rivers. Likewise, hundreds of moose, black bear, beaver and otter live out their life spans with no closer contact with humans than the drone of a high-flying bush plane. Cree

Indians still live in tepees in Ontario's north, trapping fur as their sole source of cash.

A huge chunk of this wilderness is available on a pick-your-own cabin-site basis through a plan worked out by the Algoma Central Railway Company.

For half a century, ACR trains chugging 300 miles north from Sault Ste Marie, Ontario, have provided wilderness access for loggers, trappers, prospectors, miners, fishermen, moose hunters and canoeists. The ACR line traverses canyons, lakeshores, muskeg bogs and near-endless spruce forests to reach its northern terminus at Hearst, a frontier town populated by loggers, miners and railwaymen. There are no roads or railroads beyond to the north, where forests fall away to tundra that reaches into Eskimo land.

Algoma Central Railway owns nearly a million acres of this wilderness, roughly adjoining its rail line. The railroad is encouraging 'prospecting' for your own cabin site. Most of the land is completely roadless and undeveloped, with access only via railroad, hiking, canoe or bush aircraft on some of the larger lakes.

'Prospecting' means just that. The ACR has no staked-out sites. Finding what you want is a matter of breaking new trails into wild country. There are hundreds of lakes in the lease area with no mark of human habitation. Many of these, of course, are hard to reach without great physical effort: no trails, no possibility of bush plane getting in or out.

While river systems are yet untouched by dwellings; some are seldom visited, even by hunters or fishermen. For example there's the Jimmie Cash River or the University, springing high in the Laurentian Shield north of Lake Superior. They are little explored, even today, due to the extremely rugged terrain.

The ACR land, however, does include scenic lake frontage nearer the Canadian Soo, where roads have penetrated. Also, lakes and waterways are adjacent to the railroad track, where cabin owners can drop off the train and walk or canoe to their cabins.

The railroad's lease rates vary with accessibility and desirability of the locations, but this would be in an area accessible only by rail—not by air or road.

And that is what 340 enterprising lessees have done!

CHAPTER NINETEEN

Real Estate: The City Center
Development at the Soo

The Algoma Central Railway owns 50 acres of land on the riverfront in downtown Sault St Marie, that until recently has been most inadequately used. In this area are located the headquarters offices, opposite Bruce Street, and on the river side of these are two railway tracks, extending eastward for a further quarter mile. The tracks are quite out in the open and this layout served as the ACR passenger station in the Soo for more than 60 years. At the western end a single-tracked line leads by a curving alignment to a junction with the main Algoma Central Railway yards at Steelton and thence to the north. It was scant utilization of a very valuable property, and did nothing to enhance the aspect of the downtown area of the city. Toward the end of the 1960s the Board and Management of the Algoma Central Railway gave consideration to the development of the property in a manner that would be appropriate to its unrivaled situation on the bank of the St Mary's River, and which would continue the tradition and policy of the railway in acting for the benefit of the city itself, and for the Algoma District in general.

A distinguished Canadian firm of Environmental Consultants was instructed to make a development study of the site covered by the railway property, and at the end of September 1970 they delivered their Design Report. This summarized in masterly form the various facets of the proposed development conceived originally by a number of individuals, both from the Railway Board and Management and of civic and business interests in the Soo. The report was accepted in most of its recommendations both by the railway and the municipality, and by the time I visited the Soo in April 1974 the first stage of the plan had already been implemented and successive stages were well in hand. To put the scheme in a nutshell it provides for

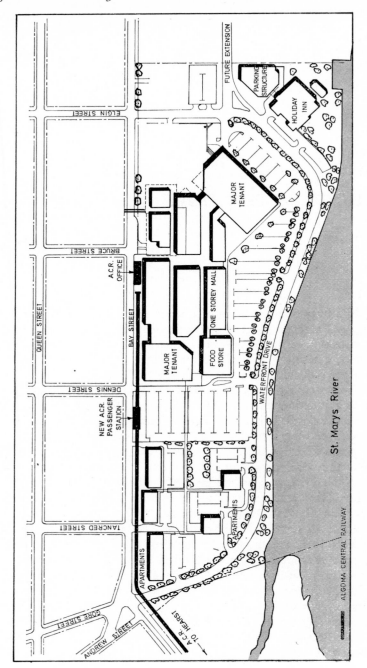

18 Sketch map showing extent of waterfront development on ACR property at the Soo

the complete metamorphosis of the riverside property from a drab, barely used expanse of veritable waste ground into a strikingly beautiful 'Center', to meet the requisites and provide amenities for a community growing in size and prosperity. It is the kind of project Francis H Clergue might well have contemplated in the business and social center of his 'empire' but had not the necessary business acumen to bring to profitable fruition.

The situation existing at the time of inception of the scheme is shown in the sketch map opposite. Its main elements were the provision, on the site, of a Civic Square; a new City Hall; a luxury apartment office complex; departmental stores and a two-level shopping mall; a motor hotel on the waterfront and a lower- and middle-income apartment complex. The disposition of the various buildings in the overall scheme has been the subject of very careful study, while considerations of user-convenience are evident in the provision of some protection from prevailing westerly winds—which can be very cold in the Soo when Lake Superior is iced up!— in the grouping of buildings around the square. There are also other forms of what can be termed 'climate control', as it affects the individual, in the form of covered pedestrian bridges from the buildings to the parking area, and the enclosed mall. The one major change from the original proposals is that the City Hall is being built on municipal land further east, but still on the waterfront.

Phase One of the Shopping Center at ground level was already in operation when I visited the Soo in April 1974. It had been opened officially by Lady Patricia Lowson, wife of the Chairman of the Algoma Central Railway, on 31 October 1973 and from my observation is a much appreciated and well patronized facility. The great variety of shops and department stores renting space have most attractive displays and the fact that one can obtain anything from a suit of clothes, a camera, an antique, or a hair-cut, to a snack, a full-dress meal, a cinema show or banking facilities, all under the one roof, with such extensive car-parking immediately outside as to create no problems in that respect, seems likely to set the seal of popularity on the entire enterprise. This however is no more than a beginning.

At the eastern end, in one of the most unrivaled sites in the entire area, the edifice of the new motor hotel was practically complete, and the equipment of the interior was in progress. By the time this book is published this splendid building will have opened, and one has only to glance at the site plan to see how commanding a prospect it will have over the St Mary's River, the attractively landscaped waterfront drive in front of the shopping mall and views to the west over the Canadian lock, the St Mary's Rapids and the great International Bridge. The motor hotel, which is owned by the Algoma Central Railway and operated by the Holiday Inns chain, has its own reserved car parking accommodation close at hand, and quite apart from the extensive public parking available for the patrons of the various activities in the mall. One can imagine that a stay at the Holiday Inn will become a very popular prelude to participating in the Agawa Canyon Tour on the railway. The motor hotel is designed to provide the highest grade facilities for conventions, civic functions, banquets and so on, in addition to its function as a hotel.

The later phases of this striking plan of development have not yet been started. The Shopping Center is to be increased by addition of a second storey, and attractive apartment blocks are to be built at the western end. The surrounding land is to be parceled out to provide individual car parking facilities for each block, set among trees and a garden *motif*.

Taking the concept as a whole, the design scheme has been prepared to incorporate such psychological and symbolic requirements as are needed to create a favorable impression in the minds of those using the Center. To this end the juxtaposition of the offices, apartment blocks and motor hotel in relation to the shopping mall is designed to create areas of distinct and differing architectural character, so that one does not head for the luxury offices or the motor hotel when setting out for one of the department stores in the Shopping Center. The report of the Environmental Consultants includes this paragraph:

> Although variation in building character is an integral part of the design philosophy, the scheme is held together by an overall architectural theme in the linking of buildings and creation of spaces within and between them. This design co-ordination is exemplified by the deliberate attempt to create an urban street scene along Bay Street.

There might have been significance in this for the present railway headquarters offices. That massive three-storey building, in the hard red sandstone excavated when the great Soo locks were made, is a 'period piece' in every way. In England it could well be scheduled as a building of historic importance, and inviolate from any attention from developers. But there are times when sentiment and history become over-ridden. In London, England, there was no more classic example than of the great Doric Arch outside the Euston Terminus: a masterpiece of architecture by Philip Hardwick, and symbolizing the immense significance of the station as that of the first main-line railway from London to the north. When that great railway was electrified and the station required complete rebuilding, the Doric Arch was not only in the way, but completely incongruous to the architectural style of the new station. And so, despite a storm of protest from many sections of the public, it was torn down.

Studying the beautiful artists' impressions of the ultimate 'look' of the development, one forms the uneasy conclusion that the old Algoma Central Railway buildings, if retained, might look strangely out of place in such a modern layout, and it was not with any sense of surprise that I read in the report of the consultants that: 'The scheme provides for the eventual phasing out of the ACR rail lines, station and office building . . .', and of course the construction, since the report was first presented, of the new passenger station referred to in Chapter 17 could have been construed as the first step toward this end. But no scheme of this kind is inviolate, and according to present intentions the old office block is happily not to share the fate of the Doric Arch, in London. Modifications, consequent upon the decision of the municipal authorities to have the new City Hall a little further downstream from where it was originally proposed, and other lesser amendments have led to some re-thinking of the plan as it affects the Bay Street frontage; and in this the historic railway office building will still stand.

So I approach the end of my story of this remarkable railway from the first flush of its enthusiastic inception, through its long years of penury, vicissitudes and struggles for survival, to the full regaining of its corporate status as a company; finally to developments and diversifications that make it one of the more prosperous companies to be found anywhere in the world. To a railway proper, shipping, lands and real estate is now added the business of trucking, though this is not carried on in the District of Algoma, but in South-Western Ontario. The diversifications of the Algoma Central bear a striking resemblance indeed—though of course on a much smaller scale—to those of Canadian Pacific, and one questions how long it might be before the ACR has also an air line! As with Canadian Pacific the purely railway function has now ceased to be the predominating partner in the Algoma Central set-up. At this stage one looks back, a little wistfully, to the man who first set the mighty organism centered upon the Soo into action, Francis H Clergue; and one salutes the infinitely stronger and abler businessmen, who salvaged what was left from the disasters of 1903, 1914 and 1933, and the financial uncertainties that prevailed, and brought the Soo to its present status, as one of the major industrial centers in all Canada.

Index